Satchfield Hall

By the same author

Magnolia House
Sometimes It Happens…
Storms Clouds Gathering
In the Cold Light of Day
The Wendy House

Satchfield Hall

Pauline Barclay
www.paulinebarclay.co.uk

Third Reprint
Originally published by AOL 2010
Second Reprint 2011

Copyright © Pauline Barclay 2010

Cover Design by Cathy Helms, Avalon Graphics
Copyright © Pauline Barclay 2016

The characters in this novel and their actions are imaginary.
Their names and experiences have no relation to those of actual people, living or dead, except by coincidence.

All rights reserved. No part of this publication may be reproduced, stored in a retrieval system, or transmitted in any form or by any means, electronic, mechanical, photocopy, recording or otherwise, without prior written permission of the copyright owner. Nor can it be circulated in any form of binding or cover other than that in which it is published and without similar condition including this condition being imposed on a subsequent purchaser.

This book is also available in Kindle format

For my husband Clive, as always with love.

Special thanks to Sue B. for all her support, patience, kindness and friendship.

To my dear friend Sandra

To my wonderful editor, Jo Field

To Cathy Helms at Avalon Graphics

Prologue

Celia stood alone in the shadows of the sweeping boughs of a willow tree. From her vantage point, she could clearly see the four people huddled together by the open grave, their heads bowed as they carried out the solemn ritual of bidding their last goodbyes. Despite it being no more than twenty yards from where she watched, the gathered mourners could not see her. She need take only a few steps forward to be visible to them, but Celia had no desire whatsoever to be seen.

Unlike the small party, she was not dressed in sombre clothing, nor was she weeping. For her, it was not a day to mourn; she had done that years earlier. Wept at the loss of the man she once believed had cared for her. He had, but not in the way she had hoped. Like everything in Henry Bryant-Smythe's life, he had viewed her as an asset, an investment, and when she had deprived him of what he believed was his insurance with a healthy dividend, he had made her pay, the price had been high; very high.

Celia shuddered. Her reason for standing silently in the cover of the willow was to witness the end of his life on this earth. She had waited for more years than she could count to see this day. She had heard it said that only the good die young: well here was evidence indeed that the evil stay on this earth for a very long time. He had celebrated his thirtieth birthday not long before she was born and she was a grandmother twice over now. You did not need to be a mathematician to work out that he had lived for many more years than his allotted three score years and ten, she mused, her lips curving in a wry smile that as quickly disappeared.

'Justice!' Celia hissed, almost screaming out the word, until she remembered where she was. But there was no justice, she thought with bitterness. Nothing could bring back what he had stolen from her. Even when he knew he was dying, he had not uttered her name nor repented. In the end nothing had changed. Instead, in a voice thick with loathing, he had told her his reasons for what he had done, confirming for Celia that he had no regrets for the pain and suffering he had caused. She recalled he had smiled at her, a sardonic smile that changed his face from haughty to malicious. Even his eyes had sparkled with malevolence, boring into her like laser beams.

'I just want you to know,' he had snapped, his voice like the crack of a whip that had cut just as deep, 'that because of your behaviour, I lost *everything*. You, with no sense of morality or filial duty, despite your lavish upbringing, were the catalyst for all that happened. You should be *begging* my forgiveness.' Celia remembered that in the corners of his mouth spittle had foamed as his anger mounted, his lips tightening with his deep resentment. 'But don't ever bother to ask for it,' he had added, 'because I will *never* give it. Now get out of my sight.'

Despite her mature years, his presence and tone had sent a shiver of fear down her spine and she had felt like a child again. Now, standing in the shadows of the willow tree, even though she knew his life was over, Celia could still feel his presence. To her horror, she realised that despite all that had happened, even in death her father still had the ability to chill her blood. Even knowing he was gone, she could not remove the hatred she had in her heart for him. It had been there for so long it was like another organ. It was part of her. It had shaped her life and the lives of all of those around her.

Her father: Henry Bryant-Smythe, the Squire of Satchfield Hall, powerful and evil, had destroyed so many and so much and had ultimately destroyed himself. Only now, as the words he had spoken echoed through the passage of time, did Celia feel a kind of pity: pity that defied all logic; the fear, the pain and suffering. She knew the words he had snapped at her as he lay dying meant that to himself, he had rewritten the past and in his own deluded mind had seen himself as the victim.

Her mother, who had suffered at his hands, had gone to an early grave. Had she only had the fortitude to stand up to the man who had taken her as his bride when she was barely sixteen, then maybe all their lives might have been different and so much pain avoided. But somehow Celia did not think so: despite Muriel Bryant-Smythe's great beauty, she had been powerless against the depredation of her iniquitous husband.

Now, wondering idly who the mourners were and having witnessed all that was necessary, Celia made to leave. Silently thanking God that it was over, she turned her back on the scene being enacted in the graveyard, but as she stepped away from her hiding place she felt a hand touch her arm. It took all of her will power not to cry out. Heart thumping, she swung round, joy and relief flooding her veins as she saw who it was.

'Jack! You startled me,' she gasped, smiling up at him and asking in a loud whisper, 'What are you doing here?'

'It looks to me, much the same as you, making sure he really *has* gone.'

Celia nodded, 'I'm so pleased to see you,' she said, linking her arm with his and wondering why she should be so startled when she'd had a feeling Jack would turn up today.

Arm in arm they walked through the concealed exit of the memorial gardens, the same one she had entered by earlier. Neither of them looked back. No doubt, thought Celia, her father was spinning somewhere between Hell and Heaven. She knew Heaven would have difficulty in taking him; there had never been an ounce of good in him. Even Hell might sniff at accepting him! Wherever he was, he would not be pleased with what in the end had been achieved. He had believed he was all powerful and had used his power to destroy and crush. It had taken the Second World War and a country desperate to rebuild and recover from its wounds, before the power he wielded was weakened and eventually removed. Yet despite being stripped of what he valued most: status, power, reputation and above all wealth, he continued to haunt those he had sought to destroy.

As Celia and Jack walked the few steps that took them to her car, she smiled, thinking that at last the chapter was closed. Her step was lighter: she was a woman who had come through it all; she had succeeded in the end, and looking up at the tall, handsome man at her side, Celia knew that despite everything, she had been blessed.

Her driver, Tony, was waiting for them in the lane. As they appeared through the thick hedge that concealed the little gate into the cemetery, he smiled and opened the rear passenger door. 'Are you ok?' he asked.

Unperturbed by his familiarity, Celia returned his smile, for whilst she was his employer and had been for more years than she cared to remember, he was also her friend. 'Thank you, Tony. Never better,' Celia stepped into the rear of the car and made herself comfortable.

Tony shook Jack's hand, 'Delighted to see you, Jack, and no doubt Celia is too. Today is a big day for her.'

Jack nodded, 'For us both,' he murmured, patting Tony's shoulder before climbing into in the car.

Once Celia's seat belt was locked into its snap, she rested her head on the headrest and closing her eyes, breathed a sigh of relief. At the same time, a tear trickled down her cheek. Even though it was over, the images sprang to life in her mind: the voices and even the smell of fear were about to consume her again. Feeling the tight squeeze of Jack's hand she pushed the memories away and looked up into his handsome face. No matter how many times she gazed at him, it would never be enough. She counted her blessings every single day. He was the image of his father; thank God there was not a trace of his grandfather in him.

As if reading her mind, Jack squeezed her hand again and smiled down at her.

'No regrets?' she asked him.

'Millions, but none anyone can change.'

Celia knew what he was referring to and he was right. If they were to list their regrets then the list would be long enough to strangle them both. She smiled at him and then laughed out loud, the memories, which only moments ago had been about to consume her, evaporating in the warmth of his smile.

'Everything ok in the back,' called Tony, looking in the rear view mirror at the sound of Celia's laughter.

She smiled at the face reflected in the mirror, 'Nothing could be more ok, Tony. I've waited a long time for this day and I intend to savour it, even if it means spontaneously breaking into maniacal laughter for no apparent reason!'

He chuckled, 'I'm glad to hear it. In your shoes I'd feel exactly the same. And if you don't mind me saying so, you deserve to laugh after all you've been through because of him.'

Approaching the T-junction at the brow of the hill, Tony slowed the car at the give-way sign before turning off to the left. As he skilfully manoeuvred the big car into the lane, Celia remembered that the road sign had not been there all those years ago when she had been driven away from Satchfield Hall. Once again, despite her exuberance, the memory slipped unbidden into her mind. She saw herself as a young woman – not much more than a girl - hunched in the back of the car and felt again the despair and misery of that day.

'*Stop it,*' she told herself, '*it's over!*' But her mind continued to replay those dreadful scenes and tears again welled in her eyes. She had never stopped wondering how one person could create so much pain and suffering in so many people's lives. She should be feeling some inner peace now, after all, in the end she'd had the last word, but she did not hear that. Instead, all she could hear was her father's voice as it thundered through Satchfield Hall all those years before.

PART ONE
1942 - 1951

Chapter ONE

What Henry Bryant-Smythe heard about his daughter sent him into a wild rage that no amount of appeasing by his wife would calm. Even as he fumed at what he saw as a dreadful scandal, he had taken steps to put a halt to it before it could do any further damage to his family's name. At the same time, he had conveniently sorted out an indiscretion of his own, but that was not something anyone else needed to know about. Thinking on his feet, he had swiftly dealt with it, using money and fear, his two principal weapons, to put right the bloody mess his daughter had laid at his door. As for the young whippersnapper who'd had the audacity to mess with his property, he had been dealt with just as swiftly and was now well out of sight; all in all a satisfactory outcome.

Henry Bryant-Smythe had little time for feelings. As far as he was concerned, emotions were for the stupid and useless and the world would be a better place if there were more people in it like him. As for sentiment and feelings: where had they ever got anybody? Over the years he had asked himself this question many times, especially when confronted with a situation that needed crushing speedily. Sentiment, he reminded himself again, was strictly for the weak and worthless. He was neither of these and God forbid anyone should dare to forget it.

With one half of the problem dealt with, he had now to finish off the other half - as if he had not got enough on his plate at the moment. Not wasting any time he had managed to get everything arranged, but it had cost him dear; far more than he had expected. 'This bloody war has made everyone greedy,' he thought, his expression bleak and forbidding as he went in search of his wife.

He did not have far to look, he knew where she would be, no doubt sitting in the drawing room patting her foolish tears and wringing her hands. She had begged him to understand how everything might be resolved more kindly, but he had not listened, he had far too much to lose. The only way to make sure everything went as he wanted was to stamp on any situation that threatened him; which is what he had done.

Now, as he pushed open the heavy double doors and stepped into the drawing room, he heard his wife's sniffle long before he clapped eyes on her. The disdain he felt for her was like bile in his throat. As he strode over to where she was sitting, she looked up at him. She had been weeping, her eyes ugly with puffiness. Seeing this added further to his resentment. He gave her no opportunity to speak: he was here to do the talking. In a low voice, verging on a whisper that not only belied his stature but his rage, he addressed her.

'So here you are, sitting and snivelling when our life is in turmoil and worse, our reputation is on the brink of being shot to pieces thanks to that disgusting daughter of yours: a disgrace at best, a whore at worst!'

He had purposely referred to the girl as *your* daughter. Henry had no time for the child, never had, not from the moment she had dropped red-faced into the world squawking her lungs out. Every now and then he had made the effort, primarily because he could see she was turning into a pretty young woman and with his business deals not always going to plan, he had begun to see her as an asset. There was no doubt in his mind that she would command a decent enough price to the right gentleman: ideally titled, but that was not obligatory provided he had enough capital assets. Now, however, her purity had been sullied and no gentleman worth his salt would look at her as a wife and mother to his heirs. The opportunity Henry had banked on as an investment in the bag had been stripped from him. Instead, her actions threatened to bring him into disrepute. He would not tolerate the disgrace at any price, which had left him with little choice but to act. And act he had. He had cut his losses and washed his hands of her as soon as had learned what she had been up to.

Looking down at his wife, his contempt oozing out of every pore, he added, 'There is no place for her here. I want her out and far enough away from me so I never have to see her face again. Is that understood?'

Muriel, tears spilling from her red-rimmed eyes, looked up at him, protesting, 'She's a child, Henry, where on earth can she go?'

'That should have been her question before she behaved like a common whore. As I said, I want you to get her out of here. Do you not think I have enough to occupy my mind without having to sort out this bloody mess?'

He did not add that the mess occupying his mind was a financial one and questions were being asked of his true worth. The last thing he needed was gossip about his family's morals, though he knew few would ever dare to question him directly. The girl's shameful, loose behaviour with that halfwit, David Gillespie, had cost him, potentially, not only a fortune but the enhancement of his family's status through her marriage into the gentry. On the other hand, albeit unwittingly, it sorted out a little peccadillo of his own - not that she or anyone else was aware of that. He firmly believed that what was not known about could not harm anyone - most importantly, no harm would come to him. By nature a ruthless man, Henry Bryant-Smythe had always believed he was untouchable: too important and far too powerful to be undermined. Despite this, he knew that tittle-tattle must be stamped on before it had even begun. He was damned if he was going to feed the lesser underlings with gossip fodder they could regurgitate to suit.

In a voice that brooked no nonsense, he said, 'While you've sat here pretending nothing is happening, I've sorted the whole sorry business out. All the arrangements have been made and she must be gone before dark. And, remember, as far as I am concerned she can never come back. Ever! I've washed my hands of her. From now on I do not have a daughter and if you know what's good for you, neither do you.'

Even as he spoke those words, Henry wondered if he was missing a trick. Was there a remote possibility that one day he might be forced to eat his words? Was it possible his daughter might yet command a price at some time in the future? Surely not! Dismissing the thought he looked down at his wife and sneered. Dwarfed by the large, leather wing chair in which she cowered, she looked even smaller and more frail than usual. He no longer saw her beauty; her weakness repelled him. Bending down he pushed his saturnine face close to hers, gratified when she flinched away from him.

'We will never speak of this again. Let me put it another way: should her name *ever* be mentioned in this house, I will send you to join her and, like her, if you dare to disobey me I will have you thrown out onto the streets. Is that clear?'

Although he kept his voice low, it made the crystal lamp on the side table resonate with its power. He could see that his wife was holding back more tears, but he did not care. She had not the faintest idea just how much more she would be weeping had he not sorted everything out. Nor was he about to tell her. He did not wait for a response, verbal or emotional, but turned on his heel and marched out of the drawing room, shutting the door firmly behind him as he left.

Watching the door close, not only onto the room in which she was sitting, but also on her role as a mother, Muriel Bryant-Smythe shook with shock and fear. How could he do this to her and to their only daughter? Disturbingly, she knew exactly what her husband was like. Over the years she had made it her business to find out what lay behind his cold exterior. She knew he had been brought up with little or no love, his parents believing that children should be seen and not heard. They had stood by those pearls of wisdom, employing a gaggle of women to take care of their offspring. Some of these women had been unkind at best and abusive at worst. The result: Henry, the youngest of five, had grown up a cold, calculating and cruel man. He had patience, but as with all of his traits he used it to get exactly what he wanted - and he always succeeded. This patience, so unexpected in a man of such ruthlessness, often lulled people into a false sense of security and only when he had snared his catch did he show his true colours. He had made fortunes from such tactics; he had also lost fortunes, although, as Muriel knew to her cost, this was forbidden territory and never to be spoken about.

So far, not once had he lost his reputation and he most certainly was not about to let an offspring of his tarnish it now. There were times when Muriel thought he would one day overstep the mark and do that all by himself, leaving total destruction in his wake. She trembled at the thought. But for now, her husband, Henry Bryant-Smythe, the Squire of Satchfield Hall, believed he was untouchable and for the time being she conceded that he was.

Muriel knew he would keep to his word and that her interference at this stage could make matters even worse for her daughter – if that was possible. With these thoughts she recalled what she had recently learnt about David Gillespie. It seemed the poor boy had been sent off to the war in what was being talked about as 'rude haste'. It was far too much of a coincidence, given the condition of their daughter. The unexpectedness of David's departure had left no doubt in Muriel's mind that her husband had somehow engineered it. The news served only to fuel her fear and an ice cold shiver slithered down her spine. She had always suspected her husband was evil, but until now she had not realised just how evil.

She sobbed at the hopelessness of the situation, knowing she must obey him to stop any more pain. Sniffing into her handkerchief, she vowed that one day she would find a way to make sure he paid for all of this. One day, Henry Bryant-Smythe would get exactly what he deserved; she would make sure of it.

Chapter TWO

Alone in the drawing room, her head aching and her heart breaking, Muriel knew there was nothing she could do to stop the inevitable and that to procrastinate would simply wreak further anguish and suffering for both her daughter and herself. Dabbing at her tear-streaked face, she got slowly out of the chair and made her way to the door, her mind filled with the image of her husband storming through it and shutting it firmly behind him moments before. For a heartbeat she hesitated, then grasping the handle, she turned it and pushed open the door.

To her dismay, Lilly Jenkins, the housekeeper, was in the hall talking to the girl who had been employed as a maid just two weeks earlier. It surprised Muriel that young women could be still found who wanted to work in the household when now, with the war raging, there were so many other employment opportunities open to them. She was, however, relieved that they did, for much as she disliked the housekeeper, Mrs Jenkins could not do everything: Satchfield Hall was a large house and to keep it running smoothly required more than one domestic.

Left to herself, Muriel would have dismissed the spiteful woman years ago, but when she had tentatively suggested doing so, Henry had humiliated her by refusing to countenance it, using the excuse that good housekeepers were hard to come by and Lilly Jenkins was worth her weight in gold and irreplaceable. 'The discussion is closed,' he had snapped, as he always did whenever she broached a subject he did not want to talk about. And as usual, she was too afraid of him to argue. Muriel was fairly sure that Lilly Jenkins provided him with a lot more services than mere housekeeping, but she preferred not to imagine what form these might take and rather than probe, she tolerated the situation. It was, after all, the least of her problems and if it kept Henry from her bed, so much the better.

As Muriel entered the hall, the new maid glanced in her direction then quickly lowered her eyes, a faint flush staining her cheeks.

'Morning Marm,' Lilly Jenkins drawled. 'Is there anything that I can be doing for you?'

The housekeeper's scornful expression made Muriel uncomfortably aware that the marks of her distress must be plain to see. Not that it mattered; at this moment nothing mattered beyond her anguish for her daughter. Forcing a look that still conveyed she was mistress of this house and not a broken woman far too old for her years, she stared Mrs Jenkins down and was gratified when the housekeeper dropped her gaze. Doubtless the woman had heard the gossip and would know not just that she had been weeping, but why. Much worse than this was Muriel's sudden conviction that Lilly Jenkins had in some way been involved in whatever arrangements Henry had made to deal so speedily with the sorry situation.

Muriel hated the very thought that her staff were used in this way, it made them believe they were above what they really were. Not that Lilly Jenkins needed encouragement on that score. What was now happening in her household gave the sly housekeeper far too much assumed power. Muriel noted the furtive look in Lilly Jenkins' eyes; the expression she always wore whenever she felt she knew something about her employers that they would prefer she did not, in particular something as juicily scandalous as this. Muriel knew her daughter's unhappy plight would make her a social outcast no matter what her class, but even more so for people of the Bryant-Smythes' standing in society. She was under no illusion that what Mrs Jenkins knew would keep the housekeeper supplied with gossip and hearsay for years to come. Muriel loathed the farce of it all. Had she not been so afraid of her husband, she would have never allowed this woman into her home, but it was all too late. No matter what she thought, nothing would change. Not yet at least. For now she had a task to do, one that was already breaking her heart. What hurt her the most was that she knew she had no choice.

'No thank you, Mrs Jenkins,' she said, 'I can manage. Maybe you could deal with the fire in the drawing room? It appears to be low.' Wincing at what she must now do about her daughter, to Muriel's surprise her voice did not betray her inner turmoil. Nor did it reveal her disgust at the sly, knowing look she received from the housekeeper - though for a moment it was a struggle. Had she not been so well bred, brought up to behave at all times with decorum, she would happily have smacked the woman squarely in the face. Instead, much against her basic instinct, Muriel held herself back and behaved like the lady she was.

Almost as if she knew what it cost, Lilly Jenkins gave a sneering smile, 'If you say so, Marm, but you know where I am should you change your mind.'

'Indeed I do.' Muriel replied and to her amazement, saw Lilly Jenkins raise her left eyebrow in a look of amused disdain. It was yet another sign the housekeeper knew far too much about what was going on. Not waiting for the rude woman to utter another word, Muriel turned and with all the dignity she could muster, headed towards the wide curving staircase that would take her to her daughter.

Half way up she heard Lilly Jenkins bark a curt instruction, 'Stop gawping, girl. Best you get that fire stoked up before it goes out.'

Glancing back, Muriel saw the housekeeper push the young maid towards the drawing room door then turn, not troubling to hide her sly smile as she looked up the stairs.

Chapter THREE

Celia lay on her bed, curled in the foetal position as if to protect herself from what she feared was about to happen. She knew her father had been more than busy, he had been manic. Now, word had reached her ears that he had arranged for her to be taken away. Whispers had resounded off the walls of the cold and draughty Hall as speculation mounted as to what would happen to the young Miss: 'Not so young, I hear,' snatched Mrs Jenkins, to anyone who happened to mention *The Situation* within earshot. 'No better than one of the common girls from the village and her with all her privileges, not that it's done her much good.' Seeing that Celia had overheard, she had smirked, her sneering expression spiked with malice.

Not only were the staff gossiping, but as if that were not bad enough, her father's rage had not taken its usual form. Normally, when Henry Smythe-Bryant raised his voice it was louder than a summer heat storm and the household would take cover, the very fabric of the building and the air in Satchfield Hall vibrating with fear. But *The Situation* did not have him bellowing, nor did he even raise his voice, and for Celia that was all the more frightening. She barely dared to imagine what he was plotting.

Terrified, she screwed her eyes tight shut, as tight as was physically possible so that she could see nothing at all, not even the little speckles that floated around behind her eyes when they were closed. With her fingers plugged deep into her ears drowning out the sounds around her, in a silent prayer she begged she could be made invisible. Celia had known her father would be angry, but she had not expected that his intervention would give her no chance to explain. Not one. He had not once spoken to her since he had learnt about her condition. It was as if she did not exist, and at this moment she wished that were indeed the case. She took a deep breath that shuddered its way down into her lungs. What she would not give to evaporate off the face of the Earth right now.

Celia had convinced herself that she and David Gillespie would be married and all would be fine, but that was ten days ago. Now, as she lay on her bed alone and frightened, she had no idea what would become of her. Since speaking with her mother her life had been plunged into silence. No one else had said a word to her, apart from some of the staff and even their tone was subdued. Mama had visited her many times, but each time she entered the room she looked increasingly strained. As distraught as Celia was, seeing her mother's obvious distress broke her heart. She knew it was all her fault. She saw the sadness in her mother's eyes and heard the anxiety in her voice, which was not the strongest at the best of times, but it now held such a mixture of pain and shame that she sounded barely normal. Despite this, Mama always held her close and continued to reassure her.

'Celia, whatever happens, you must never forget that I love you and I will always be there for you.'

This in itself disturbed Celia because her mother continued to use the phrase, *there* for you, not *here* for you. She knew by now that her father was involved and this should have concerned her. It did, to a degree, but it was overshadowed by her anxiety about David. There had been no word from him. Nothing. Not a visit, not even a hastily scribbled note. Celia could not understand it. Had he learned of her plight and abandoned her, like everyone else seemed to have done? 'No, no, please no!' But crying out in denial at this dreadful possibility only added further to her fear. Surely, she argued to herself as she sat in the solitude of her room, her father would *want* David to marry her? Then she counter-argued that there would be no need to want, because they *would* be married. They simply *had* to be. After all, the Gillespies were not only good friends, but her father's business colleagues. Had he himself not introduced David to her in the first place?

That day would be forever etched in her memory. Her father quite often brought colleagues to Satchfield Hall. On this occasion, returning home from one of his business trips in town, he had been accompanied by David Gillespie and his father, Robert. Normally, when Henry Bryant-Smythe brought business colleagues back with him, Muriel would scurry out of the drawing room taking Celia with her, but for some reason, on that day her father had insisted they both stay. 'This is my daughter,' he had said, introducing Celia in his customary dry, flat tone.

She had seen David before, of course, when he had visited Satchfield Hall, but until that moment they had not been formally introduced. She had never imagined that someone so handsome and full of purpose would ever want to pay her any attention. The way he had looked at her had made Celia's pulses race and when he held her hand, the smile on his lips mirrored in the soft blue of his eyes, it had taken her breath away. How was it possible that a man could make her feel so weak? She knew it was dangerous: she felt the danger ripple through every fibre of her body and she wanted more. She had fallen in love with David Gillespie that very moment. She had believed he felt the same way.

The first time they had met alone, he had held her and kissed her so gently she had almost fainted. Not long after that beautiful, spellbinding kiss they had become lovers. It was something she could never have imagined she was capable of doing before marriage and she had tried to resist, but he had told her that nothing was guaranteed anymore. The war was changing everything. 'We could all be killed and then we would have missed out on something so very beautiful,' he had whispered. She had believed him; she had *wanted* to believe him, her resistance crumbling beneath his touch.

But then, had not he told her how much he loved her each time he had gently and carefully stripped off her under garments? 'I love you and I hope you love me and when this terrible war is over we will sit and plan our lives so that we can be together forever.' He had kissed her senseless. How could she have resisted? She knew he loved her and that as soon as the world stopped fighting they would be married.

Celia had often overheard the servants teasing each other about their boyfriends. She knew that 'nice girls' never allowed physical intimacy before marriage, no matter how tempted they might be. At the time she had thought they were either mad or lying, but belatedly she had seen the wisdom of their words. Before David, she had been completely ignorant of that side of love; she'd had not the faintest idea how babies were made. On the rare occasions that her natural curiosity had led her to ask questions, the answers she got had horrified her. She could not bring herself to believe that people acted in the same way as farm animals. Later, when her periods started, she had asked her mother, but she had responded with a shocked and embarrassed, 'We don't talk about that, Celia!'

How differently she saw things now! Everything David had done to her she loved, except for this. Weeping, Celia placed her hand on her belly. She could feel the slight swelling. She had missed four periods. She had thought nothing about missing the first one; these things happened. They had certainly happened to her before. But in those days, she had not been making love with David Gillespie. Even after she had missed two periods, she had still allowed him do all those things to her.

Then the nausea had started. She remembered the first time she had vomited: they had made love that afternoon. David had to come to the house as normal to see her father and after the meeting he had offered to take her for a spin in his car. He had told her he had managed to get hold of some petrol and wanted to use it to take her out. The fresh air and being with David had made everything seem so normal and they had made love on the back seat. That evening she was sick, so very sick. She had put it down to going out in the car, which she was not used to. With petrol rationing, her father most certainly did not allow her to travel in his car unless it was somewhere he felt she needed to go, and even then she had to persuade him of its necessity. Hence, an outing in an automobile was very rare.

The next morning she was sick again and had been every morning since. Even with her limited knowledge, it dawned on Celia what was happening to her body and why, but she had not been afraid. Not until now.

She had planned to tell David the next time they met, but she had not seen him for several days. A shock of panic ran through her veins at the unexpected absence of her lover. Why now, of all times, was David being so elusive? She had screamed this to herself each day when he did not come to see her. It was a question that resounded round and round inside her head, but with no answer.

In the end, ten days ago, she had told her mother. It was almost impossible to hide her sickness and Celia was fairly sure her mother must have guessed. 'I think I'm going to have a baby, Mama, but you don't need to worry.' She had gushed out the words with a mixture of fear and happiness. 'You don't need to worry about anything, because David and I love each other so much. We will be married just as soon as I tell him. I know it will be a wonderful surprise to him.' But as Celia's torrent of words cascaded out of her mouth and flew across the small space that divided then, she saw the colour drain from her mother's face.

Like arrows being fired from several bows simultaneously the words had pierced Muriel's brain, sinking deep into her soul to wreak havoc. Speechless with shock, she gazed at her daughter and saw just how beautiful she was and also how very young, and worse, just how frightfully naïve. As Muriel saw all of this and her worst fear was realised, her heart lurched. She had tried to ignore the sour odour of vomit in her daughter's room over the past week. Even the windows open and the dowsing of toilet water had not masked what she had secretly feared, praying it could not be true and if she ignored it, it would go away.

Taking hold of Celia's hand, Muriel wanted to scream at her, '*Why?*' Why had she felt she could act in such a way without a care? It was not just the immorality of behaving like a loose woman, although that was bad enough, God knows, but had she not for one moment considered the shame she would bring to her family and household? But even as these words sprang to her lips, Muriel knew there was no sense in railing at the girl, it would change nothing. The damage was done. What she had to do now was to think speedily on how to protect her daughter, because she would need to do this more than anything else. Shuddering at the spectre of her husband looming over her, Muriel did her best to ignore the icy shiver that inched its way down her spine.

Trying to hold back her tears of disappointment and fear, she steadied her voice and asked, 'How many periods have you missed?' As she asked this question she begged to hear it would be no more than two, so that the pregnancy could be terminated. Nobody would need to know and all her fears would be sorted; Celia's life would not be shattered, her reputation ruined beyond repair. Her daughter was seemingly completely unaware of the pain and devastation that would follow her answer, which if it was as Muriel feared, would set in motion events that would affect so many lives and take several decades, if not a lifetime, to heal. Her own included. It did not bear thinking about.

As she waited for what seemed like an eternity for her daughter to reply, she prayed with fervour to any God who would listen that what she was about to be told was not true, for somehow Muriel sensed that it was much more than two.

Her prayers went unheard. Her poor, naïve daughter, clearly believing she was about to become Mrs David Gillespie, unashamedly replied, 'Four, Mama.'

Muriel let go of her daughter's hand, not that she wanted to distance herself, but so that she could place her own hands down onto the bed for support. 'Dear God,' she silently prayed, 'what did I not see? What was happening that I ignored and most importantly, how am I going to protect her? Because, God, if you are listening, she will need protecting.'

Staring at her daughter, Muriel forced herself to recognise the change in her. She had seen it ever since Celia had started walking out with David Gillespie, but had chosen to ignore it, arguing that it was only natural. Celia was happy; there was no harm in that. Trusting her daughter to behave like the young lady she had been brought up to be, Muriel had persuaded herself that Celia would never allow herself to be compromised. Yes, she had noticed the girl had put on the tiniest amount of weight, but had put that down to her natural growth and increased maturity. It was normal for seventeen-year-old girls wasn't it? And so Muriel had squashed any misgivings she might have had, because anything else was unthinkable.

How could this have happened? Her mind raced wildly through the last weeks and months looking for tiny details that might have given her a clue. She saw nothing, nothing at all. They were a wealthy respected family with the highest of reputations. That is what she firmly believed and her belief made the situation even more improbable. That the son of a family friend, a young man she had trusted to escort her daughter to functions and bring her home safe, had taken evil advantage of Celia's naivety and seduced her was unforgiveable. She laid the blame squarely at David Gillespie's door unable to believe that Celia could have known what was happening until it was too late.

Looking at her beautiful daughter, the word 'four' echoing in her brain, Muriel's heart began to break into tiny little pieces knowing it would be almost impossible to save Celia from the results of her unbridled passion for this despicable man. By behaving so loosely, her little girl had ruined her life. The world might be in a state of flux, but in the eyes of the society in which they lived Celia's situation was a far greater sin than anything to do with battles and war. People just about managed to cope with men not returning from the fighting, but for a girl to have a child out of wedlock was unthinkable. As at no other time in her life, Muriel knew that, as Celia's mother, she needed to form a plan that would avert a crisis. And quickly.

She tried to keep her voice calm and almost succeeded. 'Have you any idea what will happen when your father finds out?'

With eyes as wide as saucers, Celia had jumped off the side of the bed and looked down at her. 'You don't understand, Mama. David and I *will* marry. Please, just let me talk to David and then father will be as happy as we both are.'

Heartbroken, Muriel knew that even as she turned her mind to dealing with her worst nightmare, in all probability others were already determining her daughter's fate. The looks she had been getting from the loathsome Lilly Jenkins lately had not escaped her. It was unlikely that Celia's morning sickness had gone unnoticed by the staff. How long before it was brought to the attention of her father? Much as she dreaded shattering her daughter's romantic fantasy, Muriel knew she had no choice but to tell her what would *really* happen.

Holding back the tears that threatened to engulf her, she took hold of her daughter's hand and pulled her back to sit on the bed. 'Celia, nothing will allow your father to let you marry in your condition. Had you been only a month or two on, your pregnancy might have been easy to conceal. At least we could have said that the baby came early. But nothing will hide this from anyone. You know that I am afraid of your father, and with good reason. Celia, I beg you to do what I say. Because once he knows, there will be nothing anyone can do to save you.'

Celia looked at her as if she were a stranger, her mouth opening in a silent cry of protest. Before she was able to voice it, Muriel continued, 'The only thing I can do is arrange to have you sent away and then we can sort things out without him ever finding out.' Gazing into Celia's shocked eyes, Muriel could see her daughter thought she was insane.

'It has nothing to do with father,' Celia burst out. 'David and I love each other, we *will* marry. Why are you looking at me like that, Mama? You look so frightened! I thought you would be pleased. I am going to spend the rest of my life with the man I love and we are going to have a baby, your first grandchild. Surely you can find it in your heart to be happy for me?'

With a heart that felt as heavy as lead, Muriel shook her head, 'David Gillespie, will not be marrying you, Celia, he ...'

Before she could continue, Celia screamed back. 'Mama, it's the 1940s; we are liberated these days don't you see?' Her voice sinking to a whisper, she added, 'You *must* see; we *will* marry. David and I have many times talked about marriage once the war is over.' She looked down, rested her hand on her stomach, her lips curving in a soft smile, 'It will just be a little sooner than we'd planned, that's all.'

It was all just too much and Muriel with contempt thick in her voice, retorted, 'Liberation from what, girl, common decency?'

Celia looked up in horror. 'Then tell me, Mama, why did he say all those things to me when we were ...?'

'Please,' Muriel shrieked, 'spare me the details of your behaviour! Is it not enough that I have to know that you, a Bryant-Smythe, are in such a condition that our name will be dragged through the mud and beyond? Since you were born I have loved you, nurtured you, hugged you and kept you safe, Celia, but I cannot save you from this. What have I done to deserve that you should bring us all to ruin?'

'Mama, please stop worrying. It will be all right. Let me speak to David, I know he will sort this out. And please, rest assured, we *will* be married. People will soon forget that our baby came early. It won't matter ...'

Muriel held her hand up to stop her daughter's pleading. 'Dear God, child, listen to yourself! How *can* you be so ignorant as to believe that?'

Seeing the expression of shocked disbelief on Celia's face was too much: the tears Muriel had fought to keep in check spilled down her cheeks. She knew she must do something straight away to try to limit the damage, but the weight seemed almost impossible for her to carry. Even so, she must do whatever she could to help her daughter escape Henry's wrath. 'God help us,' she prayed, shuddering to think how her husband would react; in the extremity of rage he was not beyond physical violence. With these thoughts crowding her head, she got up and walked to the door.

'Celia, I will do whatever I can to get you away, but you must keep to your room until I have everything sorted out. You have disappointed me beyond words, but I am still your mother and despite all of this, I do love you.'

With this said, Muriel left the room, quietly closing the door on her daughter's anguished storm of weeping.

Chapter FOUR

Dragging her steps, Muriel walked slowly along the landing to Celia's bedroom, knowing she was about to break her daughter's heart. Several days had passed since that dreadful, bleak, black day when Celia had confided in her. Since then, her worst nightmare had come true; it seemed that Henry had already been told of Celia's condition – doubtless by the housekeeper - and had taken matters into his own hands, leaving her powerless to proceed with her plan of concealment. And now her daughter was to be banished from her home forever.

Pushing open the bedroom door, Muriel saw that Celia lay curled like a child on her bed, but hearing the door squeak on its hinges she unfurled herself and turned towards the sound. Her eyes were puffy, her face pale, she had clearly been weeping.

Muriel ached for her daughter, aware that she must have been hoping and praying to hear from her lover, unable to understand why there had been no word from him. There would be no more talk of marriage or anything at all to do with David Gillespie, for he too had been forcibly banished and to a wilderness far more dangerous than the one her daughter must now face. As hard as it was, Muriel knew it was best to let Celia believe David had abandoned her.

With Henry's cruel words still ringing in her ears, she stifled a sob. She had failed to protect her child as a mother should. In some ways it was as though history was repeating itself, for she too had been thrown to the lion's den all those years ago when she married Henry Bryant-Smythe. Her parents, completely taken in by his lies and charm had all but pushed her into his arms and she, a young girl on the verge of womanhood, had been powerless to resist. If only she had refused him their daughter would not have been born and would not now be facing a cruel and lonely future. Muriel felt as if her life had turned into a nightmare, one she had believed could happen only in novels, such as those by the gifted Brontë sisters. Not in *real* life; not here in her own home and most importantly, not to her poor, beautiful daughter.

Celia had sat up and was gazing at her as she walked across the room. 'Mama, please tell me you have heard from David?' she begged, gasping in fear as she saw her mother had been weeping and what that implied. 'Please, please tell me that you have!'

Hearing the despair in her daughter's voice, Muriel wanted to close her eyes, ears and mind to everything that was happening. The speed with which the events of the last week had taken place had frightened her beyond words. Yet she knew she must rise above her fear and from somewhere deep inside herself find the strength to do what she had to do. She looked down at Celia's taut, white face and for a moment said nothing.

'Mama, what is it? You're frightening me.'

How Muriel wished with all her heart that she could reassure her, tell her that she had explained things to Papa and spoken with David Gillespie. If only it were true. Instead, she must break the distressing news to her daughter that there was no chance of her marrying, hastily or otherwise, and that it was highly likely she would never see David again. Not only that, but her father no longer acknowledged her as his daughter and wanted her gone from Satchfield Hall forever.

With a heavy sigh, she said, 'I am so sorry, Celia, I wish I could share your naïve optimism that you and David Gillespie will be married, but I am afraid it is not to be. I know for a fact that he has gone to join the army and that even as we speak he is with his regiment on his way overseas. I am afraid you must accept that his feelings for you were not as you imagined.'

'No! No! This cannot be happening,' screamed Celia hysterically. 'It's not true! It *cannot* be true. He told me he loved me, over and over. He said we would be together. He never once mentioned becoming a soldier and going off to war, in fact he said it was not necessary, that his work gave him special dispensation from call up.' With tears streaming down her face, her fingers plucking at the bed cover, Celia's voice sank to a whisper. 'He wouldn't have gone without saying goodbye. Mama, please, Mama, tell me it's not true.'

'I'm afraid it is. I'm sorry. You have to understand that men will say anything to get what they want, Celia. Had you only resisted his advances instead of allowing him to …'

Rigid with shock, her tear-streaked face ashen, Celia clapped her hands over her ears and shook her head from side to side, a long drawn out moan escaping from her lips.

Muriel could take no more. Witnessing her daughter's misery left her feeling weak and totally drained, but she knew she had to keep her mind alert and focused. For all their sakes, she must get Celia off the bed and out of Satchfield Hall. She had spent these last few days trying to steer Henry into being lenient and though she had not won what she wanted, she had at least managed to ensure her daughter would be looked after, albeit at a distance, but a safe one nonetheless, and thankfully, Celia's whereabouts would be known to her. It could have been a lot worse had Henry had his way.

To achieve this small victory, Muriel had used all her knowledge of her husband, persuading him that his reputation would suffer were it to be known he had refused to provide for his daughter. And it soon would be, because the servants would tittle-tattle if he simply turned Celia penniless out onto the street. How would that look to his business associates? They would think he was not only heartless, but worse, financially compromised. It was the right – indeed, the only – argument that would sway him, as Muriel well knew, but she also knew that unless Celia left within the hour, he would as likely change his mind.

At the sudden knock on the bedroom door they both flinched. A look crossed the distance between them and spoke volumes: volumes of fear. Muriel turned to the sound as the door opened. Seeing it was the new maid, Lizzie Rainbow, Muriel sighed with relief.

'Do come in, Lizzie, I've been expecting you,' said Muriel in a voice that sounded more in control than she felt. The girl stepped into the room, her head bowed. Keeping her gaze on the floor, she shuffled further into the room closing the door behind her.

'Celia, get up off the bed,' said Muriel as she beckoned the maid over, 'I've asked Lizzie to help you pack.'

Shocked to her core, Celia jumped off of the bed, her mind still grappling with and failing to grasp the earth-shattering news about David. 'Pack! Why? Where am I going?'

With a small shake of her head and a look that said, 'Not in front of the servants,' her mother did not enlighten her. Dumbfounded, she watched Lizzie follow her mother into her dressing area then, in a tone that froze her heart, heard her say softly, 'Please, Celia, just let Lizzie pack your things into your trunk.'

The unexpected gentleness in her voice brought fresh tears to Celia's eyes as she stared at her mother, who looked ill and exhausted and had clearly been crying. In that moment Celia realised that Mama was on her side and had tried to help, but had failed. *She has never been able to stand up to my father*, thought Celia, certain that he was behind this. Was it surprising her mother's efforts had been in vain? *She has argued and lost, and that means so have I.*

Frozen with shock, Celia watched in silence as Lizzie scurried around, pulling clothes from the closet and the heavy chest of drawers. She could not believe this was happening to her. She wanted to scream and shout, but then, hadn't she been doing that for days, and where had it got her? She shivered and rubbed her arms, becoming aware that the room was icy cold. Just as her mind registered that fact she saw that her mother was also shivering, but from the look on her face it was as much from fear as the freezing temperature. It was the same expression she always wore when Papa was angry about something.

Wondering what lay in store for her, Celia began to tremble. Whatever fate awaited her, it could only have been arranged by her father. He had not even troubled to speak to her and she knew he must be in a towering rage. With this knowledge, her body took on a numbness that rendered her almost immobile. 'What is going on, Mama? Tell me, please,' she begged, but again to no avail.

Several moments passed, and apart from the swishing of fabric as it was being pulled from coat hangers, the only other noise in the room was the wind snapping the drapes at the open window. The longer the silence lasted, the more fearful Celia became. She had hoped that the hours and days she had spent alone since talking to her mother had meant that something was being arranged with the Gillespies. She had dared to hope Mama was wrong and that Papa, although enraged to learn the truth, would support their marriage. But as the days crawled by with no message from David, she had become increasingly confused and frightened by his silence, tiny doubts creeping into her mind as she heard again the contempt in her mother's tone. Had David, having had his way with her, shunned her because of her 'loose behaviour'?

Despite her fears, Celia had begun to hope that at the very least something had been organised to sort things out for her, but now, looking around her room, she knew that nothing could ever be sorted out. Everything she had feared had come to pass: David Gillespie had, it seemed, deserted her; he had not loved her after all, but had only wanted to make love to her and because she had let him, now she was to be taken away from her home. It was all too late to beg and plead. Lizzie, rushing around in her room packing things into the big travelling trunk, was a clear indication that the die had already been cast. Looking at her mother's taut, careworn face, Celia wanted to tell her how sorry she was for causing so much pain, but she could not speak, because she could not get out of her head that David had left her. She became aware that Lizzie was staring at her and saying something, but the words seemed to come from a great distance and she could not make them out.

Terrified of *The Situation* and afraid that Miss Celia, who looked so lost and forlorn, was about to collapse, Lizzie tried again. 'Is there anything else I should pack before I close your trunk, Miss Celia?'

Lizzie knew the goings on were nothing to do with her; after all, she was just a lowly maid in this big, cold house. Even so, she felt very sorry for Miss Celia. She had thought the family, them being so rich and powerful, would have looked after their only daughter in this situation rather than make such a fuss. It wasn't like this sort of thing didn't happen all the time. She knew it only too well: it had happened to her own sister.

Just thinking about Patsy made Lizzie want to cry. Mum and Dad had gone off at the deep end and blamed the Yanks, but Lizzie knew it was no Yank that got her sister pregnant, it was Jimmy Berry. Now, neither Patsy nor Jimmy was alive and her parents blamed themselves for what had happened. The only thing in Lizzie's mind they should blame themselves for was being so worried about what people would say they'd sent Patsy away to have her baby. 'Out of sight out of mind,' Mum had said, but tongues had wagged just the same, like they always do. Now many wished they had kept their mouths shut, because Jimmy was lying in a grave a long way from home - killed in action somewhere in France was all they'd heard – and her sister had died giving birth to a little boy. Even that poor little mite had not survived. Patsy had been sent away and like poor Jimmy Berry she would never come home.

The family's pain and sadness had driven Lizzie to leave home. She had come to work here at Satchfield Hall to get away from it all, but it had turned into another nightmare: one that frightened the living daylights out of her and stopped her from sleeping. And as if that wasn't enough, here she was caught up in the same kind of mess her own family had so recently gone through. She knew from below stairs gossip that the Squire, having told Lilly Jenkins to sort out a woman to look after Miss Celia, had washed his hands of her. It had taken Lizzie only days to discover that the housekeeper ruled the household with a rod of iron. She was a cruel and spiteful woman at the best of times. Things did not look good at all for poor Miss Celia. Why didn't her family realise their beautiful daughter was here and alive, and that she needed them? It wasn't like they couldn't afford to look after her and her baby. How could people be so stupid?

As she took in the sad scene around her, it was clear to Lizzie than both Miss Celia and the Mistress were scared stiff. The icy atmosphere in the room positively crackled with their fear. She knew that, like her, they were terrified of Henry Bryant-Smythe and that because of this, neither would be able to stand up to him and stop this terrible thing from happening. Miss Celia was being sent away to have her baby, lost and alone, just like Patsy. It didn't seem to Lizzie that the war was changing anything very much, other than to create even more misery.

She looked across at the trunk now filled with Miss Celia's clothes, hesitated, then seeing the Mistress shake her head and walk quietly from the room, pushed the lid down.

Celia, had moved over to the open window and despite the icy wind blowing through it she continued to stand there, ignoring the Arctic blast. She needed to look outside; needed to see her home. She had been born at Satchfield

Hall and loved the very fabric of the place. It was the only home she had ever known. Celia heard her mother walk out of the room, but still she stood staring out of the window.

Her bedroom was one of five, situated at the front of the house on the first floor overlooking the long, wide gravel drive. It had once been flanked by beautiful green lawns; lawns that at times looked like strips of velvet with their perfectly mown stripes. In earlier days, the gardener had, from time to time, changed the stripes to squares, creating a velvety, green chequerboard effect. The borders had once been filled with colourful bedding plants, but all that had changed. Celia could see only rows and rows of vegetables: potatoes, leeks, cabbages and carrots, but no flowers and no grass. The beautiful lawns had long since disappeared, dug over to form part of the kitchen garden in accordance with the War Office's exhortation to 'Dig for Victory'.

The war had changed so much, thought Celia, her hand moving automatically to caress her slightly swollen belly. She could not tear herself away from the window. She wanted to, but she knew as sure as day followed night, that she would never again stand in her room, let alone look out of this window. Whatever was to become of her she had no idea, but for this moment she just wanted to look at her beloved home before it was taken away from her.

The sound of the lid as it closed down heavily on the trunk made Celia turn around.

'Everything's in there Miss,' Lizzie said, as she stood at the side of the packed trunk, her chapped red hands folded over her white apron. She hesitated, looking as though she wanted to say something more, a shy, sympathetic smile lighting up her face. For a moment Celia froze, expecting to hear a word or two of comfort, but with a small shrug of her shoulders, Lizzie, who clearly knew her place, bowed her head and said nothing. It dawned on Celia that she and the new maid were about the same age, they might have been friends, yet the gulf of

Chapter FIVE

Henry Bryant-Smythe stood legs apart, hands on hips, surveying the scene in the great hall. The heavy front door was wide open allowing a blast of winter wind free reign to rush in and freeze the place, but he cared not one iota. The fact that the biting cold air snapped around everyone's face and ankles only added pleasure to his perverse mind. Apart from this minor detail, he was far too preoccupied barking orders to his driver, who was busy loading the car with Celia's trunk, to worry about such trivia.

The sounds of sniffling and the constant blowing of noses, which he knew full well were coming from his wife and bedevilled daughter, began to irritate him. Though he tried to ignore it, his patience had long since been stretched to breaking point and he turned and snarled. 'For God's sake, stop that infernal noise.'

At the same time as he barked at his wife and daughter, he spied the housekeeper, Lilly Jenkins, eavesdropping from the room next to the drawing room, where the door was ajar. This added further annoyance to his demonic temper and swinging round to leave her in no doubt as to whom he was referring, he bellowed, 'I suggest you get out here and help instead of poking your nose through gaps in doors and watching on when you should be working!'

Taking a deep breath he told himself that it was high time everyone realised that *he* was the master of this house and nobody should ever forget it. The scene now being acted out in front of him was proof that he stood no nonsense from anyone at all.

Clearly shocked at being caught out, the housekeeper scurried over to stand close to him.

'Don't just stand there woman, go and do something useful,' he hissed, gratified to see her flinch and scuttle away to stand hesitantly at the bottom of the stairs, one hand resting on the banister, the other raised to her mouth.

Turning towards his snivelling wife, he pointed at Lizzie, who was carrying one of Celia's suitcases out to the car. 'That young thing there, the one who wanders around the place frightened of her own shadow, I want her out of here. I suggest she goes too.' Not taking his gaze from Muriel's face, he added in a voice thick with contempt, 'And as for the other one ...' his eyes shifted momentarily to look straight at Celia and as quickly slid away, 'I never want to set eyes on her ever again.' That said, he looked again at the maid, who was standing rigid with fear at being addressed by the Master, her mouth hanging open. 'Yes, you, *get* in the car!' he snapped, his temper bubbling at boiling point.

His wife stared at him as at a stranger. Her look of terror gave him a small pang of satisfaction. It occurred to him for the first time that their loathing was mutual; he cared not a jot. She was powerless to interfere with the arrangements he had made to sort out the sorry mess his daughter had landed him in and she knew it. It came as a surprise when she actually managed to speak.

'Her name is Lizzie Rainbow and she belongs here at Satchfield Hall.'

With a look that could freeze a hot summer's day, Henry raised an eyebrow, 'I don't give a damn what her name is, she is going and that's all there is to it. And from now on, as far as I am concerned, *she* ...' for the first time since they had arrived in the great hall, he met Celia's gaze, part of his mind noting that she looked like a rabbit caught in the headlights, 'does not exist.' Seeing his daughter wince as if he had struck her, he again regarded his wife, allowing her to read in his eyes the hatred he felt for her. '*You*,' he snapped, the word erupting like the crack of a whip. 'You,' he repeated, 'will make sure she is taken care of, whatever that entails, but rest assured, she is no daughter of mine.'

At this point he turned to the housekeeper and shouted as if she was at the other side of the Hall instead of still lingering just a few feet away. 'Earn your keep, woman, and help Miss Celia into the car. And don't forget to check that no bags have been left behind.' He added this because as useful as Lilly Jenkins was - and she was very useful – from time to time he needed to remind her exactly what her position was: he told *her* what to do, much as she liked to imagine it was the other way around.

Jumping almost to attention, Mrs Jenkins rushed over to Celia and grasped her elbow. 'Come now, Miss Celia, Mr Brand will be driving you. It doesn't do to keep him waiting. Believe you me, it's for the best.'

Celia looked at her, a cold, steely look, before she spoke, 'Is that so?'

Mildly amused by this interchange, not that he would ever allow it to show, Henry watched as his daughter shoved Lilly Jenkins out of the way and ran to her mother, who was visibly broken.

Henry tapped his toe in annoyance as the two women sobbed and hugged, 'That's enough, Muriel,' he shouted, 'let the girl go. I want her out of here and out of my sight right now.' Turning on his heel, he strode back into the hall, confident that not one of them would ever dare to disobey him.

Her eyes blurred with tears, Muriel held her daughter as they walked to the car that waited to take her away. 'Celia, you must go, but as soon as I can I will come to see you. Trust me, it is for the best and you will be safe. I will not abandon you. I promise, but please do as you are told and get in the car before your father goes back on his word and turns you out into the street.'

 Moments later, the large car, loaded with all Celia's belongings and a very frightened Lizzie, whisked away her daughter from Satchfield Hall. Shivering, Muriel stood and watched until the car was a black speck in the distance then turning she went sadly back into the house.

Chapter SIX

As the car, driven by George Brand, travelled along the winding empty road flanked by barren hedges and leafless trees that bowed in the cold winter wind, Celia sat ramrod straight gripping the edge of the leather seat. Even the jostling and lurching of the car on the uneven surface of the road did not manage to dislodge her position. She glanced at Lizzie, sitting next to her and staring straight ahead, her eyes unblinking as though she were afraid to move.

Turning to gaze unseeing out of the car window, a constant flow of salty tears slipping down her face, Celia thought through the events of the morning. Nothing her mother had told her made any sense: she simply could not accept that David had forsaken her, but if he had not, then where was he? Why had he made no attempt to contact her? Perhaps he had tried to write to her and her father had intercepted his letter. If so, David must think she had not troubled to reply. Gripped by panic, Celia's mind raced between where he might be and where on earth she was being taken to. Why could her mother not have told her and set her mind at rest? Was it because Papa had told her not to? It would be just like him to want to frighten her in this way.

Celia gasped with fear as she wondered if her destination was to be one of those 'hide-in-the-hole homes' she had overheard the staff talking about. Places that did barbaric things to girls in her condition, relieving their families of any further embarrassment – quite often relieving the girls of their lives at the same time! With her knees pushed tightly together, Celia shuddered at the thought of the torture she might have to endure. Was this to be her punishment? Was she to have an abortion? She tried to tell herself that surely her father would never do such a thing, but by now she could believe anything of him. She hoped against hope that she was wrong, that he was not so cruel and inhuman.

Closing her eyes, Celia prayed that her father had been persuaded by Mama to contact distant relatives and ask them to care for her; she cast about in her mind trying to remember other members of the family she knew, but could think of nobody, distant or otherwise. Only her brothers, and they and gone to fight in the war. She prayed for their safety every day, but just now the dread and terrifying uncertainty that awaited her overshadowed thoughts of them. Her mother had told her not to worry, that everything would be taken care of. *Taken care of!* It was these three words that worried Celia the most. Despite her mother's reassurance that she was not to worry, what else could she do? Here she was with the new maid and no idea where the road she was being driven down was leading too. Her head was dizzy with worry and her whole body was shaking with fear. But even as her mind raced with all these thoughts, a tiny voice in her head tried to make itself heard. Deep down, in the midst of all her pain and confusion, Celia knew she must try to calm herself, if not she might lose the baby: hers and David's baby. Whatever her mother had said about David's feelings, Celia knew with absolute certainty that her baby had been conceived in love. More than anything, whatever the future held for them both, she did not want to lose the child she carried. With a sudden wave of shock she wondered if that was what her father intended to happen after all. Was that why he had sent Lizzie with her so that she could tidy up the mess afterwards?

With this new thought added to her worried mind, Celia turned to look at the only person it seemed she now had in her life. To her dismay she saw that Lizzie looked even more petrified than she felt herself, if that was possible. Whatever was going to happen it was clear they were both as frightened as each other. Celia felt a sudden qualm of guilt: if it were not for her, Lizzie would still be safe at Satchfield Hall. Gently, she reached out and took hold of the young maid's cold, chapped hand and squeezed it tight.

Lizzie turned to look at her and whispered, 'Thank you, Miss.'

Holding hands, they sat in silence as the journey continued, the car turning left and right many times as it travelled along roads Celia had not realised existed, so rarely had she left her home and then only to be taken into the nearby town to visit her mother's seamstress and be fitted for dresses.

When they had been travelling for almost an hour by Celia's reckoning, although it seemed much longer, the road began to climb steeply as if it led up the side of a mountain. At the top it levelled out again and the driver eased the car over to the side of what was nothing more than a dirt track. They bumped along here for about a further mile before he finally brought the car to a stop and turned off the engine.

Without looking behind at his passengers, George Brand got out of the car, walked stiffly to the rear door and opened it. Nodding his head in a slight bow, he spoke in a gentle voice, 'Miss Celia, we are here. Please would you kindly get out of the car?' He did not offer his hand or arm to help her out. Despite having known her since she was a child, he was far too nervous and embarrassed. George was fully aware of the condition of the young Miss and whilst it was nothing whatsoever to do with him what the gentry got up to, nonetheless he was shocked. 'Who'd have thought such a young and pretty thing could get up to such things?' He had foolishly said this to Lilly Jenkins, who had added more than she should have. He had ignored the housekeeper's barbed tongue, moved to pity for Miss Celia's plight.

Now, waiting for her to get out of the car, he felt even sorrier for her. Underneath her puffy features and sad, swollen eyes he could see she was beautiful and somehow that made it all the sadder. From now on life was going to be very different for the poor lass, gentry or no. As these thoughts flickered through his head, George realised that his own life, for the moment, would also change. He was going to be doing a lot of running around for Miss Celia, but he had been told by the Master to forget that he knew anything about her whereabouts. He was no fool: he could keep his mouth shut with the best of them, especially when paid to do it. He was also wise enough to know that should he utter a word, he had far more to lose than Miss Celia ever would have. Nobody crossed the Squire who did not live to regret it.

Holding the door open, George stood and patiently waited until his charge had fully alighted. He noted her hand, white knuckled, gripping the top of the door as if she were afraid to step away from it. Thinking to give her a moment to collect herself, he made his way to the back of the car and opened up the back, leaned into the cavernous boot and with all the strength he could muster hauled out the young lady's trunk.

Standing by the car, swaying slightly, Celia heard George Brand struggling with her belongings: his laboured breathing echoed around in the still air as he dragged at her trunk. When she heard the thud as it dropped to the ground, she let go of the car door and walked slowly round to the other side, aware that Lizzie had followed her.

Celia stared all around in the hope that something might tell her where she was. It did not, though her eyes widened in amazement at where she had been brought. It was as if she had been hauled to the top of a mountain and the whole world was laid out before her. The view was not only breathtaking, it made her sway and to catch her balance she clutched the car for support. If she had not felt so frightened she might have laughed, because for a strange moment she thought she had been dropped outside the gates of Heaven, since the height from which she could look down onto the world below was so incredible. The hilly countryside, dotted with sheep and distant clumps of woodland, stretched out beneath her, misty and forbidding. She could see no house in the immediate vicinity, just a closed wooden gate at the side of the track and beyond it a cinder path that seemed to lead to nowhere. Shivering, Celia pinched herself to confirm that she was still awake and not caught up in some dreadful nightmare. She became aware that Mr Brand was speaking to her.

'This way, Miss Celia,' he beckoned and trod across the frosted grass verge towards the gate. Standing in front of it, he reached over and pulled back the large bolt that kept it shut. The gate creaked softly as he pushed it open and Celia, at last moving away from the car, saw that the path curved round to a cottage. It was long and low, tucked into the side of the hill and blended so well with its surroundings that she had not noticed it until now. As she looked, fingers of apprehension clawing at her stomach, a ruddy-faced woman came into view, walking towards them along the cinder path. She was smiling and in a cheerful voice called out, 'Good afternoon, Mr Brand, you've made it up here all right then.'

Gladys Thrift had met George Brand for the first time less than a week ago, and what a whirlwind time it had been. Her hectic days had all been down to the rushed arrangements organised from Satchfield Hall. Plucked from a nice little job looking after two bonny children in the village, to suddenly be living in a pretty cottage that sat on the top of the world, her feet hadn't touched the ground since Lilly Jenkins had sought her out. Mind, she wasn't complaining. The price for this lovely set up was simple; she had to look after the needs of a Miss Celia Bryant-Smythe. It was all a bit complicated, but she would do her best and life for her had unexpectedly improved.

Now, as she saw George Brand again, her heart skipped just a tiny extra beat; she hoped things might improve there too. There was something very charming about him, she thought, as he answered her.

'Glad we've got cars these days, a horse and cart would struggle to get up here.' George Brand gazed down onto the valley and then back at her as if he wanted to say something else, but he did not get the chance because just then the young woman, whom Gladys assumed to be Miss Celia, came to stand beside him. Gladys was sure she saw a flash of disappointment in George Brand's eyes before he looked away, which made her smile with delight.

'Hello Miss Celia, welcome to Ridge View Cottage,' chirped Gladys at the sight of her new charge. The poor girl looked frightened to death and had been crying so much her face was all puffy and pink. Just behind her stood another slip of a girl, presumably Miss Celia's maid since she was carrying a suitcase. She too looked petrified.

'No doubt you are wondering just where you are,' said Gladys. 'Well don't you be bothering yourself too much on that score at the moment, best we get you inside in the warmth, then we can do the proper introductions.' She bustled towards Celia and without hesitation took hold of her arm as if she was a long lost friend, then carefully guided her along the path and into the open door of the cottage, the maid, as if she were Miss Celia's shadow, following meekly behind.

Once indoors, Gladys pointed to the blazing fire, which roared and crackled up the blackened chimney. 'You two girls wait there a moment and get warm and just as soon as Mr Brand's got your things in, I'll make you both a nice cup of tea.'

As Celia and Lizzie moved gratefully towards the fire, Gladys nodded to George that he should bring in the trunk. She would have liked him to stay, but knew it was best he did not linger. 'I'd ask you in for a cup of tea, Mr Brand,' she said, keeping her tone cheerful to hide her disappointment, 'but I think it best if you leave us to settle in.'

Walking over to the scrubbed table top she picked a bag of homemade biscuits and a thermos flask filled with hot, sweet tea, which she had put together earlier. 'This should keep you going until you get back.' She smiled at George, her fingers brushing his leather-gloved hand as she handed over the goodies, 'Though I'm sure we'll be seeing plenty of you in the coming weeks,' she added, hoping it was true. Gladys knew she had enough to be doing, settling in Miss Celia and the maid, whom she had not been expecting, without being distracted by the driver, but nonetheless she wanted him to return as soon as possible.

George nodded and accepted the gift. 'Thank you, most kind of you I'm sure. I'll go and fetch Miss Celia's things in then.'

Gladys waited, holding the door for him. Moments later, with much huffing and puffing, he was back carrying the heavy trunk, his face flushed with the effort. 'Where do you want it?'

'Just down there will be fine,' she said, watching as he carefully placed the trunk on the floor where she indicated.

'I'll say goodbye now, then,' he said and turning to leave, gave her a shy smile, adding in an undertone, 'I'm right glad you'll be taking care of the young Miss.'

At Satchfield Hall, Muriel, oblivious to the freezing blast that whistled in through the open door, had watched as the big black limousine slowly made its way down the long drive to the great ornate gates. She had stood stock still, yet in her heart she had wanted to run as fast as her legs would carry her after the car and snatch back her daughter, hold tight and tell her just how much she loved her and that she would always be there to care for her.

She had wanted to scream at her husband and tell him just how lucky he was having a daughter and what on earth was he thinking about, sending her away? She had so wanted to do all these things, but even though her vision had been blurred with desperate tears as she watched the car grow smaller and smaller, she had known that what she wanted most of all was for all this madness to have been stopped in the first place. Surely marriage would have been the obvious solution? David Gillespie should have been forced to do right by her daughter. How she wished she'd had the courage to speak to the Gillespies, but it was no use; her husband had forbidden it and he was far too powerful to go against or stop. Others had tried and failed, to their cost, in the past.

Muriel acknowledged her own weakness; her husband frightened her witless, he always had, but no matter how long it took, for as long as she drew breath she would strive to find the strength, and one day she *would* stop him. She said this to herself in a soft, but determined whisper as she watched the car pass through the gated opening and disappear. Only then, when there was nothing left to be seen, had she slowly turned away and closed the heavy door.

Bowing her head with sorrow and sadness, as the tears rolled down her powdered cheeks she asked herself again and again, why did this have to happen? She had borne four children: three sons - all of them away fighting in the war - whom she might never see again. And, if that was not enough, her only daughter had been banished from her home, and if Henry Bryant-Smythe had his way, banished completely from their lives.

Chapter SEVEN

'Sit down, dear,' Gladys Thrift said in a soft voice, as she ushered Celia to an armchair by the fire. 'My name is Gladys, Gladys Thrift, and I've been charged to take care of you. You're safe here with me.'

The woman's cheerful kindness stopped Celia from shaking. Soon after entering the cottage, she had realised her greatest fear had so far been unfounded, for this did not appear to be a 'hide-in-the-hole home'. Now, sitting in the chair as directed she gave Gladys Thrift a wan smile, not because she was happy or afraid - in fact every emotion in her body had frozen, she simply felt numb - but because she had never been called 'dear' before. Of late, she had been called many things, none of which she wanted to dwell upon, but until now, never that. Of course, she had heard the household staff in Satchfield Hall calling each other 'dear', but never once had anyone said that to her, not even Mama.

Celia found, in a strange way, that she liked the sound of it. Here she was in the middle of heaven only knew where, and a complete stranger had spoken to her kindly. For the past week no one, with the exception of her mother and Lizzie, had shown any kindness to her. The rest of the household, along with her father, had completely ignored her unless it was to tell her what to do, usually Lilly Jenkins, and always in a frosty tone. Whenever she had ventured from her room, the staff, who in the past had always been friendly, had walked by her in silence and refused to meet her gaze.

It had seemed to Celia that ever since the day she had told her mother she was pregnant, believing that it would have a happy and celebratory outcome, she had become invisible to the household in Satchfield Hall. She had asked herself, during those long, silent hours in her room, what was worse: the snarling, clipped tones that occasionally came her way or the wall of silence that had apparently been erected against her. It was a pointless question, one that did not deserve an answer because her life had become so unreal. It was as if she were living in a time capsule, suspended in the worst possible nightmare and unable to do anything to change what was happening. Gladys Thrift's unexpected kindness was almost her undoing, bringing fresh tears to her eyes as she struggled to stifle the sob that lodged painfully in her throat.

The sight of Celia sitting huddled in front of the fire made Gladys Thrift's heart melt. Nothing had prepared her for such a frightened young girl. She had been told all that was necessary, but it changed nothing as far as she was concerned. She could see the girl looked desolate and scared out of her wits.

'You're shivering, come on now, let's get your coat off and then you can get yourself comfortable. I made sure the fire was as big as the grate could take. It always makes me feel better if I can feel the heat from the flames, especially when it's on my face,' Gladys said in an attempt to comfort the poor lass.

She took the coat from Celia's trembling hands and was surprised to see that despite the girl's loose clothing, she was clearly in the family way. Lilly Jenkins had not said how far on she was, no wonder she looked so pale and drawn, poor lamb, her life was not only a mess but likely ruined forever. Gladys had seen far too many girls lose their families once they had got themselves into trouble; cast out like last week's rubbish. These thoughts made Gladys sigh and shake her head. Had she been a different person, one from the privileged classes, then she would certainly have told that Henry Bryant-Smythe a thing or two: how he should be thankful not only that he had a beautiful daughter, but that she was safely at home and alive. There were so many families in pieces with the war and what it was doing to them, who had no choice. In Gladys' view, the Bryant-Smythes' reaction to their daughter's pregnancy was not only heartless, but stupid. Money and power such as the Squire had at Satchfield Hall created cold, selfish people who cared for nobody but themselves. Gladys could only hope that all the suffering everyone had to endure right now would eventually ensure that the Henry Bryant-Smythes of this world got their comeuppance. He certainly deserved it, she thought with disgust. She was just considering what retribution should be handed out to the likes of him when the sound of sobbing sound broke into her thoughts. To her dismay she saw Celia shaking and tears rolling down her pale, thin cheeks.

Bending over her, Gladys took hold of the girl's cold hand, 'Come on now, dear,' she said, keeping her tone soft and gentle, 'it's not going to be all that bad. You've got me now and I'm going to look after you right until you have that baby.'

'You mean I *can* have the baby? Thank God!' the girl cried, her voice choked with relief, her tears spilling unheeded as she stared up at Gladys. 'You have no idea what terrible thoughts have been going through my head, but now I know everything will be all right. David will come back from the war and see his beautiful child and we will be a proper family.'

For the first time since she had arrived, Celia's face lit up in an involuntary smile. It transformed her features and seeing her true beauty, Gladys' heart melted. She didn't know anything about a David or anyone coming back from the war. All she knew was that this young girl was too far gone for an abortion and she was to be kept here for the remainder of her pregnancy. Gladys had been tasked to see her through to the birth and then make sure the baby was taken to a family as would be arranged; not an orphanage where it could be traced. Gladys did not have the heart to mention this now. Pleased to see her young charge calming down, she had no intention of putting right any misunderstanding at this stage. Time enough for that later.

With the young Miss settled for the moment, she bustled away from her, anxious to see about getting the maid settled and her chores sorted out. Just a slip of a girl she was, standing motionless, still clutching the suitcase and staring at the floor. What she was doing here, Gladys had yet to learn, but keeping her occupied was what was needed. She beckoned the maid into the kitchen and set about making her feel at ease. 'First things first, you can call me Miss Gladys,' she said kindly, 'and what should I call you?'

Hearing the low murmur of voices coming from the kitchen, Celia, watching the flames dancing up the chimney, settled back in the large chair. The fire enveloped her in a comforting heat that made her feel drowsy. 'I'm going to be allowed to have my baby,' she kept repeating to herself. 'I should have trusted Mama. Everything is going to be all right.' For the first time in over a week she felt a sense of calm drape itself over her like a warm, soft blanket.

The room was filled with the mouth-watering smells of home cooking, which appeared to be drifting from a small wrought iron cupboard, like a tiny oven, at the side of the fire. She had never seen anything like it before. 'It must be one of those bread ovens I've read about, like they have in old cottages,' she mused, surprised that she found the aroma so appetising when usually the mere thought of food made her feel queasy. She had not eaten properly in days, the few morsels she had managed to keep in her mouth and eventually swallow had rapidly returned. Yet whatever was cooking in that cupboard, it smelt so good that for the first time in ages she actually felt hungry. She was just debating with herself whether it was because of the shock of everything that was happing to her, or simply the result of the country air, when a large mug of steaming hot tea was thrust into her hands.

'Take this, it will calm you down and warm you through at the same time,' smiled Gladys as she handed over the pot of hot liquid.

Celia had never held a mug in her life. Tea had always been poured from a bone china teapot into delicate matching cups, which sat perfectly in their saucers, with sugar lumps in a silver bowl and silver tongs and teaspoons. What she stared down at was not china nor did it have a saucer, but all the same, she lifted the heavy mug to her lips and sipped the tea. It was milky and sweet the way she liked it, but as it slipped down her throat and warmed her insides, Celia was gripped by a pang of homesickness and once again began to sob.

At Satchfield Hall the door to the drawing room flew open and Henry Bryant-Smythe strode in, rubbing his hands together as he made his way over to stand in front of the fire. 'Thank God for those bloody trees,' he barked. 'If we'd not got them felled when we did, we'd be sitting here freezing to death.'

As he spoke he turned so that his rear soaked up the warmth from the blazing logs. He gazed into the room avoiding looking at his wife, but he knew what she was doing: weeping again into her linen handkerchief. It was a soft weeping, but he heard it nonetheless and the noise annoyed him. Grimacing his disgust at her feeble behaviour, he added in a voice thick with contempt, 'You'd have a lot more to cry over if this fire was out, that's if your teeth would allow it with all the chattering they'd be doing with this bitter weather we're having.'

A sardonic smile crossed his lips at his attempt at humour as he turned back to face the heat. By good fortune he had managed to sort out three nasty problems in one fell swoop. There were others to do the legwork, of course: he had them all jumping to his tune with his power and influence, but then, he was Henry Bryant-Smythe, the Squire of Satchfield Hall and, most importantly, he was the Master.

Pleased with himself, Henry's smile grew wide with self-congratulation. His daughter's sorry state disgusted him, but he had sorted her out, and as for the cheeky young buck who had messed with her in the first place – the gall of the boy! – well he had been dealt with too. Henry was not stupid enough to publicly associate that peacock with his daughter's condition; oh no, he was much too clever for that. After all, the Gillespies were far too useful to him to create any ill feeling with that family. Instead, their son David, having demonstrated his capacity for lust, had fitted the bill perfectly for sorting out another tricky situation in which Henry had found himself. At the same time he had taught the young whippersnapper a much needed lesson.

He swayed back and forth on his heels and grunted with satisfaction. No one would ever suspect that he, the Squire of Satchfield Hall, had anything to do with the sudden and unexpected call-up of young Captain Gillespie. Had his original plan worked, of course, the Bryant-Smythes and the Gillespies would have been united by marriage and his financial problems a thing of the past, but thanks to the loose morals of his daughter that had not come to fruition, for it was simply not to be countenanced that his daughter should *waddle* up to the altar, her shame clear for all to see and remark upon! Not that he cared what they said about her, aside from the fact that it reflected on him as her father.

As it so happened, nothing had been lost in the end. Indeed, messy as it was, it had worked out better than he could have hoped. His smile grew wider at these thoughts as he stretched his hands to the fire, warming them against the flames. It was a shame he would no longer have that little kitchen maid in his bed: a scrubber in every sense of the word; young, tight, and naughtily frisky. He was going to miss her; she had been just perfect, wriggling around and so willing to learn, but stupid too, threatening that unless he elevated her status and pay she would announce what playing around with him had brought her to. He had soon put her right on that score. With Lilly Jenkins' help it had been simple enough to pack her off and ensure nobody believed a word she said about who was responsible for her condition - and that was where David Gillespie had come in. Henry smirked, murmuring under his breath, 'How convenient. What perfect timing, Captain!'

For the coming night, sadly, his bed would be cold, for he had also got rid of that frigid shadow, Lizzie Rainbow, who despite acting like a timorous mouse, had refused point blank to take the other's place, until in the end his patience had run out and he had forced her, damn the girl! Once upon a time, Lilly Jenkins had kept him satisfied, but not any more: he liked his flesh young and sweet and with her it would be like sucking a lemon, the raddled old tart. But she had her uses and would doubtless find another willing girl to share his bed before too long - if she knew what was good for her.

A smirk lingered around Henry's mouth as he considered all he had accomplished in so short a time. The self-satisfied expression sat perfectly on his handsome features, as natural to him as the piercing quality of his cold, dark eyes. He turned to glare across the room at the weeping woman who had so reluctantly borne him four brats. He had liked not one of them. Had he ever liked her? No, never: she had been the means to an end; a step up society's ladder and a way of settling his debts, that's all. With her wealth, good connections and delicate beauty it had been a feather in his cap when she agreed to marry him. Occasionally, he still insisted she provide him with his conjugal rights; her loathing afforded him a perverse kind of pleasure, but not often. She was frigid and fragile: no better than the silly little maid he had sent packing along with that loose daughter of his. He sneered at the irony of it; Celia clearly did not take after her mother!

Regardless of her tears, Muriel flashed a look of pure hatred at her husband. She had never liked him, but once, long ago, she had thought she loved him; it was impossible to believe that now. How could he stand there discussing the merits of the trees being chopped down or that her teeth might chatter, when their only daughter had been whisked away and if he had his way was likely never to return?

She wanted to say something that could change all of this. She wanted to tell him what she truly thought of him, but none of this would bring her daughter back home. Muriel knew she would be wasting her breath; whatever she said, he never listened. It was a bitter pill to swallow. Yet even as these thoughts tumbled around in her head, deep within herself she could feel a stirring, one that had lain dormant for years and was slowly, very slowly awakening: a feeling of inner strength. Broken woman she may be, but despite her heart being shattered, she began to hope that all was not entirely lost. Her thoughts turned again to her daughter, in her mind's eye seeing the cottage where Celia had been taken and which, until she had reminded him of it, Henry had forgotten he owned.

Gladys Thrift was sitting at the scrubbed wooden table, trying to get acquainted with Lizzie, who was without doubt a frightened little thing. Glancing across at her charge from time to time, Gladys noticed that Miss Celia's eyelids were getting heavy. Not surprising, she thought, what with all the stress and then the hot tea and the warmth from the fire. It had all been too much for her. Gladys smiled with satisfaction when the young woman's eyes finally closed. It was good to see the tortured expression being replaced by a soft glow of contentment as Miss Celia gave in to much needed sleep. She'll be wanting all the strength she can muster in the coming months, poor lass, thought Gladys, turning back to Lizzie.

'There's no need to look so worried, Lizzie, though for the life of me, I don't understand why you've been sent here.'

Squeezing her hands tightly together, Lizzie, bent her head to gaze down at her lap and mumbled, 'Nor do I, Miss Gladys.'

'Well, no doubt the Squire and his lady had good reason, and no doubt they'll be wanting you fetched back when Mr Brand comes with the rest of Miss Celia's things the day after tomorrow.'

Gladys had no idea if that was true, but assumed it was what the girl wanted to hear and hoped it would serve to dispel her fear. Contrary to her expectation, her words had the opposite effect. Gladys was brought up short by the sheer horror in Lizzie's eyes as the girl looked up at last, her mouth working, but no sound coming out. 'Ah ... well, maybe not,' she added hastily, 'it's likely you've been sent to help Miss Celia for the duration. Don't look so worried, girl, I only bite when I'm hungry,' she added with a chuckle, pleased to see Lizzie respond with a nervous smile. It quickly disappeared; the girl was biting her lip, clearly trying to stop herself from crying.

Gladys was no fool. She had been in service long enough to know what went on both above and below stairs. With that knowledge she drew her own conclusions as to why Lizzie Rainbow was petrified of being sent back to Satchfield Hall. For now, Gladys knew she would get nothing out of the young maid, but she would in the end, once the girl unbent a little. For the time being she needed to be kept busy and her mind far away from whatever had scared her half to death back at Satchfield Hall. With this in mind Gladys said, 'Well now, best you help me sort out what's in Miss Celia's trunk.'

'It was me packed it for her,' said Lizzie raising her chin with pride, a little of the nervous tension leaving her taut body.

Relieved to see this, Gladys smiled, 'Well in that case it will make emptying it all the more easy, won't it. Come on then, we'll let Miss Celia sleep and you and I can get to know each other a bit better.'

As Gladys pushed herself up from her chair, she wondered just what she had been asked to take on: a young lady pregnant and ruined and a maid of much the same age, who had been abused or else sent away because she had refused to give in to the Squire's demands. Either way, she too was likely ruined. These important snippets of knowledge had in the last hour changed Gladys' mind about the two people who now shared the cottage with her. Miss Celia was nothing more than a girl. She had expected some bossy little madam who would have plenty to say, but the young woman who had gingerly walked into the cottage was a long way from that.

Gladys had been paid well to carry out her duties. She would do as she had been instructed to do, but it was not going to be as easy as she had thought. In the short time, less than an hour, in which she had become acquainted with Miss Celia Bryant-Smythe and her maid, Gladys had already begun to warm to them, finding herself sympathising with their plight. Essentially maternal, she knew she would grow to like and no doubt love them both in different ways. These thoughts worried Gladys, who knew people were going to get hurt.

Never mind, she told herself, time will sort it all out in the end, but nonetheless, she was disturbed. Pushing these concerns to the back of her mind, she bustled across the rag rug that covered the stone floor and made her way to the back of the cottage where the rooms for sleeping were.

'Come along, Lizzie,' she said over her shoulder, 'follow me, and don't trip over the mat!'

Chapter EIGHT

In the five months since Celia had been brought to Ridge View Cottage, she had grown to an enormous size. Her daily walks with Lizzie had ceased over a month ago and now, lying on her bed, she felt tired and sickly. Increasingly unable to do anything active, she had kept herself from going completely mad with boredom by writing in her diary. Recording what was happening to her during her absence from the world had become the most important task of each day.

From the moment she had arrived at the cottage on that bleak day, which now seemed like a lifetime ago, Celia had logged every detail of her days, including her conversations with Lizzie and Gladys Thrift and the exchanges she had with her mother. She also wrote down her silent conversations with David, which somehow, just for a moment or two, seemed to bring him closer. 'Where are you?' she cried soundlessly, feeling as though her heart was breaking.

As the weeks dragged by, Celia thought back over the times she and David had spent together – all too few - and the words of love he had spoken to her, which continued to echo in her head. She had not had an opportunity to tell him she was carrying his child, so it could not be for this reason that he had left her. Had someone else told him? But surely, had he known he would not have deserted her? It was unthinkable! She was devastated that he had never once written to her, not even penned the briefest of notes, nor left any message to explain why he had so hastily gone off to the war. Try as she might, she could not understand it and night after night she tortured herself by imagining all the dreadful things that might have happened to him.

As these thoughts raced around Celia's head each day she continued to wonder if her father had had something to do with it. That he could be cruel she knew for a fact, but despite his cold and callous treatment of her, she did not believe even he had the power to make David Gillespie disappear.

Not long after she had settled into the cottage, her mother had come for a visit, arriving in the big limousine driven by Mr Brand. Delighted to see her, Celia had begged for news, 'Mama, please tell me about David. What happened? Why did he go so suddenly? Please find out about him for me, I beg you.'

It was hopeless: her mother had just gazed blankly at her for a moment then changed the subject. Not once did she so much as mention David Gillespie's name, not then and not in all her subsequent visits.

All of this and more, Celia entered into her diary in the hope that one day she would see David again and then she would be able to tell him all about how she had lived, perched at the top of the world while their baby grew inside her. The hope of seeing him again never left her. She *had* to believe it.

During the last two months of her pregnancy, Mr Brand, who mysteriously seemed able to obtain an endless supply of petrol despite the constraints of rationing, brought her mother on frequent visits to Ridge View Cottage. Celia, surprised that her father allowed it, soon discovered that Mama always waited until Papa was away from Satchfield Hall on business. Fortunately for them both, whatever dealings he was involved in kept him fully occupied and absent for much of the time. Celia was thankful for this; had she not been able to see her mother as frequently as she did, her spirits would have sunk without trace. Even knowing that her mama had not forgotten her and went out of her way to see her, Celia's heart would not mend. It seemed to be shattered beyond repair at the absence and silence from the father of her child.

As time went on, her mother grew increasingly worried, 'Oh, Celia, I so *wish* I could take you back with me,' she would fret as she got ready to leave.

'It's all right, Mama,' Celia would reply. 'I am quite content here. Mrs Thrift and Lizzie look after me very well, you must not worry,' she would say. And it was true: as much as she missed her home, Celia knew that life would be intolerable for her at Satchfield Hall and despite her increasing physical discomfort and the shame of her banishment, she had settled into her new, simple life at Ridge View Cottage. It suited her quite well.

Today, an hour or so after her mother had been driven away, Celia, even more uncomfortable that usual and convinced the baby in her hugely distended belly was wearing hobnail boots, struggled to pen in her diary the tiny details related by her mother about life at Satchfield Hall in her absence. Her back had been aching all day and she had barely written half a dozen words when she was forced to put down her pen, no longer able to ignore the waves of sickness and pain that seemed to be taking her over. She closed her eyes and tried to construct an image of David's face, but to her dismay his features eluded her. 'Oh, my love, I can no longer see you,' she cried silently. 'What has become of you? Where are you? Why do you not reply to my letters?'

Gripped by another spasm of breathtaking pain, Celia gasped. She let go of the diary and heard it fall with a thud to the floor, her hands balling into fists as she lay back and stared unseeing at the ceiling. She had written so many letters to David since she had been here; Mrs Thrift had assured her they were given to Mr Brand to be sent on to wherever Captain Gillespie was stationed. Had he received them? There was no way of knowing, for she had heard nothing from him. Hot tears of despair trickling down Celia's face; it was clear to her now that she had been brought to a place where no one could reach her, not even the man she loved so much. It hurt so badly that he could have no knowledge of where she was and what she was going through.

As another bout of pain attacked her, Celia let out an involuntary cry: this time it was unbearable and she had no idea how to stop it. Panic seized her. She tried to get herself up off the bed, but it was impossible without inflicting more torment on her body. Even though her heart was beating loudly in her ears, she could still hear Mrs Thrift and Lizzie working in the kitchen. The noise threaded its way through her door, left open this last month to enable her to see the two women and, more importantly, so they could keep an eye on her. Clattering about with pots and pans, baking tins and china plates, they had not heard her cry and neither of them looked her way.

Busy in the kitchen, Gladys was baking: she had a special cake to make. She had learned a few days ago that it was George Brand's birthday and although the event had passed, she wanted to surprise him with one of her delicious sponges. She knew he would be calling at Ridge View Cottage later that day and she wanted to have it baked and wrapped ready for his arrival.

Gladys was always in her element when she was in her kitchen, she loved cooking and baking, and George's birthday had given her a good reason to put on her apron and roll up her sleeves. These days her activity in the kitchen was more out of habit than need: Lizzie ate barely enough to keep a sparrow alive and Celia played or picked at most things offered to her. Because of this, Gladys found that a big pot of stew and a loaf of fresh bread, with the odd batch of biscuits, were about as much as she was required to do. Their needs were so few that rationing had very little impact, particularly since George Brand was always bringing her fresh eggs and other things which, because of the wretched war, were almost impossible to get hold of these days. To her great shame, there had been times when the birds had finished off the bread and the local scavenging wildlife had polished of her meaty stew.

Gladys had been attracted to George Brand from the start, but over the months her attraction had grown into fondness, which she now knew to be mutual. Once things were sorted here, she would be free to spend some time with him. She had told him so only last week when he had asked if he could take her to listen to a local band playing in the village hall. It was on that occasion she had learned about his birthday and decided to make him a cake, wanting to be sure he had something special from her.

As she stirred her cake mixture to a perfect consistency, she thought about Miss Celia, whose pregnancy was causing a great deal of concern. The girl was frequently sick and suffered from bouts of dizziness, which the Doctor had said on his last visit were down to high blood pressure. Gladys didn't like the sound of that at all. Grimacing, she shuddered at the thought of anything bad happening during the birth. Pushing the alarming idea to the back of her mind, she added more vigour to stirring the cake mixture.

Although not a qualified midwife, Gladys had helped many women bring their babies into the world. This experience, along with her reputed loyalty and discretion, was why she had been asked to live at Ridge View Cottage and care for Celia Bryant-Smythe until after the birth. Gladys' own circumstances were ideal for the job: her husband, Fred, had long since disappeared - to where, she had no idea and if she was honest, did not care – and with no children of her own to bring up she had eased her frustrated maternal instincts by becoming a nursemaid. Even at such a ridiculously short notice, she had been happy to accept this job when it was offered by her sister-in-law, Lilly Jenkins, who had been told by the Squire of Satchfield Hall to deal with the family's embarrassing situation.

Gladys knew it would likely be a temporary position, but it made a pleasant change for her and the money was good. She had been warned to keep her mouth firmly shut: Lilly had told her in no uncertain terms what would happen to her if she didn't! Well she need have no worries on that score: unlike her sister-in-law, Gladys was the soul of discretion and whatever Henry Bryant-Smythe had in mind as a threat would most certainly not affect her. Thankfully, she had not met the man, nor would she. Lilly had made it clear from the beginning that he wanted nothing more to do with the situation. A cold, heartless bastard, thought Gladys, but he was paying her for her duties and that was all she needed to know.

She had never liked Lilly; thought her brother's widow a vicious, nasty woman if the truth were told, but it did not do to make unnecessary enemies and although she had kept her distance, out of a sense of duty she had always made sure her sister-in-law knew where to get hold of her should she need to. And it seemed that she had on this occasion. It was a very different job from those Gladys was used to, but it offered far more than she normally received, not just in terms of a wage, but in giving her the opportunity to be mistress of her own domain, no longer at the beck and call of various housekeepers. It was a comfortable cottage and she enjoyed the country life.

Gladys knew that looking after Miss Celia would have its share of heartbreaks. She had been informed of what she must do and what would happen in the end, but tried not to dwell on this aspect. Despite this one bleak side of the job, here at Ridge View Cottage she was free to do what she wanted and as long as she did as she had been told and kept her lips sealed, she would be sufficiently rewarded.

Now, having been at Ridge View Cottage all these months, Gladys not only felt as if she was living in her own home, but she had grown very fond of Celia. She had known from the start this might happen and it disturbed her. Celia could have been the daughter she might have had, had her feckless husband been more interested in her than in all the other women in the neighbourhood. Why he had married her in the first place she could not fathom and sometimes she wondered if her father had paid Fred to take her off his hands; it would not have surprised her. But that was in the past and it did not do to rake over old memories. They were all out of her life now.

Taking the job was not a mistake, but getting too fond of the young Miss was. Hearts would be broken, and Gladys knew hers would likely be one of them in the end. Just as she had predicted, she had even grown fond of Lizzie Rainbow: a decent young lass, hard working and never complaining about having to cycle five miles down to the village for supplies. It made Gladys smile that Lizzie never stopped talking about the wonderful ride down the mountainside or being out of breath pushing her bike back up the hill, the basket brimming with groceries.

Sticking her finger into the cake mix to taste it for sweetness – she had been a bit low on caster sugar and had made do with granulated - Gladys thought through the arrangements that had been made for when the baby came. It would not be long now. She had never enlightened Miss Celia, who still thought she was keeping her child and only had to wait for its father, David Gillespie, to come home from the war. None of this was going to happen. Gladys had wrestled with the problem of how she was going to break the news to the poor young woman and still had no idea. She had been putting it off, deciding to wait until after the baby had arrived before Miss Celia had to be told that not only was she not going to keep the bairn, but the man she loved was dead. The thought of what it would do to her brought tears to Gladys' eyes and she dreaded being the one to tell her. She just hoped the poor lass did not find out what her David had been up to before he went off to the war. 'Well I'm certainly not going to tell her *that*,' thought Gladys, remembering what Lilly had said about what had actually happened.

Evidently, Henry Bryant-Smythe had caught David Gillespie messing about with one of the chambermaids from the village. The girl, who according to Lilly was nothing but a tramp and a liar, had faced instant dismissal, but the Squire, enraged by such goings on under his very nose, had informed the boy's father. Appalled, Robert Gillespie had lost no time in buying his son a commission in the army. No doubt he thought that with David bundled out of sight and out of mind, the ugly rumours would die away before he came home again. Except that he never would come home, for within a week he was dead; killed in action somewhere overseas. It was perhaps no more than the wayward young man deserved, but it was a tragedy for the Gillespie family and also, Gladys supposed, for Miss Celia. Just how many people were going to be hurt beyond repair by this terrible war? And how much misery could be laid at the door of men like Henry Bryant-Smythe? Thinking about the hypocrisy of the gentry and the sadness of it all, Gladys sighed.

She was weighing out the flour to add to her mixing bowl when she thought she heard something, though the maid was making so much noise washing up the pots and pans she could not be sure. 'Hush, Lizzie!' she ordered.

The sound came again: a cry of pain. Still clutching her wooden spoon, Gladys rushed along to Miss Celia's room and saw straight away that the young woman was in labour. Fortunately, the doctor was due later that day. He called in three times a week and had been paid handsomely, both to deal with the girl and to keep quiet about it.

From her experience of birthing first babies, Gladys knew at a glance that it would be some time before he was needed, but she was relieved even so when, some three hours later, having ordered a frightened Lizzie to fetch clean towels and put pans of water on to boil, she had rubbed Celia's back during the contractions and done what she could to keep both girls calm, she heard the now familiar rattling of the doctor's old car as it pulled up outside the cottage.

As Doctor Black brought his Austin 7 to a stop in front of the gate at Ridge View Cottage, he was not thinking about the unmarried Celia Bryant-Smythe. He had too many other thoughts on his mind. The midwife who brought most of the babies into the world in his district had a serious bout of influenza. This worried him on two counts: firstly, the flu was spreading rapidly around the area and secondly, he had no fewer than eight women due to give birth in the next week. Getting round to them all was proving a headache and he just hoped that each household was able to cope with the birth until he could get there, because even he could not be in two places at once and it was sod's law that they would all go into labour at the same time!

Pushing open the creaking driver's door he stumbled out of the car. He was exhausted: lack of sleep and too many sick people to care for was taking its toll. Clutching his heavy medical bag in his right hand, Doctor Black walked down the now familiar cinder path to the front door. With the knuckles of his left hand he rapped on the door, but did not wait to be asked in, he did not have time for such courtesies. Instead, he turned the doorknob and entered the cottage.

The heat from inside hit him straight in the face; it was like an oven. Instead of closing the door behind him, he left it open to let some of the heat out, wondering what Gladys Thrift was thinking of, letting the place get like a furnace. But even as he asked himself this question, the shrieking coming from Celia Bryant-Smythe's room gave him the answer: Mrs Thrift had far more on her mind than the temperature of the cottage; the girl was in labour.

He smiled at the sound, because with all he had to do in the absence of his dedicated and capable midwife, he knew these screams would save him yet another trip back to Ridge View Cottage later that day - or worse, that night. From what he could hear, the baby was well on its way, which meant he would be able to take the little mite with him and straight to its waiting new parents, as had been arranged. Despite his weariness, this cheered him, he had enough to do and if all went to plan it was one less thing to worry about. Though if truth be told, he was unhappy that he had to take the baby away from its poor young mother, but that was what had to happen and he knew better than to argue with the powerful Henry Bryant-Smythe, who had given him a handsome fee.

Two hours after Doctor Black had entered the cottage, Celia's little boy was born. She had never experienced pain like it and with her body covered in sweat and every part of her aching with the effort of pushing her baby into the world, she was exhausted and yet elated. Breathless, she gazed at the miracle Gladys Thrift held in her arms; saw the fuzz of hair, the perfect little face screwed up with anger at being born, the tiny fists waving. She reached out for him, aching to feel the sticky, soft skin of her newborn beneath her hand.

Her fingers closed around nothing. Gladys, never once meeting her eyes, whisked the baby out of her reach, wrapped him in a brand new white towel and handed him over to the Doctor. With a nod and a smile, the little white bundle held carefully in the crook of his left arm, Doctor Black picked up his bag in his other hand and left the room.

'My baby ...' Celia gasped. 'What is wrong? Where is he taking my baby?'

'Nothing is wrong, love. Just let me get you cleaned up, Miss Celia. There's no need for you to fret, the Doctor is looking after your baby, he will be fine, but you need to sleep just now. You must get your strength back.'

Gladys proceeded to wash Celia, talking soothingly all the while, hoping that her voice would mask the cries of the newborn child, which echoed throughout the little cottage and beyond as the doctor carried him out of Ridge View Cottage. Even though she had been complicit in the arrangements, Gladys hated being a part of this. Celia Bryant-Smythe had been denied the most important right known to mankind and that was to hold her baby. But it was better this way. Everyone knew a mother would grieve less if she had never felt her newborn's body against her own.

Working quickly, she rolled the protesting young woman onto her side and pulled out from under her the bloody towels and protective rubber sheeting. Tossing them to the floor, she replaced them with fresh ones then, with capable hands, she stripped off Celia's wet nightdress and proceeded to sponge her body, hoping that for the minute, exhausted and in pain, Celia would not realise her baby had been taken away from her forever. This shock awaited her, Gladys thought, grimly, but by the time she became aware that her pleas to hold him were being ignored, the baby would be well on his way to the family who would bring the child up as their own. Gladys hoped Lilly had chosen carefully and that they were good people, but her anxiety was all for the young woman, whose voice was rising in panic as she continued to plead for her baby.

'Lizzie, where's that fresh bowl of hot water? Hurry up, girl,' Gladys called, seizing a large, fluffy towel and wrapping it around her charge. 'Hush, now, Miss Celia, we'll soon have you comfortable,' she soothed. 'Ah, there you are, Lizzie. Put the bowl down over there and help me with your mistress. There's a clean nightdress and another towel on top of the chest. Quickly now.'

Hearing the rising panic and distress in Miss Celia's voice, Lizzie did as she was told, all the while silently praying as she smoothed the wet rats' tails of hair back from the young woman's face and helped to ease the clean nightdress over her head and down around her body. Not wanting to meet Miss Celia's fear-filled gaze, Lizzie kept her own eyes averted afraid she might break down and weep, because even through the young woman's anguished pleas, begging to see her baby, Lizzie had heard the doctor's car drive away. She could not bear what was happening to her mistress, who over the months had become her friend. She was very fond of Miss Celia; they had grown close in the time since they had arrived at

Ridge View Cottage and it had begun to seem to Lizzie that they were almost like sisters. So much so that at times she forgot that she was employed to look after Miss Celia, who never spoke to her like she was just the maid.

Miss Gladys had never once mentioned what would happen after the birth and nothing had been said about any arrangement for the future. Until Lizzie saw Doctor Black carrying the baby out to his car, it had never crossed her mind that it would be taken away. Both she and Miss Celia had believed the infant would be brought up at Ridge View Cottage and Lizzie had imagined herself filling the role of nursemaid, living happily in the cottage with the child's mother and Mrs Thrift. Nothing had prepared her for what had actually happened. She sniffed and tried to swallow her tears, becoming aware that Miss Gladys was glaring at her.

'Stop snivelling, Lizzie, and finish off here while I go and make Miss Celia a hot cup of tea.' That said, she picked up the bundle of dirty linen from the floor and carrying it in front of her, bustled out of the room.

Lizzie could not help noticing that Miss Gladys' eyes looked moist as if she was trying not to cry, but she did not mention this. Instead, she forced a smile and tried to sound cheerful. 'I've got to get you looking like your old self, Miss Celia. If I don't I'll have Miss Gladys after me.'

Celia shook her head, 'Please go and tell Mrs Thrift to bring in my baby, Lizzie. The Doctor must have finished by now, I'm sure I heard his car go. Why has my baby stopped crying? My breasts are leaking with milk for him and I intend to feed him myself. Go and get him for me, Lizzie, please. I need to hold him.'

Lizzie turned away; she could not hide her sorrow anymore. She rushed out of the room her eyes cascading with hot, salty tears. As she ran into the long living room that served as the sitting room, dining room and kitchen - a far cry from the opulence of Satchfield Hall - she saw Miss Gladys walking back through the front door from the garden: she had clearly been crying.

At the sight of her, Lizzie dashed her own tears away, wiping her eyes on her apron. All she could think of was the milk oozing out of Miss Celia and no baby to take it. It was a crying shame.

'We had no choice, Lizzie,' Miss Gladys said in a choked voice, as though reading her mind. 'The Squire ordered right from the start that the baby had to go. I can tell you it is going to a good home, Doctor Black assured me of this. I do not know where, so there's no point in you or anyone else asking. We must trust the Doctor to ensure the babe is well looked after, so dry your eyes, child. We have to be calm and cheerful for Miss Celia, for I'm afraid there is more. She is never to be allowed back to Satchfield Hall, not ever. Her father wants nothing more to do with her. She has to stay here and so do you.'

Lizzie, her mouth open, dropped into a chair at the scrubbed wooden table and covered her face with her hands. What would become of them all? Poor Miss Celia, she thought, to go through all that and not have her baby at the end of it, and then to lose her home. It was all too much. In a way it was even worse for Miss Celia than it had been for Patsy, because at the end of the day her sister and the babe had died. They didn't have to suffer like Miss Celia was going to. With that thought, Lizzie burst into a storm of weeping.

Chapter NINE

Celia's tortured cries made Gladys want to put her hands over her ears. She had sent Lizzie down to the village for a bag of flour; she did not need any, but it would not be wasted and she had wanted the maid well out of the way before she broke the devastating news to the young woman in her care. As Gladys had anticipated, Celia Bryant-Smythe quite forgot she had been born into a privileged class where decorum must at all times be observed. The girl behaved like any natural mother would when told that her baby had been taken away: she screamed and howled like a wounded animal. Her cries were loud enough to be heard several miles away, had there been anyone to hear, but perched halfway up a mountainside, here in Ridge View Cottage, there was no one except the sheep that huddled on the hillside and they cared not at all. Not for the first time, Gladys was made ruefully aware that the cottage had been well chosen by the Squire; so isolated they never saw a soul from one day to the next.

With the heartbreaking cries piercing her eardrums, she held Celia close, feeling the girl's raw pain and anguish and wishing with all her heart that it did not have to be this way, but knowing it was for the best. The world was not ready for unmarried mothers of Celia's background. Were she to raise her illegitimate child, she would become a social pariah as would her infant. The stigma of bastardy would stick to him all his life. Sad as it was, Gladys knew that in time the distraught girl would get over it – or at least, learn to accept it - but for now, Celia clung to her like a limpet, all the while screaming and begging for her baby.

Eventually the screams died away to an agonised moan. Only then did Gladys gently loosen the girl's grip and move her hands away, helping her to lie down and pulling the covers up around her. Still sobbing, Celia allowed herself to be tucked in like a child and Gladys, forcing back her own tears, murmured, 'Hush now, dear, you will make yourself ill. I'll go and warm a nice drop of milk for you. Things will look better when you've got your strength back, you'll see.'

With a long look at her charge to ensure she was not going to become hysterical again, Gladys bustled out of the room and went to prepare the sedative Doctor Black had left for emergencies. Sleep was the best medicine and in Gladys' view, this was an emergency. Best to keep the girl sedated for the next few days, she decided.

Celia could not remember ever feeling as exhausted as she did now, her whole body throbbed and ached, her hands were bleeding where she had scratched and clawed at them in despair, her throat was raw and she had no more tears left to cry. Worse than any of this was the ache in her heart; she felt as if it had been shattered into tiny pieces that were too small ever to be put back together again.

At first she had not been able to bring herself to believe that her baby, her beautiful, perfect son, had actually been taken from her. She yearned for him, her whole being tormented by his loss. As the reality of what had happened sank in, Celia knew that only one person could have arranged it: her father.

'He has won,' she whispered. As this knowledge penetrated Celia's tired mind, she realised he would not only have made sure the baby's identity remained a closely guarded secret, but paid handsomely to be absolutely certain her child would never be found or known to her. She knew, as sure as night follows day, that her father would have gone to any lengths to ensure her child – his own grandson – disappeared from the face of the Earth as though he had never been born and she would never know if he was alive or dead.

This certainty terrified Celia, sending her into the depths of despair from which she knew she would never recover. Yet even as she sank deeper into depression, she vowed that no matter how long it took - if it meant her entire life - she would find her son and take revenge on her father and those who had betrayed her. She was crushed and broken, but one thing sustained her: she would make sure they paid for what they had done.

When Gladys reappeared carrying a mug of warm, sweet milk, Celia dutifully swallowed the comforting liquid, welcoming the oblivion that quickly followed.

Less than twenty-four hours after Celia had given birth to her son, a message arrived at Satchfield Hall informing Henry Bryant-Smythe that everything had been dealt with as per his instructions, which had been carried out to the letter. Not that he had expected anything less, but it was a relief even so. The money he was paying – and the threats - to those involved, guaranteed their tongues would be stilled and now he could forget the entire episode as though it had never happened.

Alone in his drawing room, Henry walked over to his drinks table and poured himself a generous brandy, knocking back the fiery liquid in one large gulp. Banging down the glass, he lifted the decanter and poured another large one. Catching sight of himself in the mirror over the mantelpiece, he grinned, raised the glass, extended his arm and said, 'Well done, Henry; here's a toast to the nasty business that is now sorted.'

He smiled at his reflection as he swirled the golden liquid around the crystal glass and celebrated his success. He did not need or want company. He just wanted the disgusting episode to be forgotten and now it would be. He brought the warmed glass to his lips and gulped the second large brandy as greedily as the first, content in the knowledge that he had once again resolved a tricky situation.

Pouring yet another drink, he carried it thoughtfully to his dimpled leather armchair and sat down, reflecting that the silence he had paid for was not about protecting his worthless family; he cared not a jot for his daughter or his wife - or anyone else for that matter. He knew Muriel considered him to be brutally cruel and that many others thought his behaviour bizarre, but they did not know that he lived on a knife-edge of fear and uncertainty. Nor would they, by God! He was aware that at times his actions might be considered heartless and callous, but he was not concerned about that. He was driven by his fear that 'the underlings' – as he dubbed everyone beneath the status to which he aspired - would behave in a manner that could undermine everything he had achieved. All his life, from the time of his miserable childhood, he had striven to put himself in a position where nobody could hurt him ever again, as his beautiful mother had done in casting him aside when all he had yearned for was her love and approval.

At times, as now when in a reflective mood, Henry was aware of what drove him. Money was power and power was a drug to him. He would do whatever it took to maintain his status as a member of the respected landed gentry, even if it meant crushing those in his way; hence why Celia had had to be dealt with. *Nothing* could be allowed to destroy the position he had achieved. Looking around at the rich display of his material wealth, the valuable antiques, the precious ornaments and priceless paintings, he smirked with satisfaction. Nobody could come here to Satchfield Hall and not be impressed. He alone knew how vulnerable it all was; the lengths to which he had to go to maintain this show of opulence; the ever-present danger from people who knew too much about those of his business dealings that were not entirely legal.

On top of this, although he would never admit it, this war was causing him a good deal of concern. Not that

Adolf Hitler – that twice-damned fascist - bothered him. Henry was convinced the Nazis had no chance of ever setting foot in Britain, let alone winning the war and taking all the spoils of the greatest empire the world had ever known. No; what worried him was what would happen after the war when the enemy was here on his doorstep: the men who came back from the fighting. Too much had been sacrificed to keep these shores free from invasion. There would be a price to pay for this: social order would be overturned and he was in the firing line.

Uncrossing his long legs, Henry, his glass again empty, inched forward in his chair to gaze out of the tall windows at the sweep of the drive beyond, in his mind's eye seeing the horde of the poor, the working classes, the masses who would want their say and the right to exercise it, marching to his door to expose him as one of them. The image brought a qualm of panic and he shuddered.

'Am I being paranoid?' he asked himself. Possibly, and yet he could never quite dispel this overriding fear of exposure. It was why he had arranged to keep Celia at Ridge View Cottage, away from anywhere where she could cause a problem. Her tongue like the rest had to be stilled. Should others get to know that he, Henry Bryant-Smythe, Squire of Satchfield Hall, had sired a daughter who had the morals of an alley cat, advantages could be taken. He could never allow that. Crush and kill if necessary, but nothing would stand in his way. Whatever it took, he would continue to maintain his position and wealth, both of which fed on each other and gave him the ability to wield the power that kept him safe.

With the brandy settling in his veins and warming him, Henry pushed his paranoia to the back of his mind, reassuring himself that nobody could touch someone of his standing in society. Lives were lost for less, he thought, his warped humour reasserting itself. Lives like that of David Gillespie!

Pushing himself up and out of his chair, the taste of fine cognac on his tongue and his lips twisted in a sardonic smile, Henry went in search of his miserable wife. He was looking forward to seeing her face when he told her the good news.

Flinging open the door of her room, Henry stood for a moment enjoying her startled gaze. He could tell from her expression that she was expecting the news he brought her and he waited a moment, prolonging her suspense, seeing her draw in a deep breath, her fingers fluttering to her throat.

'You'll no doubt want to know that the whore you call a daughter has given birth to her bastard. It was born alive and has been dealt with.'

'Dealt with ...?' she repeated.

He did not trouble to hide the malice of his smile as he watched Muriel struggle with this information. He stood just long enough to see the horror at what she was imagining creep into her face, which only fuelled his repulsion of the woman he had to call his wife.

'What of Celia ...?' she faltered. 'Is she ...? Henry, please tell me she is alive!'

He waited a moment longer, watching her face grow pale; the ever ready tears springing to her eyes, then with a curt nod he snapped, 'Yes,' and watched with glee as tears of relief flooded down her flawless cheeks. He could play her emotions like a fiddle!

Henry knew she believed he had no idea she had been visiting Ridge View Cottage – was she so stupid as to imagine Brand did not keep him informed? Apparently so. He had not stopped the visits, enjoying the fact that it destroyed her a little bit more each time she returned to Satchfield Hall alone. He wanted to see her suffer for allowing their *daughter* – not that he any longer thought of her as such - to disgrace the family name. Muriel should have prevented it. He might have known she would allow Celia to run amok. He would teach them both that he was the Master.

The resentment Henry felt for the high society lady he had married burned deep inside him. It was a thorn in his flesh that he had needed her then, but not anymore. She alone knew that the image he so carefully projected was built on a house of cards. For that as much as anything he wished her dead and there were times when he was tempted to hasten her end - were it not for the scandal that would ensue.

As he made to leave, Muriel spoke in a tone that surprised and momentarily shocked him. 'I promise you, Henry, that you will pay for what you have done and believe you me, I will do whatever I can to make sure you do.'

He bent back his head and roared with mocking laughter, but to his discomfort, an ice cold shiver shot through him as he turned away.

Chapter TEN

Tom and Jean Hargreaves were shocked into a flutter of anxiety and excitement when they received the telegram. The young boy who had delivered it, having pedalled his bicycle from the Post Office as fast as his legs would go, was red-faced and out of breath as he solemnly handed it to them.

Even though they had been expecting to receive it, Tom's hands were shaking so much he had difficulty in slitting open the envelope. In two brief lines of type, the cryptic message conveyed all he needed to know. It was the communiqué that for months they had been waiting for. He looked up, thanked the boy and assuring him there was no reply, tipped him a sixpence and watched as he got back on his bike and pedalled away. Tom then passed the telegram to his wife, who read it out loud, her voice cracking with emotion.

'*THE BOUGH IS BROKEN AND THE SUN IS SHINING, NO DAWN AFTER ALL, DELIVERY LATE TODAY.* Oh, Tom! It's a boy and he's on his way,' she cried, decoding the words they had been told to expect. 'A little boy,' she repeated, clapping her hand over her mouth, tears of joy slipping down her face.

Tom knew she had only ever dreamed of receiving this news. It seemed that not only had her dreams come true, but her prayers had been answered. At long last, after the years of disappointment, they would not be childless after all, but were going to have a child of their own. Swallowing his own rush of emotion, Tom hugged his wife close and voiced his sudden anxiety, 'This will change our life forever.'

She laughed, 'Of course it will, Tom, change it for the better. We've talked about this endlessly and whatever the future holds we are prepared for it, you know we are.'

He nodded. 'A son ...' he whispered, squeezing his wife just a little bit tighter. 'I love you, Jean Hargreaves.'

She leaned back in his arms and looked into his face, her eyebrow raised in surprise. Tom grinned down at her a little sheepishly. He was not normally the kind of man to put his emotions on display, but this telegram had opened up a little window and for the moment his feelings were too strong to hide.

'I still can't believe it,' she sobbed, 'it really *is* going to happen: we are going to have a little baby of our own.'

'I know,' Tom answered thickly, clearing his throat. It was odd that he felt so emotional when he had harboured so many doubts about taking on someone else's child. When they had been offered the baby all those months ago, he had known he could not say no. Jean had wanted it so badly; she needed to be a mother. Now, as he looked at her, his heart swelling with love, he knew it would be the making of her. He too was thrilled by the thought of having a son, but he was also saddened, though only in a selfish way. He knew that from now on he would always come second. Despite this, he could not deprive Jean of what she needed. He blamed himself: he had let her down in being unable to give her a child. He could not let her down again by denying her this chance.

The telegram had arrived just as he had got back home for his dinner, a late dinner time break today: it had been mid-afternoon before he had managed to get back to the cottage. Despite the late hour and the momentous news, Tom knew he had to get back to work. He must tell his boss what had happened. It was hard on the farm just now, what with all the younger men gone off to the war, but he needed to be here when the precious delivery was made. He knew he was needed at the farm too. It was a bad timing because it was a busy time of year, but then, when was farming any other these days?

The clock sitting on the mantelpiece ticked loudly and glancing at it, Tom saw to his horror that the hands were sitting on the new hour. The news of the baby's imminent arrival had taken over every second since he had got home. He had not even eaten the thick, hot soup Jean had made for him. It still sat in the bowls on the worktop in the kitchen, no doubt with a thin skin over the top and cold, but even had he the time to eat it, he had no appetite now, there were too many responsibilities fighting in his head. He had to go back to work so as not to lose his job, but the baby was likely to arrive at any time and Jean wanted him here when it came. He had to act quickly; the adrenalin was pumping fast and strong in his veins and making his head hurt.

Gently disentangling himself from his wife's embrace, he looked into her eyes that were bright and sparkling with joy, and smiled. 'I know you don't want to be left alone, love, I'm sorry, but I must just ride back to the farm and tell Mr Collins. The last thing we need is for me to lose my job with a baby on the way.' Realising what he had said, he laughed, adding, 'I promise I'll be straight back. I'll be here when our baby comes, don't worry.'

Tom did not wait for Jean to say anything; instead, stopping her mouth with a soft kiss, he strode across the clean linoleum-covered floor to the front door. As he opened it, letting in a cold breeze, he turned and called, 'I'll be back before you've even missed me.' He threw her a kiss, it was not something he normally did, but with the news of their son arriving he felt so jubilant he could not help himself.

After he had gone, Jean stood for several seconds staring at the back of the closed door. The door her husband had just walked out of was the same door through which their baby would enter their lives. She could hardly believe it was about to happen. Her hands trembling, she picked up the telegram and read it again.

She wanted to cry out with her joy and tell the world of her good fortune, but that was something she could never do, not ever. They had been told to keep the whole thing quiet. Laying the telegram back down on the table, Jean walked over to the window and peered out. She saw nothing but bare fields and emptiness. Secretly, she had hoped she would see Mrs Green walking down the path with their son, but knew she had to be patient just a little bit longer. Turning away, she bustled over to the chest of drawers and for the hundredth time began turning out all the things she had collected for when their baby came.

As Tom pedalled at speed down the narrow lane to the farmhouse, he could not believe they were really going to be given a child today. Despite being breathless, his lungs almost bursting and hurting from the exertion, he still managed to call out, 'Thank you, God!' And as he watched his white breath clouding the air, he repeated, 'Thank you, God. Thank you so much. My wife will make the best mum you could ever wish for and I'll try to be a good dad, I promise.'

Even the cows in the field, huddled against the brown-twigged hedge in an attempt to stand out of the wind on this cold November day, turned their heads at the sound of Tom's shouts of gratitude. Chewing the cud, they watched in bovine curiosity as he pedalled past at speed towards the farm. Tom was oblivious of their interest. He was far too busy silently thanking everyone he could think of, because he found that despite any misgivings he might have had, he was now so grateful for what he was about to receive.

These last months he had been afraid that the mother-to-be would change her mind when she saw what she had spent nine months carrying. Thank goodness she had not, though it would be only natural, for what mother could give away her baby? It was one of the reasons he'd had doubts at first, knowing that should this happen his Jean would be devastated and he had wanted to protect her from that. Of course, he had never mentioned this to her, but had silently prayed that what they had been offered all those months ago would actually come to pass. And today, it was about to! What a strange old world it was to be sure: him and Jean desperate for a child and unable to have one, and this unknown woman having one she did not want and giving it away. Shaking his head at these thoughts, Tom cycled into the yard, skidded to a halt and jumping off his bike, propped it against the wall of the cowshed. Then, cap in hand, he made his way to the farmhouse and knocked on the door. Sam Collins was a good boss; Tom had already told him in confidence that he and Jean were going to have a baby. He would understand.

Jean sighed with relief when, within the hour, she heard her husband arrive home; he had been as good as his word. Always dependable was her Tom, she thought fondly.

'There's a lot on at the moment,' he said, walking into the living room, his breath coming in short bursts from pedalling fast up the lane, 'but Mr Collins said he fully understands and told me to get back to you straight away. I said I'd make up the time and he was satisfied with that. He told me to say he was pleased to hear the good news and he'd send Millie down in the morning to see you and the baby and help you out.'

Jean nodded, hearing what he said, but not taking it in, she was far too busy bustling around, her arms full of baby things. 'We must check everything is perfect for when Jack arrives,' she said, then saw her husband roll his eyes and knew he was trying not to laugh at her. 'What?' she said.

'You're like a cat on a hot tin roof,' he grinned.

'Well what do you expect?' she retorted, 'It isn't every day I have a baby!' She knew she was fussing, but she could not sit still, it would only add to her anxiety. Keeping busy was her way of coping.

'Jack's a fine name, I'm glad we picked that one,' Tom said, wandering over to hang his jacket on the back of the door then returning to check on the wood burner. 'I'll get you in some more logs in a bit,' he said. 'It's bitter cold today.'

She nodded, smiling up at him as he watched her pick up various items of miniature clothing, holding them up to the light to inspect them before placing them back in the same position. Jack was the name they had agreed on for a boy, they both liked it.

'I wouldn't have minded if it had been a girl,' she said, examining one of the many white matinee coats she had knitted during the last few months. 'I hope it will fit him,' she said, hugging it to her. 'Jack is just as beautiful a name as Jacqueline. You never know; we just might get lucky and have a girl next time.'

Jean knew there would never be a next time. She didn't even know why she had said what she just did. Nerves and excitement, she told herself, her silent voice trembling with it all. With the name of their new son still ringing in her ears, she turned her attention to all the things they had ready for their baby's arrival, needing to check everything was perfect. Still hugging the tiny knitted jacket, she looked around, but while her gaze feasted on all the beautiful clothes and the new wooden crib Tom had made, her mind kept racing, she did not know what to do first.

Tom poked the fire to keep the logs burning evenly and to give his hands something to do. For the first time that he could remember, time was ticking away very slowly as they waited for the most important knock they would ever have on their door. Turning from the spitting logs, he watched as Jean walked round and round their little cottage. Everything was prepared for the baby, but neither of them could settle. He looked on as she fussed around with the things they had made, bought or been given. His heart melted for this wonderful woman. She so needed to have a child snuggling down in her arms. She had ached for a baby all the years they had been married, but never once had she made him feel inadequate when at last they had plucked up the courage to seek medical advice and been told he had a very low sperm count. 'It's not impossible your wife will conceive,' the doctor had said, 'but I'm afraid it is unlikely.' Tom had been devastated, but Jean had accepted it philosophically. 'I'd rather be married to you than to anyone else, childless or no,' she had told him and he had loved her all the more.

He continued to watch her folding and re-folding the soft baby garments; placing the mound of towelling nappies in a neat pile together with the large safety pins, balls of cotton wool and a pot of ointment; checking and re-checking the feeding bottles and teats, and the large brown bottle of steriliser they'd got from the chemists, along with a lidded bucket for the dirty nappies. Then lifting down from the shelf the cans of evaporated milk, bottles of orange juice and rose-hip syrup and putting them back again, before inspecting the large, soft towels, the baby bath, soap and talcum powder. And then there was the cradle, and the pram standing waiting in the corner, second hand, but good and clean. The list of all the things Sam Collins' wife, Millie, had told them they would need had seemed endless. Tom had wanted to wait until they were certain about the baby – it all cost quite a bit and his wage was not that great - but Jean had insisted they get everything ready just in case and he had not had the heart to refuse.

'Everything is ready, Jean,' Tom protested, 'it has been ready ever since we were told about the little one,' but he could see she wasn't listening. He couldn't blame her; she had talked of nothing else since they'd learnt about the chance of getting this baby. She would settle down eventually, once they got into the new routine.

'I just want everything right for him,' Jean whispered, looking at Tom helplessly, tears again welling in her eyes.

Putting the heavy poker back into its holder, Tom wiped his hands on his backside and walked over to her. 'I know, love.' He brushed her tears away with his thumb then kissed her softly. Nothing could describe his joy in her: the only person he had ever loved was his beautiful Jean. 'Our son is one lucky baby, for you are going to be the best mum that ever was,' he murmured. 'And he'll be here very soon, so dry those tears now and make us a cup of tea, eh?'

It was dark when, just three hours after receiving the telegram that was to change their lives, they heard the knock on the front door they had been listening for. It was not a heavy rat-a-tat, but a gentle tap, and instead of rushing to the door, they both stood motionless staring at each other.

As the knock came again, Jean gasped, 'Oh!' Covering her mouth with her hand she looked up at Tom, her eyes wide. Only then did he take the few steps to the front door and open it.

A smartly dressed woman stood outside holding a cardboard box in her arms. The sound that came from it was a soft whimper and Tom, gazing down at it, felt his heart melt.

Chapter ELEVEN

The woman known to Tom and Jean Hargreaves as Mrs Green had called on the couple twice before, but this time she was not here to ask questions. Her task today was to complete the deal they had arranged months earlier. She stood in front of the little cottage ready to hand over what she had been well paid to deliver. Her instructions had been clear from the beginning: get rid of the child and remain silent and anonymous, hence the assumed name, Mrs Green.

From Doctor Black she had got the names of several suitable foster homes, but when he had handed her the new born barely an hour ago, he had said he had no wish to know which she had chosen. Fair enough, the fewer who knew, the better. In fact, only George Brand knew where she had brought the baby - simply because he had driven her here - and she was confident he would never reveal what he knew, aside from the money he had been paid, it was more than his life was worth.

Looking at the couple who had agreed to take the infant, Lilly Jenkins was pleased at what she saw. After careful probing she had ascertained they were desperate for a child; so desperate they would keep their mouths shut and not ask questions. It was why she had chosen them, not because they seemed kindly; she did not give a tinker's damn for that. What concerned her was the price she would have to pay if the child's whereabouts were ever discovered. She had made sure the Hargreaves understood the baby would be taken away from them if they ever talked. Not that there was much for them to talk about since they had not the remotest idea of the child's identity, but the least said about how they had come by it, the better. They had been told to tell anyone who persisted in asking that it was a foundling whose parents had been killed in the Blitz and that they knew no more than that. It was not so far short of the truth, after all, and these days it was a common enough problem.

Lilly, satisfied that she had organised everything so that even the good Lord himself would have trouble locating Henry Bryant-Smythe's first grandchild, smiled to herself, thinking that at the same time she had taught that hoity-toity Miss Celia and her equally haughty mother a lesson or two. Lilly had not been in the least surprised when it became obvious Miss Celia was in the family way. She had seen the girl behaving like a trollop with David Gillespie for weeks, but for her own amusement had neglected to warn the Squire. He would have half killed her for not telling him if he thought she had kept quiet about it, but it was worth the risk just to see his face when she later told him his daughter was pregnant. It had sent the fool into such a towering rage Lilly had thought he was going to have a fit! She had narrowly avoided a beating just for being the messenger, but as it happened, she had been able to divert him by suggesting a way out of the tricky situation he had got himself into with a housemaid, which had earned her a pat on the back instead. The reward for her little deed had been a handsome one, and one day she would spend it, but not until she knew she could get no more out of Henry Bryant-Smythe – and that would not be for some time yet, or so she fervently hoped.

She had been his mistress once; had even loved him. Not anymore. He was evil, she knew that, he had used and abused her for more than a year before he had tired of her and cast her aside. But Lilly was cunning: instead of weeping and wailing as he had expected, she had made herself useful to him. She kept him informed of everything that was going on in the household and the village. She had also made sure he had a constant supply of young housemaids: girls selected for their ambition, whose morals were questionable or whom she knew would be easily seduced by the promise of higher pay and an easier life. She had made the odd mistake - Lizzie Rainbow for one, stupid girl - but most of them knew which side their bread was buttered on. So long as Lilly got what she wanted from Henry Bryant-Smythe in terms of her position and the money he gave her, she was more than happy to oblige. It did not take a genius to work out that aside from the Squire himself she, Lilly Jenkins, was the most powerful person in Satchfield Hall; far more so than that milksop wife of his.

Now, looking at the Hargreaves silhouetted against the light from the cottage doorway, Lilly was aware that they were staring at the box she held in her arms, both so transfixed they seemed to have forgotten their manners until, in an apologetic voice, the woman gushed, 'Sorry to leave you standing on the doorstep, Mrs Green, please come in.' Jean Hargreaves dabbed at her eyes with a handkerchief and repeated, 'Please, come on in. You have no idea what all of this means to us.'

'Mrs Green' knew exactly what her visit meant to this anxious couple, which is why she was here, but all she said was, 'Ah, but I do,' and smiled back at them. It came easy to her, this playacting, she reflected. They were not to know that her smile conveyed her pleasure at the misery they were helping to inflict on the child's mother and grandmother.

Jean and Tom Hargreaves stepped aside and despite the cold night air, opened the door wider so she could walk through with her precious cargo. Stepping over the threshold into their home, Lilly looked around and knew the child would most likely have a happy life here, for what it was worth. The Hargreaves were poor, but she could tell they were good, honest folk. The cottage was homely and although sparsely furnished, she could see that next to the fireplace, a new crib had been made in preparation for the baby's arrival. There were small piles of hand-knitted baby clothes on the kitchen table and on the wooden clothes horse were hung several clean, white towelling nappies airing by the wood burner, which was casting a warm glow around the threadbare but spotlessly clean living room.

Lilly Jenkins' smile grew wider. Not that she particularly cared, but in her view she had done this fatherless mite an enormous favour. It would never have to know the evil man who was its grandfather, nor be raised in the fraught atmosphere of Satchfield Hall with a grandmother constantly weeping and a mother who was too young to know the first thing about raising a child and would in any case have had a succession of nursemaids to look after it. Things had gone very well indeed, she reflected. Celia Bryant-Smythe would never find her baby and if she did, it would need more force than the pull of gravity itself to prise the child away from these two people. You only had to look at their faces and the trouble they had gone to, to know that.

Jean could not tear her gaze away from the box held in Mrs Green's arms: it looked like a normal every day carton you would get at the grocer's shop. It could have contained anything from groceries to kindling for the fire, but she knew it held none of these: its content was far more precious than anything else ever could be. Hearing the slight whimpering coming from the box, she lifted her arms to take it from Mrs Green's grasp. Her heart was pounding like a drum: the moment she had been waiting for had at last arrived and once again she thanked God, as she had a thousand times and more, for bringing her this baby.

Although they had been told, during that first visit from the woman now standing in their home, that her name was Mrs Green, for some reason that Jean could not quite put her finger on – maybe it was the sight of the luxurious limousine in which the woman had always arrived - she did not believe for one moment that Mrs Green was her real name. Nor did she care. Whoever she was, it was of no consequence; the woman was offering something she and Tom were desperate to have. It seemed that this dreadful war was not just killing and wounding people, it was also producing unwanted babies. Young girls enjoying their freedom and young soldiers not sure if they would ever come home. It was a dangerous cocktail and one that had consequences neither couple fully understood until it was all too late. For her and Tom it was a blessing; they just wanted a baby and a baby is what they now had.

Right from that first meeting they had been told that anything to do with *Mrs Green* and the cardboard box *delivery* was something that should never be discussed with anyone, ever. That had been the stated condition. It was a condition with which they were both more than willing to comply. It went without saying that their need for a child would always guarantee their silence. Jean's only anxiety had been for the mother, but Mrs Green had assured her that the child was most definitely not wanted. The father was a soldier, possibly an American, but the mother did not know which soldier, hence her reason for giving the child away. That was all they needed to know, she had said.

With her outstretched arms aching to hold their son for the first time, Jean took the box carefully from Mrs Green and then looked down. What she saw, snuggled in a white towel, was the beautiful face of a newborn baby. She was so overcome with how blessed they were to receive this gift from God that her eyes filled with fresh tears and she could no longer see.

Mrs Green turned to Tom, who was gazing in awe over his wife's shoulder, and handed him a sealed envelope. 'This is for you and the baby and to remind you that you take this child as your own and you must never allow it to look for its family. Not ever! You are its only family now. Please remember this. There has been enough pain, we don't want any more and you don't want to lose him.'

Tom nodded and took the envelope, though did not open it, 'You need have no fear on that score, Mrs Green.

This is our son; we are the only family he will ever know. You can be sure of that.'

Jean heard what was being said, but it meant nothing. Whatever was in the envelope would not change anything. They wanted nothing but this baby and he was now theirs. She gripped the box more tightly. Nothing or nobody would ever take him away from her, not now, not ever, she thought fiercely. She was aware of Tom at her shoulder, both of them gazing down at their new son. The babe had stopped whimpering almost as if he knew he had come home. The little newborn face with unfocused eyes seemed to gaze back at them and Jean, her tears dropping onto the towel in which he was swaddled, loved him instantly and from the expression on her husband's face, she could see he felt the same.

Confirming her thoughts, Tom whispered, 'Hello Jack, welcome home.'

Lilly Jenkins did not trouble to break into their rapture. Her task was accomplished, the baby and the envelope were handed over and there was nothing more for her to do here. She turned away and without even saying goodbye, quietly let herself out of the front door and walked up the path to the lane where George Brand waited in the car. Seeing her, he leapt out and opened the door for her, much as he did for the Mistress. She acknowledged him with a satisfied smile. It had been a touching scene back there in the cottage, watching the new parents so completely absorbed in Celia Bryant-Smythe's baby. 'I wonder how long it will be before they even notice I have gone,' she thought, settling back into the rear passenger seat. Then she put the Hargreaves out of her mind and forgot them.

Chapter TWELVE

For several days after the birth, Celia's milk had continued to seep through every garment she wore. Her breasts were hot and painful and the odour was just one of the reminders that she had recently given birth to a baby; a baby she had never held in her arms, let alone suckled. The bitterness of what had really taken place burned deep into Celia's soul and the only thought in her head was of vengeance.

She had screamed the place down until her throat bled and her body was so exhausted she could no longer move let alone utter a word or a cry. The day she had been told her baby had been taken away now seemed like a lifetime ago, but the words were branded on her heart and continued to reverberate around in her head.

Doctor Black had returned to check on his patient, warned Gladys to watch out for mastitis and to send Lizzie to fetch him if necessary. Because Miss Celia was so distraught he had left whole box of sedatives for her, but the drugs had only worked for a few days. It seemed that in her adrenalin-driven state she had the energy to resist them and five days after Celia had given birth, Gladys Thrift and Lizzie Rainbow were at their wits end. Nothing they did made any difference to Celia's behaviour. She wept and sobbed until her eyes were sore. She could no longer scream because her throat was too raw, but the persistent moaning she still managed to make morning, noon and night, was heartbreaking to hear. The cottage was plunged into gloom and despair and with Gladys and Lizzie both suffering from exhaustion it could not go on.

Reluctantly, Gladys felt compelled to do something she did not agree with, but in light of Celia's hysterical distress, she felt she had no alternative and doubled the dose of the tranquilizers. It worked, but only for a few more days, three to be precise, but they were a blessing for everyone. For those three days Celia was barely conscious and when she finally awoke, it seemed that the long, deep sleep had calmed her emotions. At first Gladys was pleased to see this, but it wasn't long before Celia's behaviour caused further worry.

The regular visits from Muriel Bryant-Smythe did nothing to help. The woman was clearly distraught at the sight of her daughter, though confided to Gladys that despite the harrowing scenes, she felt it was the best thing all round that the child had been fostered. She did not ask where her grandson had gone, not that Gladys could have told her, she simply asked for reassurance that he was to be well taken care of, which Gladys, who had asked Doctor Black the same question, was glad to be able to do. She was pleasantly surprised when Muriel thanked her for her care of Miss Celia and went on to say that despite the girl's present distressing state, she was in the best hands. It was not often the gentry bothered with words of gratitude and it helped to mollify Gladys somewhat.

Two weeks after the birth, looking in on her charge, Gladys could see the physical scars Celia had suffered were almost healed: she had needed only a few stitches, her milk had dried up with no sign of mastitis and the self-inflicted wounds to her hands and arms had faded to pale scars. To all intents and purposes she appeared back to normal, except that from morning till night, she lay prone; not speaking, barely eating, her expression vacant. It was as though she had disappeared into herself and nothing Gladys tried brought her back. She could only hope and pray that the girl's emotional state would eventually settle down and that one day she would find peace, but if truth be told, Gladys was beginning to fear this might never happen.

In the weeks after the Hargreaves had taken possession of their son, Jean quickly learnt to cope with his needs while Tom caught up on the hours of work he had lost during those early days after the baby had arrived. Along with the pleasure Jean derived from her son, the more she got to know and love him, the more worried she became. Her fear was an ever present black cloud hanging over her that at any moment a knock would come on the door and their baby would be snatched away from them.

'It's not going to happen, love,' Tom reassured her, time and time again. 'Mrs Green told us that nothing of the sort would happen so long as we keep to our side of the bargain.' But still Jean fretted: it had all gone too smoothly and for her, a little too secretly. For simple country folk, which is what they were - and proud to be - this was not the normal way of things. The arrival of a baby was shouted out from the rooftops; everyone wanted to know about it and to look. It was the most natural thing in the world to want to show off your baby, but she was so anxious about the need to keep everything quiet that instead of pushing her babe out in the pram, which is what she longed to do, she stayed at home lest she meet someone. The chances of that were few, of course, since where they lived was a few miles from the village down in the valley and aside from the two or three farm workers' cottages further along the lane, they had no near neighbours. She had begun to wonder if that was why Mrs Green had selected them. There was something about the whole business that did not feel quite right and this, along with her fear, clouded her joy.

One day, while Tom was out at work and she was nursing little Jack, she had an idea. The more she thought about it, the better it seemed. What if they were to move away from here, somewhere where nobody knew them and Mrs Green – whoever she was - would not find them? It would mean Tom finding another job, of course, but so long as it came with a tied cottage like the one they had now, what did it matter? And farmhands were in short supply just now, it shouldn't be difficult. Thinking it through from every angle, Jean was certain it was a solution. Now all she needed to do was persuade Tom.

Tom had worked as a farm labourer, right from when he had left school. He loved the life and knew no other. If he was not driving the tractor he was herding the cows in for milking or doing one of the hundred and one other jobs that needed seeing to on the land. His days were long and became even more so as fewer and fewer hands were left to do the heavy work. The Land Army girls helped enormously, but he knew they could not be doing some of the heavy, dirty and at times dangerous work he did. When they had first arrived most of them had not known one end of a cow from the other, he thought with a smile, but they were getting better as time went on.

Tom liked his boss, Sam Collins, who owned the farm. He was a decent man and each day he asked after Jean and the baby.

Just two weeks after their son had arrived, Sam sought him out. 'When you've finished milking the cows, Tom, I'd appreciate a word over at the house.'

Even though he spoke in a tone that implied nothing more than a friendly chat between employer and employee, Tom was nervous. His lack of sleep since the baby had arrived and Jean's constant worrying about the child being snatched back, had him bone weary and fretful, which was not like him at all. He knew his tiredness was affecting his work and though he had tried very hard not to let it show, there had been moments when he had needed to slow down just a tad. He now wondered if his boss had noticed. Thinking about that, Tom sighed heavily. The last thing he needed was to lose his job.

Finishing his work in the cowshed, he left two of the girls to finish washing down in the dairy and wiping his hands on his jacket, made his way round to the back of Home Farm, where the door was always open. Leaving his boots on the large doormat in the porch, he walked gingerly in his socks to the kitchen door and rapped against it lightly.

'Come on in, Tom,' Sam called. He was sitting at the long kitchen table, a jug of beer at his elbow and two glasses. 'I thought it was high time we wet the baby's head,' he announced with a chuckle. 'Seems to us there's an air of celebration in your household these days, how's the littlun settling in?'

This was the last thing Tom had expected, but with so much happening to him and Jean these last weeks, it was hardly surprising his mind was not functioning properly. Pulling out a chair he sat down at the table, grinned at his boss and answered, his voice betraying his mixture of relief at the hospitality and his pride at being able to talk about the baby. 'He's got a good set of lungs on him that's for sure, but apart from that he's not doing too badly at all. Jean's a natural, but she worries so.' Picking up the glass of beer Sam had poured for him, Tom took a long, grateful gulp then wiped the froth from his upper lip with the back of his hand.

As he was speaking, Millie had walked into the kitchen. She wandered over to her husband and rested her hand lightly on his shoulder. They had been married for twenty-five years and their affection for each other was lovely to see. She was like a breath of fresh air, thought Tom, smiling up at her. There were no airs and graces with Millie, she was a farmer's wife and to her that meant helping out with whatever needed doing, which she regularly did.

'Nice to see you, Tom, I'm glad Sam's got round to getting you up to Home Farm because we've both got a few things we want to talk to you about.'

For a brief moment, Tom forgot the jug of beer in front of him and the glass he held in his hand, his mind jumped back to work and his worry that he had been brought here to be sacked. Was this cosy chat a way of softening him up to give him the bad news? But before he could let his imagination run away any further, Millie continued speaking.

'Firstly this, I've got these for you.' She handed over a large box filled with baby clothes. 'This will keep the young man warm and looking bonnie for a few months. Some are hand-me-downs but most are new, I knitted some of them myself.'

Silently, Tom berated himself for even thinking bad thoughts. He really must be tired because these people had only ever shown him and Jean kindness. Looking at the box filled with all manner of things for the baby, he didn't know what to say, but one thing he knew, Jean would be thrilled to have these. 'Thank you, I know my wife will be very grateful.'

He picked up his beer to hide his embarrassment and glanced at Millie as she helped herself to a glass of water then joined them at the table. Seeing his expression, she laughed, 'I might help out on the farm, Tom, but I draw the line at drinking ale!'

Sam cleared his throat, 'Now I don't want you to take this the wrong way, Tom, but we've heard a few things and it's worrying us. We think we know what you might want to do, and before you say anything, we do have some idea about the problem, so we've come up with a proposition.'

Tom's heart sank and he bowed his head, he just hoped that what they had heard was not what he and Jean had been talking about lately. Since little Jack had arrived, Jean had changed. The baby was everything to her, and because of this, her fear of him being snatched away was spoiling the joy she should be having. She kept on at him about moving away and to calm her he had agreed to look for work elsewhere, but as yet he had not had the time – never mind the energy - to do much about it. He was not ready to mention this to Sam; he dreaded letting his boss down, leaving him in the lurch when he was so short of manpower. Yet it seemed Sam and his wife somehow knew it was what he was thinking of doing, for what else could it be? Forcing his weary mind to work, he wondered how they could possibly know about it; they weren't mind readers! Had Jean said something to Millie? He hung his head, ashamed to be sitting here with a glass of ale and a box of bits for the baby and thinking about running away with his new family.

'We know how it is for Jean, Tom,' added Millie, 'we know what she is thinking. And in her shoes, I'd be feeling much the same, believe me.'

Perplexed, Tom stared at her, wondering how she could possibly have any idea what his Jean was thinking and feeling, but before he could work that out, Sam nodded and said, 'Which is why we want to put this idea to you. My brother owns Top Farm over the other side of Pendleham, and his farmhand needs to be away from there. Don't ask me why, because I'm not entirely sure myself, but to help out on both sides, I've suggested a swap: you for him.'

Tom looked first at Millie and then at Sam. He was shocked. 'Why would you do this for us?'

'Because we think you and that baby deserve a chance to be a real family. Tom, we know Jean is fretting about the baby being taken back. As do one or two other folk round here. For a start we never see her about with the babe, which isn't natural and word spreads in a small village, as you know. But that's not the point. This war has changed so much and people have changed too. And I think for Jean and the baby, somewhere fresh would be a good thing. Somewhere where nobody will be any the wiser about your son, and whoever brought you the baby won't know where you've gone either, because we'd tell nobody. Not a soul. You understand what I'm saying?'

Tom looked from Millie to Sam, then back again, grappling with what Sam had said. He wondered what they had heard, and from whom, but whoever, or whatever it was, he knew that these good people meant only to help. He wanted to ask who had told them and what they knew about the baby, but he couldn't, maybe he really didn't want to know. Like Sam said, the community they lived in was small so tongues were bound to wag; it was the norm, especially given the secrecy surrounding the sudden arrival of a new born. He supposed it would not have taken folk long to work out there was something a bit odd about it, which would have aroused their curiosity all the more. Even so, Tom was taken aback by Sam and his wife knowing so much about what was going on in his household and for the second time that morning he did not know what to say. He knew his panic must be showing in his face, because Millie leaned across the table and reached out to pat his hand.

'Don't look so worried, Tom. Sam and I understand a lot more than you think. You - and everyone else come to that – only see us as a settled family here at Home Farm and imagine that is how it has always been for us, but things are not always as they seem ...' she broke off, glancing at her husband, who frowned and gave a slight shake of his head. 'Well, anyway,' she said softly, 'suffice it to say there are things in our past that help us to realise how it is for you both and why your Jean is fretting so. Just think about what Sam is proposing, Tom, will you?'

Tom was amazed, he had not a clue what Millie was talking about, but it was none of his business; he wasn't one to pry. He didn't need to think about what Sam had suggested, he knew without even asking what Jean's answer would be. 'I don't know what to say. You are both so kind. I don't want to leave your employ, Sam, I never did. It is only because of the baby. I thank you for your concern and I can tell you now, the answer is yes.'

'We'll miss you, Tom,' said Sam. 'You've been the best man I've ever had working for me, but I think that with this opportunity it will help you and Jean both to settle with the little one.' He grinned suddenly, 'And it will keep my brother happy into the bargain. So we're all sorted, yes?' With this, Sam raised his drink and with a hearty click on Tom's glass he took a swig of the strong home brew and smacked his lips, 'Mm, nothing like the taste of good ale when there's something to celebrate!'

Tom drank his beer and looked appreciatively down at his empty glass, 'It's a good brew this one, Millie.'

She laughed, 'Ugh! Horrid stuff. I just make it, I never taste it.'

Pushing back his chair, Tom looked at them both and smiled, 'I know just as soon as I get the words out, Jean will be packing. Have you any idea when your new man will get here?'

'As much as we don't want you to go, I think we'll be looking at a few days,' said Sam. 'My brother wants the exchange sooner rather than later. I reckon as how this new chap's got himself into a spot of trouble dipping his wick where he didn't ought to!'

'Sam!' Millie exclaimed. 'That'll be enough of that sort of talk. Whatever his reasons for wanting to leave Pendleham, it's no business of ours.'

Sam rolled his eyes and winked at Tom, who grinned back, feeling more relaxed after the strong ale he had just downed and his relief that out of the blue had come a solution to his problem with Jean and the baby. 'I don't know how to thank you,' he said again. 'You'll never know just how grateful we are for this.' He got up from his chair, pushed it back to the table and picked up the box of things Millie had given him for Jack. 'I'll get off home now then and tell Jean the good news, and thanks again for these.'

After he had gone, Sam and Millie sat there in companionable silence for a while, Millie thinking about Jean and how she was feeling. The sudden arrival of the Hargreaves' baby had brought back so many memories for her. It was so long ago she had almost forgotten that her and Sam's oldest son was adopted. Not so much adopted, rather that he had been given to them by a distraught family who had more children than they knew what to do with. Tom Junior, as they had called him, had been the family's fourteenth baby. The poor souls had simply been unable to cope with another mouth to feed. Nobody around here had known he was adopted because at the time she and Sam had been in the process of buying Home Farm. So when they moved here, Tom Junior was simply their son to anyone who asked - and he would pass any day of the week for their son, Millie reflected, for if nothing else he had Sam's walk and ways.

They had never told their boy he was not their natural son, and as the years went by and brothers and sisters had followed, there had seemed no need. Maybe it was wrong of them, but it was too late now, it would break his heart to find out after all this time, which is why Sam had not wanted her to say any more. Millie suspected that Tom would work it out, but she was utterly sure that even if he did, he would never mention it to anyone. He was a good, solid, honest man was Tom. She would miss having him around.

She and Sam had been at Home farm for twenty years or more now – good heavens, how time flies, she thought - and in that time Tom Junior had become a carbon copy of the man he knew as his father, but it had been a very long time before Millie had stopped being afraid that his blood family would one day demand him back. Oh yes, she knew exactly how Jean Hargreaves was feeling.

She smiled at her husband, 'I'm glad we were able to help Tom and Jean Hargreaves, I think they'll be happy over to Pendleham.'

Chapter THIRTEEN

When the news reached Henry that David Gillespie had been killed in action, he was not surprised, nor was he particularly sorry, in fact, he reflected, if he felt anything at all it was thankful that the whole episode concerning his profligate daughter was done and dusted. She was exiled, her bastard child was gone, where he neither knew, nor cared, and its father, who might have caused a problem had he returned, was dead.

It had to be said that the boy had been a most useful scapegoat. Lilly Jenkins had done a good job blackening the housemaid's name so that not even her father believed her claim that the Squire had raped her – not that he had; she had been only too willing as he recalled; little tramp! – and the rumour Lilly had fabricated that David Gillespie was responsible for her pregnancy had been believed. It was fortunate indeed that the girl had miscarried or her father might have claimed compensation from the Gillespies had their boy refused to marry her, which might have led to a more detailed examination of the facts. As it was, nothing could be proved, though it had been a close call. Henry congratulated himself that he had managed to throw up a smoke screen around the whole episode and could happily feel he had done the right thing. Indeed, the best all round for everyone, but most importantly for himself and in particular in respect of his dealings with Robert Gillespie.

The Gillespies and Bryant-Smythes had been friends and business colleagues for many years. The relationship between the two powerful families went back at least three generations, though how it had begun Henry had not the slightest idea. What he did know was that when his grandfather, James Bryant-Smythe, had lost a massive sum of money on unwise investments and died leaving the family impoverished, it had been Robert Gillespie's father who, out of the goodness of his heart, had kept Henry's own father from going under, enabling the Bryant-Smythes to hang onto Satchfield Hall - if only by a thread. The debts had continued to mount during his father's lifetime; a fact of which Henry had been made painfully aware while he was growing up, always forced to maintain the outward appearance of wealth and status, when in fact they were as poor as church mice. Indeed, it was why, when his father had left this mortal coil leaving him with a crumbling house and a mountain of debt, Henry had set his cap at Muriel, whose family had amassed a fortune from their South African diamond mine. It still enraged Henry that he had been forced to concede ownership of half of Satchfield Hall to his wife. Her family had insisted, as collateral for the enormous amount of money they had given him to clear his debts in return for the hand of their daughter. Since then, he had rebuilt the family fortune through a variety of successful business ventures – and almost lost it again, but nobody must know about that, least of all the Gillespies!

All in all, the relationship between their two families had served them both well in business, and in other areas too, when it was necessary to keep the lower echelons under control and their own landed status intact. 'I may be an arrogant bastard,' thought Henry, his mouth twisting in his customary sardonic smile, 'but I'm proud of it. It goes with the territory.' He had often said as much to anyone who had the gall to question him; few, of course, ever did. Only now, in the privacy of his own room, did he admit to himself that despite his apparent pomposity, he was all too aware that this war was creating changes that threatened his very way of life. In common with many other people in his position, those of the landed gentry who were struggling to maintain their grip on their wealth, he needed to court new business colleagues and keep all his acquaintances and contacts - as well as his enemies - in his sights. Friends too: Robert Gillespie as much as anyone could be classed as a friend, Henry supposed; his neighbour at least, since their lands were adjoining. It was this very fact that was currently occupying Henry's mind. He had a scheme up his sleeve which, if he could pull it off, would solve all his financial problems.

Wandering over to the portrait of his grandfather that hung over the sideboard, he stared up at it for a moment. 'You useless old fool,' he muttered, his mind turning back to the Gillespies. It occurred to him in passing that by using their son to cover up his own misdemeanours he had indirectly contributed to the boy's fate, but Henry felt no guilt. David Gillespie should have kept his trousers buttoned up! Besides, his own three sons had given their lives fighting for their country, killed in action at *El Alamein*, so why not Robert's son too? It seemed only fair. The pity of it was that all these young men had been killed for a cause that instead of sorting out a few megalomaniacs had escalated into the mass destruction of human lives.

'I suppose I should call on Robert and Zilda Gillespie to express my deepest sympathy,' he reflected. 'It will be expected. Muriel too, I will insist she accompany me.' His wife had taken the loss of their boys hard, which was only natural, but it was not just that. She had been acting strangely of late, speaking up to him in a way she never used to. Damn the woman, it was unsettling. He knew she had not forgiven him for refusing to allow their daughter back to Satchfield Hall, but she had no idea just how difficult a position Celia had put him in with her loose ways. Despite his efforts the staff had talked. People knew she had messed around with somebody, though not who, fortunately. He imagined the whispers that would spread like wildfire if she came home, all directed at himself: 'There goes the Squire who can't even control his own whore of a daughter,' they would say behind their hands, mocking him. It would undermine his authority and was not to be borne. Shuddering at the thought, Henry swung away and strode to the door, calling for Brand to bring the car to take him and the Mistress to Rookery House. He then went in search of his wife.

Muriel was shocked. 'Do you really expect me to speak to those poor people and express my great sadness at their loss, when our own daughter has recently given birth to their own grandchild? The only one they'll ever have now their son has gone ours too quite probably. We should tell them.' Muriel tried not to weep, but it was hopeless; the tears kept coming, the pain in her heart was too much to bear.

'There are times when you surprise me beyond belief, Muriel,' he said coldly. 'The Gillespies have just lost their only son; the last thing they need to hear about is our disgusting daughter and what she has been up to. We need to offer them our condolences and I *insist* you ready yourself straight away.' Turning to leave, he swung back, 'And be sure to keep your mouth firmly closed on anything to do with *you know who* or I will not answer for the consequences!'

Watching her cold, calculating husband striding away, Muriel wondered if she was dreaming because if not, she was living a nightmare. Henry had not once referred to the loss of their own sons, completely ignoring her when she had tried to broach the subject. It was as if what had torn their lives to shreds had not happened. She knew how evil he could be, but this was something beyond her comprehension. Over the passing months she had noticed a change in him; one that teetered on a wickedness that was beyond her experience and for the first time she wondered if he was going mad, for what sane person could behave as he did? What sane man would show no emotion when told that all of his sons had been killed?

'My boys,' Muriel whispered, her throat aching with sobbing, 'my three boys ... all gone. Well I'm not going to lose my grandson too!' she exclaimed, vowing in that moment that whatever it took she was going to find Celia's baby and Henry Bryant-Smythe could go to Hell where he belonged.

Twenty minutes later, dressed in a dark grey costume, Muriel descended the stairs. She had applied copious amounts of face powder in an attempt to hide the dark circles around her eyes, but the face that looked back at her in the mirror was like a death mask.

No invitation having been given, Henry and Muriel Bryant-Smythe arrived at Rookery House unannounced, but in the circumstances that was perhaps not unusual. Sitting by the fire in the drawing room, Zilda Gillespie heard the crunch of tyres on the gravel drive. She looked up at her husband, who had walked over to peer out of the window. 'Be brave, my love,' he said. 'It's the Bryant-Smythes. I am afraid we must expect people to come and offer their sympathy. They will have heard about David.' His voice broke and swaying, he put out a hand to grasp the back of her chair.

Hearing the butler open the front door and voices echoing in the large, draughty hall, Zilda's heart sank, but she controlled the urge to flee from the room and hide, steadied by her husband's reassuring presence. A tap on the door and moments later the butler announced the Squire of Satchfield Hall and his lady.

'Thank you, Dawson, show them in if you please.' As Robert walked forward to shake Henry's hand, Zilda got up from her chair and embraced his wife.

'Thank you for coming, Muriel,' she murmured, 'especially given your own recent loss. I'm so sorry. It is such a shock. We can hardly believe it. Please; come sit with me on the sofa.'

Zilda was appalled by the sight of Muriel, who looked positively ill and so frail. The death of her three boys on top of that dreadful business with Celia had clearly aged her. It was heartbreaking to see. 'You and I have quite a lot in common, it would seem,' she said, horrified to see

Muriel's eyes swimming with tears. Zilda bit her tongue; she should not have said that. The poor woman was so patently close to the edge.

It was true, nonetheless: their own son had been embroiled in a scandal, trifling with a girl in the village, and according to rumour, Muriel's daughter had been similarly indiscreet with some young man, packed off to the country to give birth and not allowed to come home again. Zilda felt she could hardly blame the Bryant-Smythes when she and Robert had reacted in much the same way, sending David off to war when, as a farmer managing their estate, he was in a reserved occupation and could have stayed at home. It had been for his own protection: the last thing they had wanted was David being blackmailed into marrying the poor man's pregnant daughter, particularly when there was no proof he was responsible. David had strenuously denied it and Zilda believed him, but Robert had insisted it was best he go away for a while. Nothing could have prepared them for the fact that he would never come home. That was something that happened to other people; not them. Not to their only son.

Feeling her own tears welling, Zilda looked across at Henry and experienced an unexpected surge of sympathy. Whatever one thought of him – and indeed, he was a loathsome man – he had a lot on his plate just now. Perhaps they had misjudged him. Arrogant he may be, but he had always ensured that their shared business interests prospered. She saw that he had released Robert's hand and was patting his shoulder in a brotherly way. 'We are here to convey our deepest sympathy for your loss,' Henry said, his tone calm and firm. 'We of all people understand how you feel.'

'Yes, of course. Your own loss is insupportable,' her husband replied. 'Come, sit down and we old friends can perhaps be of comfort to one another. Can I offer you a glass of brandy?'

As he ushered Henry to a chair, Robert exchanged glances with Zilda and grimaced. She gave him a tremulous smile then returned her attention to Muriel.

Chapter FOURTEEN

Celia had taken to going out walking each day. She would walk for hours, often round and round the large gardens of Ridge View Cottage which, aside from the vegetable plot tended by Lizzie, were largely uncultivated. During these meandering walks, she encountered nobody. The only breathing souls she saw were the flocks of sheep grazing in the lush fields that looked down on the valley below, and all she could hear was the excited twitter of the birds in the trees. These sights and sounds soothed her and helped to ease her troubled mind.

Learning about the death of her brothers had only deepened Celia's depression and yet it seemed so unreal, as though it had nothing to do with her. Most of her waking thoughts were confined to her baby, how he was; where he was. It was torture to think he might be quite near; it was equal torture to think he might be far, far away. She imagining him growing, losing the tiny newborn features that had been her only glimpse of him before he had been snatched away from her. There was no room in her head to think about much else, apart from David. The pain of his betrayal had dulled to a lingering ache and the image of him had begun to recede from her mind until she could no longer remember exactly what he looked like. Recording the details of her life each day assumed greater and greater importance and because writing seemed to calm and absorb her, her mother brought her a supply of exercise books and pencils, for she had long since filled her original leather-backed diary.

Celia treasured her moments alone away from Lizzie's constant chatter and the sharp-eyed gaze of Gladys Thrift. She needed solitude to think and to work out a plan to find her son. Being out in the fresh air and the wilderness of the garden helped, but it did not answer any one of her questions. Whenever she mentioned her baby, Gladys ignored her and immediately changed the subject. It was the same with her mother and even Lizzie simply shook her head and looked away, her face taking on a closed, anxious expression. A wall of silence had been erected against anything to do with him and Celia was incapable of understanding why. It was as though she had imagined the whole thing and never given birth at all. As the weeks turned to months and the physical signs faded, it occurred to Celia that perhaps she had suffered some sort of illness that had rendered her insane and the pain that had ripped through her body during the trauma of birth was all part of some vivid dream. Yet although her mind might be in turmoil, she had only to read the entries in her diary to know she was not insane; that it had been no dream. She reflected that whoever had coined the phrase, 'Least said, soonest mended,' had been very wrong; she was not mending at all; quite the reverse.

Eventually, during one of her quiet moments alone in the garden, Celia realised that she could not go on torturing herself in this way, but must learn to cope; either that or go mad. She was aware that what she wanted was very different from what her mother, Gladys Thrift and Lizzie Rainbow *thought* she wanted – in other words, what they thought was best for her. It wasn't; but for the time being, she must lull them into thinking that it was and over time their vigilance might relax and allow her more freedom, which was essential to her plan.

Harnessing these thoughts, Celia became increasingly secretive, beginning to feel she had a measure of control, if not over her life, at least over her mind. Determined to recover her health so that she would be strong enough to search for her baby, she began to eat the nourishing food that Gladys prepared for her and went through the motions of normality, feigning interest in the minutiae of day to day life at Ridge View Cottage. She put on weight and gained colour in her cheeks and slowly, as the outward signs of her recovery progressed, the three people in her life, her mother, her maid and her minder, began to relax as she had hoped.

Muriel Bryant-Smythe had kept the knowledge of David Gillespie's death from her daughter, not because she did not want her to know, but because she felt that as yet, the state of Celia's mind was far too fragile. As time slipped by, Muriel fretted constantly that gossip might reach Ridge View Cottage and Celia would learn the tragic news without her being there to help and comfort her. She waited anxiously for the right moment, which came not long after her daughter's health had begun visibly to improve.

Arriving at the cottage one afternoon, she asked Gladys Thrift to remain in the living room rather than going out to the car to talk to George Brand, as was her habit. 'I have come to deliver some sad news to my daughter, Gladys,' she said, 'and I would appreciate your support. I fear it will be too much for her.'

'Yes, Marm, of course,' Gladys replied, her brow furrowed with concern. 'Miss Celia's in the garden helping Lizzie to sow the broad beans, I'll fetch her in.'

'Thank you, Gladys.' Muriel seated herself at the table and waited nervously, rehearsing the words in her head.

'Yes, Mama, what is it?' Celia asked, coming in and washing her hands in the sink before taking her place at the table, her eyebrow raised in query.

Muriel hesitated then drew a deep breath. 'There is no easy way to say this, Celia. I am so sorry to have to tell you, but I regret that David Gillespie has been killed in action against the enemy.'

To her horror, instead of collapsing in a storm of weeping as she had expected, Celia went into peals of maniacal laughter. Muriel grasped her daughter's hands to still them; they were as cold as ice. 'Celia, please, it is no laughing matter. Do you understand what I have just said?'

As suddenly as it had started, the laughter stopped on an indrawn sob. 'Yes, David is dead. You say the enemy killed him, do you? And who might that be?' Celia's features twisted into an expression of scorn that was so like her father's, Muriel shuddered. Worried that as she had feared, the news had driven her daughter over the edge into a nervous breakdown, she exchanged a fearful look with Gladys, pleading silently for her help.

Gladys, hovering at the table, anxiety written all over her face, responded to the plea. 'Well, the Hun - or are they called the Jerries this time around? Whatever their name is, it were the German soldiers what killed him, Miss Celia.'

'Really? You don't say, Celia snapped. 'How strange, for I would have said the Germans had little to do with it!' Pulling her hands away she looked from Gladys to her mother. 'In my book it is the family that are the *real* enemy. They alone are to blame for David's death.'

A shiver prickled Muriel's spine as the words spun round the tiny room. Trying to keep her voice even, she said, 'There is no one to blame, Celia, that young man was only doing what thousands of other young men are doing in this terrible war – his duty.'

For a long moment nobody spoke. The silence was broken by Gladys, who bustled over to the kitchen sink and filled the kettle before placing it onto the hob at the side of the roaring fire. The hob sizzled when the cold water from the bottom of the kettle splashed onto its hot surface. 'I think we all need a hot cup of tea,' she called over her shoulder.

'Thank you, Gladys, that would be lovely,' Muriel said automatically, trying hard to stay calm. She was aware that her hands were shaking and she felt swamped by a wave of fatigue. Her daughter had unerringly homed in on the fear Muriel had harboured ever since David Gillespie had been unceremoniously packed off to the war, that Henry had somehow engineered it.

Breaking into her thoughts, her daughter asked, 'Is this what was planned?'

'*Planned*? Whatever do you mean? Surely, Celia, you cannot think for one moment that anyone had anything to do with this?'

'I am sure of nothing anymore. I wanted to believe in fairies and Father Christmas when I was a child. Then when I grew up, I wanted to believe in love, but none of these exist.' Celia's face was without emotion when she added in a whisper, 'What did he tell you?'

'What did who tell me about what? You are not making any sense, child.'

'I am no longer a child, mother. You know very well that I am referring to my father.' Celia spat out the word 'father', her eyes steely cold. Muriel could almost taste her daughter's hatred. 'What did he tell you about David Gillespie after you found out I was pregnant?'

'I don't know what you mean.' Aware that Celia was searching her face, Muriel dropped her gaze, afraid that her fear would show in her eyes. 'Your father may at times behave in a way that is hard to understand, but rest assured, nothing in this mad world we live in could bring him to do anything that would hurt anyone, particularly the Gillespies, who are old and dear family friends, as well you know. Indeed, we had both hoped that one day, you and David ....'

Muriel's voice trailed away. It was all too late and too cruel. She could not admit to Celia or anyone else what she feared. The rumours about David and their sacked housemaid had all been a little too convenient, as if invented by someone who wanted to cover his tracks and dispense with David Gillespie at the same time. Someone? Henry, of course; who else? For years she had closed her mind to the goings on in her household, aided and abetted by Lilly Jenkins, but this time, Henry had gone too far. She was increasingly sure he was to blame and it sat like a canker in her mind, but she had no intention of airing this to anyone, let alone her troubled daughter.

She lifted her gaze and forcing her voice to remain steady, said, 'Well, anyway, you know what we had hoped, but it was not to be and there is no point in thinking about it now. What's done is done and as impossible as it may seem to you now, in time you will come to terms with it and make a life for yourself. For now you must concentrate on regaining your health and stop imagining that anyone is to blame for what happened. David was doing his duty; he is only one of the thousands of young men who have lost their lives in this dreadful war, and that includes your brothers.' Despite her good intentions, Muriel's voice broke as she said this. She fell silent, unable to control the tears seeping out of her eyes.

'I'm sorry about my brothers, Mama, you know I am, and I am sorry to distress you so, but you cannot imagine what it's like for me. Not long ago I had a baby; David's son. It is all I have left of him and I need to know where my baby is, but nobody will tell me anything. Will you?'

Helplessly, Muriel gazed at her daughter, thoughts tumbling around in her head. Not sure what to say, she shook her head.

'No, I thought not!' Celia then turned her attention to Gladys Thrift. 'You knew all along about the baby and that it would be taken away, didn't you. How much did he pay you to arrange it all?'

Muriel glanced in horror at Gladys, who flushed red, clapping her hand to her face as these words assaulted her. Turning back to the stove, she ignored the question and taking hold of the whistling kettle, poured the boiling water into the teapot.

'Celia,' Muriel gasped, 'have you gone mad? Mrs Thrift is here to look after you. How can you possibly make such cruel accusations when she has cared for you so well? I beg of you to try to forget about the baby. What sort of a life could you have offered him? If you care about him at all then consider his best interests. It is you who must now regain your strength so that we can look ahead to you being back to your old self.'

Even as the words left Muriel's lips she knew they were pointless, her daughter was never going to forget the child any more than she could herself. For the last few weeks she had been making discreet enquiries; not that she wanted at this stage to do any more than discover the child's whereabouts and ascertain that he was being raised in a kind and gentle home. To that end, she had been leaning on Gladys Thrift to impart what she knew and had discovered in so doing that the woman was related by marriage to Lilly Jenkins, which was a shock. As soon as she knew this, Muriel had stopped asking questions for fear that it would get back to Lilly, who, as she had long known, told Henry everything. As much as Muriel wanted to find out about her grandson, there was no way she would ever risk his welfare, which was what she would be doing if Henry even *suspected* she was looking for the boy. It had, however, given her another lead. If Lilly Jenkins was involved, it was highly likely that George Brand would know something, since he was often asked to drive the woman hither and thither. George was a kindly man; scared of her husband – as weren't they all – but he had a soft spot for Celia and also, he was a bit slow. Muriel felt she could most likely extract information from him without his even being aware of it, and so she would, as soon as things had settled down.

Reflecting on the tragic events of the past year and looking at her daughter's pale, set face, Muriel found herself wondering if Celia ever would return to her old self. Sadly, she feared not and to her sorrow realised that nothing, not even her daughter, would ever be the same again.

Chapter FIFTEEN

'Beggin' your pardon, Marm, but it aint just my job'll be on the line if Mrs Jenkins finds out I've brought you here. All due respect, but she'll tell the Master and he's said as 'ow he'll ruin my family if I ever so much as breathe a word, and my sister and her husband have got troubles enough without that. It'd kill our old ma and pa if anything happened to them.' George Brand had opened the car door for his Mistress, not the limousine today, but an old Ford that was less eye catching, and stood to one side, his kindly face taut with anxiety.

'Please, Mr Brand, the housekeeper is not going to find out and nor is my husband. I will not tell a soul and neither will you. Now be so good as to wait in the car and please stop worrying.'

He touched his cap and nodded, but his eyes were bleak and his hands were shaking as he helped her from the car. Not for the first time, Muriel inwardly cursed her wicked husband who could turn solid, dependable people like George Brand into shivering wrecks, herself included.

She pushed open the latched gate and walked along a brick path that led between tidy and very pretty flower borders to the front of the cottage. Her heart was racing with anxiety and anticipation as she raised her gloved hand and knocked on the door. She meant to do no more than see for herself that her grandson was being well cared for. From the look of the neat cottage and garden, the outward signs were good.

Nobody came to the door. Muriel knocked again, hearing the sound echo hollow and empty within; as hollow and empty as she felt. After the strain of working herself up to the point where she had the strength to come here, Muriel's disappointment was acute to find nobody at home. She moved away and walked around to the window to peer inside. Her heart sank ever further: there was no sign of habitation; she could see the living room was empty of furniture, the place bare, swept clean, but lying on the floor by the door, as though it had been dropped unnoticed, was a small, hand-knitted Rupert Bear. Unable to help herself, Muriel burst into tears.

Gladys Thrift had begun to think that since learning of the death of David Gillespie all those months ago, Miss Celia had, in varying degrees, lost her mind. She was obsessed about the baby and not a day went by that Gladys was not forced to field a barrage of questions. Her patience was wearing thin: she had things on her mind that were bothering her and could do without this continual assault on her emotions. The atmosphere in the cottage these days you could cut with a knife.

She gazed at the young woman who, as she did every day, pleaded to be told what Gladys was unable to tell her. 'Trying to wear me down is not going to make any difference, Miss Celia. As I keep telling you, it's not that I *won't* help you; it's that I *can't*. You don't believe for one minute they would have told *me* anything do you? They knew only too well I'd have had to say something to you.'

'I don't believe you. My father arranged it and he paid for your silence too,' snapped Celia, her eyes blazing with frustration. 'You pretended to be my friend when all the time you were betraying me.'

'I'll ignore that, Miss, like I always do. I've told you all I know: Doctor Black was to take the baby to be fostered in a good home - a *good* home, mind; he assured me of that. I do not know where and he would not tell me and nor will he tell you. Even your mother does not know, so you might as well give up asking. It's not my fault, so there's no point in your looking at me like that. I didn't betray you. What else could I have done? I was paid to see you through the birth and look after you and that's what

I've been doing to the best of my ability.' Sighing wearily, Gladys tried to hide her irritation. Of course she felt sorry for Miss Celia, but at the end of the day, despite the disgraceful behaviour that had led to her being here in the first place, she was being more than well looked after, as she had been from the start, and Gladys felt it was high time the girl remembered her breeding and showed a little gratitude.

'I want to believe you,' Celia cried, 'but I can't. There must be *something* you could tell me that would help me to find my baby, please, Gladys, I beg you.' She broke down and wept; it was the same every day and always ended like this.

'Miss Celia, for your own sanity and wellbeing you must forget all about that baby. Like your mother told you, you should consider his welfare and stop thinking only of yourself. By now he will be settled in his home with his new parents, a childless couple who will love him and raise him as their own. You must put this behind you, because if you don't you'll spend the rest of your life lonely and stuck up here, halfway up a mountain. And I'm sure that is the last thing you want. As far as I'm concerned there never was a baby. And once you start thinking this way too, you will be able to get on with your life again.'

Relieved when the young woman turned away, Gladys watched her lift her coat from the hooks inside the door; off on one of her country walks, thank goodness. Gladys realised that under pressure, she had given a little more away than usual by mentioning a childless couple, but so what? There must be hundreds of married folk who were desperate for a baby and unable to have one of their own. It was true what she said, she knew no more than she was telling. George must know, of course, but Gladys had not asked him because she really didn't want to know and thankfully, it had not occurred to Miss Celia that he was the one to ask. Not that he would say anything; the Squire of Satchfield Hall had him by the throat, judging by what George had told her.

That poor girl, she sighed again, watching as Celia wended her way out into the garden. Telling her to get on with her life was one thing, but what sort of a life would there be for her now? If she married at all, only someone well beneath her station would have her and what would that be like for a woman of Celia Bryant-Smythe's delicate sensibilities, born with a silver spoon in her mouth? With the war in Europe to all intents and purposes over and the men coming home, things might change, but Gladys suspected that girls like Celia would never fit into this world, changed or otherwise. These thoughts upset Gladys; she had become very fond of her charge in the eighteen months or so that they had lived in Ridge View Cottage. She could only hope the girl's father would relent and find in his heart a nugget of compassion, enough to pay someone of his own class to marry his daughter. Without that, Gladys feared Celia Bryant-Smythe would end up an embittered, lonely old maid, her chances of happiness lost forever.

Gladys' fears grew daily because in all likelihood, she herself would be leaving Ridge View Cottage in the coming months. She and George had been stepping out together and their relationship had become increasingly serious. She remembered the first kiss. It had all but stopped her heart! Then last month he had proposed. Even though she had imagined the moment and wished for it, it had taken her completely by surprise.

'You've got me all flustered,' she had answered, feeling the colour rise in her cheeks. It was her day off and they were in the little café next to the cinema in town – a rare treat for Gladys; it had been a very long time since she had been to such a big place - and after they had sat through the afternoon matinee of *How Green was my Valley*, they had gone for a cup of tea. With Walter Pidgeon's voice still ringing in her ears – what a marvellous actor he was, she thought, and what a sad film

- Gladys had barely put the cup of steaming hot tea to her lips, when George placed his hand on hers, looked into her eyes and said, 'Will you marry me, Gladys? You're very special and if you'll have me, I'd like you to be my wife.'

As his words had spun around in her head, it seemed for a moment that everything suddenly stopped and the only thing Gladys could hear was her own heart pounding in her ample bosom. It was six years since her feckless husband, Fred, had run off and left her and she had seen neither hide nor hair of him since that day. Technically, they were still married, but she knew he was living with another woman and divorce for his adultery would be a formality even if they hadn't been apart all these years.

'Well, what do you say?' George's voice had been uncharacteristically shaky as he added, 'I love you, Gladys Thrift; I've not felt this way before with anyone else and I'm glad about that, for if I had, I'd not be sitting here now feeling all soft inside about the wonderful woman sitting opposite me. Please say yes and you'll make me the happiest man alive.'

It was quite a long and emotional speech for the normally taciturn George and Gladys, with her mind trying to take in what he had just said and her heart beating unusually fast, knew there was only one answer. 'If the courts will let me be rid of Fred after all these years of him being gone, then I'd be more than happy to say yes.'

Since that day, Gladys had worried more than ever about what would become of her charge. Although she did not hold out much hope that Miss Celia would be allowed back at Satchfield Hall, she knew she had to talk to the girl's mother and ask what could be done. Muriel Bryant-Smyth visited once a week and had done since her daughter had first arrived, but Gladys could see the strain of what had happened was taking its toll. The poor woman looked more ill and frail each time she saw her. Even so, Gladys did not intend to forgo the chance of happiness presented to her by George Brand and was determined to talk to Celia's mother about arrangements for the future.

Before then, however, on her next day off she would catch the weekly bus from the village into town and see a solicitor. Once her divorce was underway, then she and George could start to plan for the future. It may take some time and would probably use up all her savings, but she could wait, so long as they were together at the end of it. She wondered where they would live once they were man and wife. In some ways she would be sad to leave Ridge View Cottage, it felt so much like home it was like she had always lived there.

As each day passed, Gladys' excitement about her future mounted, as did her concern about Miss Celia. When Muriel Bryant-Smythe did not arrive on her usual day that week, she was in a fever of anxiety and at her wits end. The sinking feeling in her stomach told her that something must be wrong, but there was nobody to ask, so she tried to carry on as usual and not let her worry show.

Chapter SIXTEEN

As Jack, with plenty of huffing and puffing blew out the three candles on his birthday cake, Tom and Jean Hargreaves looked at him and then each other and beamed with pride.

Tom had managed to scrape enough money together doing extra hours to buy a little Brownie camera; it was second hand, but it worked and he was taking several pictures of the happy day. 'Smile Jack, watch the birdie,' he cried.

The little boy, his face smeared with red jelly, laughed excitedly as the shutter clicked. 'More, more,' he shouted.

'Come on Jean, let's get you in the picture too,' Tom said, as Jean hugged their son, planting a kiss on his tousled hair.

'The birdie!' Jack shouted, as the camera clicked again. Fascinated, the little boy called again for more, and so Tom clicked away until the last of the twelve frames on the roll of film were used up.

'That's it son, all done, now we just have to get them developed and you will see yourself all in black and white, blowing out your candles.' Under the boy's avid gaze, he rewound the film in the camera before opening up the back and taking out the roll. 'Next time you go into Pendleham, Jean, perhaps you'll take it in to Jerome's,' said Tom, placing the precious roll of film on the table. 'They're the best in town; we'll have the photographs back within a fortnight.'

'Of course, love,' she said with a smile, thinking as she watched Tom empty the camera and listened to the gurgling laughter of their son, that it was as if they had always been a family, like this. Those first twelve years of their marriage without a child had melted away and now, as they enjoyed jelly and a cake topped with three thin, blue candles, Jean had never felt so happy; everything was perfect.

Later, after Jack had been bathed and put protesting to bed, Jean, not wanting to wake her husband who, worn out after the busy day was dozing by the fire, tiptoed around the living room, tidying up Jack's things. It was a nice cottage, this: quite similar to their last home. She could not believe they had already been here at Top Farm for almost three years. Her fear that Jack would be snatched away at any moment had receded as time went on, and nobody round here knew she had not given birth to him. Only occasionally, as now with her hands in the washing up bowl, did she glance out at the shadowy garden and remember how hard it had been living with constant anxiety; always waiting for a knock on the door or a face at the window. She still thought about Jack's birth mother at times, they had been told so little about the girl who had given life to their son, other than that she had not wanted to keep him. What concerned Jean was that people often changed as they got older. What if one day his mother came looking for him? The thought of that sent cold shivers up and down her spine.

She and Tom had talked about whether they should tell Jack he was adopted, and if so when. 'Not yet, obviously, he would not understand; maybe when he's about ten,' Tom had said. 'Leave it any longer and he'll think we've been dishonest with him.'

Jean was for not telling him at all. 'Why does he ever need to know?' she had asked, dreading that Jack would want to find his *real* mother and might turn against her and Tom. 'He is *our son*,' she had added fiercely, deciding then and there that if it was up to her, he would never know.

'We have no right to keep it from him, Jean,' Tom had argued.

It had led to a rare quarrel between them and since then, by tacit agreement, they had not talked about it again.

As always, when she thought about this other woman, Jean wondered about her. Was she pretty? Jack was growing into such a beautiful looking boy, she must be. Did she think about her baby or care that she had given him away? Did she miss him; long for him? Jean did not much like the thought of that, but whatever Mrs Green had said, she could not imagine a woman giving up her baby willingly and the thought of his birth mother's pain made her feel guilty. Where did she live, this woman? Had she had another child? For some reason it upset Jean to think Jack might have a brother or sister he would never know. So many questions, she thought, smiling ruefully at her reflection in the kitchen window. She reached up to draw the curtains; it got dark so early at this time of year. Soon it would be Christmas and with Jack now at an age where he could really enjoy it, what fun it would be.

Drying her hands she glanced back at Tom; his mouth was open and he was snoring slightly. He worked all the hours God sent; up at five o'clock to milk the cows and on the go all day, it was not surprising he fell asleep the moment he sat down in the warm. He was a wonderful father, she could not have wished for better. She kept all her thoughts about Jack's birth mother to herself, not only because she did not want to worry Tom , but she knew he would not want to hear such talk. It had taken all her powers of persuasion to get him to consider taking on someone else's child in the first place; the last thing she wanted was to remind him that their son was not really theirs - and why.

Since coming here to Top Farm, Jean had taken to keeping a diary. She told herself it was for Jack, so that he could learn about his childhood, the early years: the ones, he would not be able to remember. It was more than that, though. Behind the seldom opened doors in the deepest recesses of her mind, she knew Tom was right and that their son deserved to know the circumstances of his birth.

It was only natural to want to know who had brought you into the world, even if they had not wanted you in the first place. Maybe one day, when she and Tom were old and Jack was grown up and understood about life – perhaps with children of his own - she would tell him. By then, Jean reasoned, no one could be hurt and then, if he ever found his birth mother, the diary would tell her how he had grown up. 'One day' was a long, long time away and Jean, having salved her conscience, continued to keep her diary and tried never to dwell on the reason why.

She retrieved it now from the drawer of the dresser and took it to the kitchen table, smiling when she saw the blob of jelly she had missed. How her little boy had enjoyed the celebrations, she thought, seeing again the big grin on his sticky face as he blew out the candles, totally unaware of all the happiness and trauma that his little life had already brought.

She opened the diary to today's date: the 19th. November – Jack's birthday – and took up her pencil. She wanted to capture all the tiny details of the day and add them to her little book.

Forty miles away as the crow flies, Gladys Thrift sat at her kitchen table dismally contemplating the way things had turned out. For whatever reason, her divorce from Fred was taking a long time; primarily, her solicitor told her, because they had not yet succeeded in locating him to serve him with her petition. This was hardly surprising with so many men being repatriated and so many families on the move; everything was in a state of flux in the aftermath of the war. 'Be patient,' he had advised her. 'If we fail to locate him we will file for him to be pronounced dead *in absentia* and then you will be free to remarry. He has be missing for seven years for that, so we must establish precisely when he could be said to have disappeared,' he had smiled, 'but we are working on it, don't worry. A year or two more at the most I would say.'

A year or two? She was trying to be patient, God knows, but it seemed so unfair to have to wait so long. She had not yet broached the subject of Celia's future with Muriel Bryant-Smythe, who had been bedridden for months after a severe bout of illness brought on by nervous exhaustion, or so George had told her. Not that it mattered as much as it had, since their plans were on hold for the time being. He was a calming influence, was George, but even he was beginning to show signs of impatience, his goodnight kisses become so fervent as to take her breath away. They were neither of them spring chickens anymore, but it seemed that passion did not dim with age! Thankfully, he always took no for an answer or Gladys feared she would be no better than Miss Celia, unable to resist the man she loved, though at her age there were unlikely to be consequences. Even so, she wanted to be married before she went down that road and no mistake.

At least Miss Celia was much better these days. The young woman had persuaded George to teach her to drive – not in the big limousine, but in the little black car he was allowed to borrow on his days off. Gladys had not been sure about it at first, but as George had said, what harm could it do? It wasn't as if she could go anywhere without them and it seemed to cheer the girl up immensely to have something else to think about. At long last, thank the Lord, she had stopped asking questions about the baby and seemed well enough in herself to take the occasional trip down to the village, which was fine so long as Lizzie went with her to keep an eye on her. The two girls had become friends and when Lizzie wasn't attending to her chores, they were more often than not in each other's company. Lately, Gladys had even seen Miss Celia laughing, which would have been unheard of a few months ago. Times were changing much as Gladys had predicted and these days it seemed to matter less that their backgrounds were so different.

This was all well and good, but it did nothing to help Gladys' mood. She was anxious to become Mrs George

Brand and not waste all this time awaiting. Life was too short.

At Satchfield Hall, Muriel had slowly begun to recover; not fully, but enough to get out of her bed and at last recommence her visits to Ridge View Cottage, although she was left quite breathless and weak from the effort. The doctor had diagnosed a mild heart attack and prescribed morphine and bed rest. Muriel knew precisely what had brought it on. David Gillespie's death, coming so soon after losing her own sons, along with her dread that her husband - albeit indirectly - was responsible, had weakened her both mentally and physically. Seeking out her grandson had been the final straw. She was foolish to have attempted it when her emotions were so heightened, but she had listened to her heart and not her head.

Some weeks after her abortive attempt to locate the baby's whereabouts, she had continued her search, her enquiries leading her eventually to Home Farm. The farmer and his wife, who had introduced themselves as Mr and Mrs Collins, had seemed very nice people, but clearly overawed by her manner – or perhaps by the shiny black Daimler in which she had chosen to arrive. They had invited her into their rarely used front room and served her a cup of tea and a slice of homemade cake, Mrs Collins all the while apologising for their humble dwelling. As far as Muriel could see their home was spotlessly clean and it was their manner rather than their home that was humble, but their obvious respect for her had suited her purposes.

Without divulging her name and having ascertained in a roundabout way that the empty cottage did indeed belong to Home Farm, she had explained that she was a distant relative of the father whose orphaned child had been fostered there last November – not true, of course, but it was her attempt at a smoke screen - and was merely making enquiries on the family's behalf to ensure the boy was being well cared for. Mr Collins, assuming from this that she knew far more than she actually did, had unwittingly given away the name of the couple who had taken in the baby, going to great lengths to reassure her that Mr and Mrs Hargreaves were the kindest, most hardworking people he knew and the child would certainly be receiving the best possible care. However, the Hargreaves had moved away and were now living near Pendleham.

Muriel was conscious of Mrs Collins casting warning glances at her husband as he imparted this information and was not surprised when, try as she might, she was unable to persuade him to give her an address. In the end, thanking them graciously for their hospitality, she had asked George Brand, who alone knew what she had been doing and would never speak of it, to drive her home. Arriving back at Satchfield Hall, she had promptly keeled over and been put to bed.

Now, some months later, Muriel still wondered what to do with the information she had obtained that day. It would not be difficult for a private detective, furnished with the couple's name and approximate area of residence, to find the child, but she was hesitant to go that far. Her husband did not appear to suspect what she had been doing - indeed, he had been so shocked by her sudden collapse he had hardly come near her these last months, which was almost worth having a heart attack for! However, there was no question that if she were to hire a professional to locate her grandson, Henry would inevitably find out. There was not much went on that he did not know about.

Aside from this, Muriel was mindful of her daughter's much improved mental state. Gladys had assured her that Celia had mentioned neither the baby nor David Gillespie in weeks, and it seemed to Muriel, who could not bear the thought of upsetting her daughter all over again, that perhaps it was best if she let the matter rest. At least she knew that her grandson was in good hands and maybe that was enough for now.

Returning home from a visit to Ridge View Cottage and in light of her recent health scare, Muriel thought long and hard about her decision to keep what she knew from

Celia, who surely deserved at least to know that her son was being well cared for and by whom. It then occurred to Muriel that if her heart suddenly gave out, which she knew could happen at any time, what she had discovered would go with her to the grave. In the end, she compromised by writing a letter to her daughter then putting it with her personal papers, the envelope marked: '*To be delivered to Celia Bryant-Smythe in the event of my death.*' Having done that, Muriel then thought about her will; it had been drawn up a very long time ago. With the death of her boys, so much had changed; maybe she should think about amending it and at the same time adding a codicil to make some provision for her grandson. The idea gave her peace of mind and determining that tomorrow she would visit her lawyer, Muriel retired to her bed.

Waking the following morning, feeling more rested and clear-headed than she had done for some time, Muriel was about to inform George Brand that she needed him to take her into town, when she received news so devastating that it wiped all thoughts of visiting her lawyer from her head.

Chapter SEVENTEEN

More than three years had passed since the sad news of David Gillespie's death had come to Satchfield Hall, but his name was once again being whispered around the rooms and in the hallways of the large manor house. Rumours had been circulating for days, believed by some, denied by others. 'About as likely as Hitler being our Prime Minister,' Lilly Jenkins had remarked sourly to her mistress, but her voice had been unusually subdued and her forehead creased in a worried frown, which gave Muriel pause for thought even as she dismissed what people were saying as hurtful gossip.

A few days after this brief exchange, sitting at her satinwood writing desk, positioned beneath the window to take full advantage of the sunlight that flooded into her room, Muriel clutched in her nerveless fingers the letter she had just received and contemplated the joyous news it contained. She read it through several times hardly daring to believe what was written, until at last her mind absorbed the earth-shattering words.

The rumours were true: David Gillespie was alive and coming home!

At the same time as she rejoiced at this wonderful news a cold hand touched Muriel's heart as she considered the implications. Not just that the old scandal about David would be revived and her husband's part in it quite possibly revealed, but how Celia would react when she learned the good tidings, which she would, for of course she must be told.

Robert and Zilda must be overjoyed, thought Muriel, quickly suppressing a sudden spike of envy. Their son had been gone for such a long time, where had he been and what had happened to him? Who had posted him as dead and why? The letter provided no answers. With her head full of questions and her heart filled with joy for her friends, Muriel folded the letter and placed it on her desk making no attempt to wipe away the warm tears that flooded her face. There had been times in the past three and a half years when she had wiped not only her tears away, but when her mind would allow, all the other distressing events that had taken place. It was the only way she had been able to survive without descending into madness. Not just the death of her own three boys, but the scandal that had led to David Gillespie being sent away, along with her daughter's disgrace and banishment and the subsequent birth and disappearance of their illegitimate son. All of it could be laid at the door of Henry Bryant-Smythe; the wicked man to whom she was shackled for life and as the tears rolled freely down her face and her weak heart sent pains thudding into her chest, Muriel knew she could no longer wipe away the past; a past that to her eternal shame, she had done nothing to prevent.

The news she had just received, that against all the odds the father of her grandson had miraculously survived the war and come back from the abyss, was a reprieve. A chance for her to put things right. The thought brought with it an unexpected surge of strength and Muriel was forced to take several deep breaths to steady her shaking form. The doctor had said, 'No stress!' Almost she had laughed in his face as he had stood beside her, his fingers grasping her wrist to check her fluttering pulse. It bewildered Muriel that she was still alive. Given the strain she had been under she had expected to meet her maker long before now and for the first time since taking on the mantle of Henry Bryant-Smythe's wife, she realised that her fortitude was far more resilient than she had imagined.

Muriel picked up the embossed headed notepaper and once again read the fine, handwritten letter, wanting to confirm she was not imagining any of the news therein. And, of course, she wasn't. The joyous words brought stark reality to the enormity of what lay ahead, for Muriel knew the letter had the power to change so much. Certain things must be done to help those who had been hurt and it was down to her to ensure that something good was salvaged from the wreckage of people's lives and no more pain and devastation added to what had already been done. Muriel knew her days were numbered, but if she could only achieve that before she left this mortal coil, she would die content.

With her mind clear on what she must do, she picked up her pen to respond to the letter, but just as quickly put it down. It would be futile to attempt to convey in faceless words everything she wanted to say. What was needed was for her to go immediately to Rookery House and from there to her daughter at Ridge View Cottage. Even as Muriel organised these thoughts in her mind, she heard Henry's booming voice echoing throughout the Hall and her resolve started to melt, as it always did when he was near. Silently castigating herself for her weakness, yet visibly withering as her bombastic husband flung open the door to her private room and marched in, Muriel, her hands trembling, slid the letter out of sight beneath her blotter and waited for the axe to fall.

'Good God,' he bellowed with mock disbelief, 'you will never believe what I've just had confirmed!'

The letter about David had been delivered to Muriel unopened, so she failed to see how he could yet know what it contained and assumed his intrusion and outburst concerned a member of the household, or more likely some business deal. She knew he had embroiled himself in a variety of so-called 'money making deals' since the end of the war. Henry was a gambler; always so certain the risks he took would pay off, but without the wit or the skill to ensure they were calculated. Sometimes it had worked for him, enough to keep his head above water, but not lately. Muriel knew a good deal more than her husband realised, in particular that if he continued with his hairbrained schemes he would soon be penniless. It meant little to her, not now that her sons could no longer be affected by it. Because of her late father's foresight, she herself had independent means and financial security, about which, thankfully, her dissolute husband knew nothing. Inwardly shrugging, since she was not interested in anything Henry had to say, Muriel gazed out of the window and practised taking deep, calming breaths as the doctor had instructed.

'Look at me when I'm talking to you!' Henry roared, striding towards her and slapping his bunched fist down on the desk with such force that her fountain pen jumped onto the floor and splattered ink onto the pale green carpet.

Reluctantly, Muriel turned to face him. He stood, legs apart, staring down at her, the sunlight from the large, south-facing French windows casting a shadow on his still handsome face. As soon as he saw he had her attention, he smiled at her: a smile that would sour the freshest cream and darken the brightest day.

Worried by her husband's unexpected exuberance, Muriel's thoughts turned swiftly to concern as he repeated, 'You simply will not believe what I have just heard.' This time he did not wait for a response, 'That young buck Gillespie has turned up at Rookery House - seems he wasn't killed after all, just badly wounded.'

Muriel gasped, raising her hand to her mouth in distress as her plans for the day tumbled around her ears. She had so hoped to delay her husband's receipt of this news, but she might have known it was not possible; little escaped him, she thought bitterly. She heard his derisive laughter as from a distance and wondered if he was deliberately trying to shock her, maybe even hoping she would have another heart attack so he could get his hands on her half of Satchfield Hall. Had she not already received the letter, the news would indeed have shocked her coming as it did in so brutal a fashion.

'Nothing as dramatic as death it seems,' he laughed again. 'One just needs to ask where the hell he has been these last few years. Running away from it all no doubt.

Bloody coward should've been shot at dawn and I for one will make sure the world knows about it!'

Grunting, Henry directed a sneering grin at her, his enjoyment at her distress patently obvious as he lingered for a moment, his dark eyes searching her face. Then, with a final mocking laugh, he turned on his heel and strode out of the room, slamming the door shut behind him.

After he had gone, Muriel sat for a long while, breathing deeply until her heart had stopped hammering. Almost she believed that Henry was disappointed to learn of the Gillespies' good fortune; as if he had *wanted* their son to be dead, which in the circumstances, she reflected, was not altogether surprising. How annoyed he would be had he known she had received the news before him. Her husband had always been callous, but until now she had barely realised how much worse he had become over the years. His cruelty and selfishness knew no bounds it seemed. Was he now going to blacken David's name even further by publicly questioning the young man's courage under fire in an attempt to keep the old scandal from re-emerging? If she asked him, her husband would doubtless claim he was simply attempting to protect their daughter's reputation. The extraordinary thing was that he would not just claim it; he would *believe* it! It was as though Henry's obsession with keeping his status intact blinded him to reality, to the extent that he was losing his grip. Not for the first time Muriel wondered if his mind was unhinged. He rode roughshod over anyone or anything that got in his way, whatever the consequences and it seemed that his latest target was David Gillespie - again.

'Where will it all end?' Muriel asked herself, but even as the words hung in the silence of her room she knew that it would not. The pain and devastation would continue until someone brought him down. As God was her judge, she would find a way; whatever it took, she would live for long enough to bring about his downfall.

Muriel retrieved Zilda's letter from beneath her blotter and read it again. Henry had said David had been wounded, but his mother did not refer to that at all. To have been missing for so long, it must have been severe. Not for one moment did Muriel believe he was a coward. Shuddering at the thought of what might have happened to the poor young man, her thoughts turned back to Celia and how she would be affected by this news.

Chapter EIGHTEEN

No sooner had her husband slammed out of her room than there was a knock on her door. Before Muriel could gather her wits the door flew open and Lilly Jenkins stepped into the room, stared straight at her and with no preamble announced, 'Mr Brand has a need to speak with you. I've told him I didn't want to disturb you as I know you are busy, what with one thing and another.'

Muriel bristled, 'I was not aware that I told you to enter,' she snapped.

Ignoring the reprimand, the housekeeper looked pointedly at the sheet of notepaper still clutched in Muriel's hand, then her expression changed and she seemed suddenly and uncharacteristically subdued. 'I'm sorry, Marm, he said it was important. I didn't stop to think,' she said, her tone less strident.

'Clearly not!' Muriel was used to the odious woman's rudeness, but she was still reeling from Henry's callous outburst and Lilly Jenkins had caught her on the raw. It was apparent the housekeeper was aware she had received a letter from Rookery House and judging by her changed manner, feared the consequences. As well she might, thought Muriel grimly. The very sight of the woman irritated her intensely and added a brusque, cold edge to her voice as she added, 'Let him enter, if you please.'

Lilly Jenkins, clearly taken aback by her mistress' curt tone, turned and beckoned George Brand into the room. She then hovered in the doorway and with defiance radiating from every pore, held on to the door handle.

'Please, Mr Brand, do come in and take a seat.' Muriel smiled up at George and pointed to a chair close to her desk. Clutching his cap in one large hand, he walked to the seat she indicated and gingerly sat down, but to Muriel's annoyance she saw that Lilly Jenkins was still lingering by the open door. The audacity of the woman! Turning to her driver, Muriel said loudly, 'I imagine, Mr Brand, that you wished to have a *private* word with me, is that so?' Flushing, he nodded and looked at the floor.

Muriel stood, eyed the housekeeper and outwardly keeping her composure, said sharply, 'That will be all, Mrs Jenkins, thank you. Kindly return to your duties – and close my door on your way out if you please. In future, you will wait until I call you to enter before barging into my room. Is that understood?'

Jaw dropped, the housekeeper froze for a moment then, with a quick nod, dropped her gaze and backed away, almost tripping over her feet in her hurry to leave the room. In a final act of defiance, she banged the door shut behind her.

With her departure, the atmosphere immediately lightened. Breathless, her limbs shaking, Muriel sank back into her chair. Never had she quite had the courage to speak to Lilly Jenkins in that way and the effort had exhausted her. At the same time, she felt an immense sense of achievement: mistress in her own house and not before time! She was well aware that her dislike of the housekeeper was mutual. Lilly Jenkins' attitude towards her had deteriorated considerably since Celia had been banished from the Hall. Indeed, the woman treated her with a contempt that seemed at times to verge on unadulterated hatred. Muriel had no idea why and could only assume it stemmed from jealousy. At one time she had both feared and distrusted her: she still did not trust her, but no longer was she afraid. By some strange alchemy, she had somehow got the upper hand, though had no idea how. Perhaps it was the very fact that she *did* no longer fear her. The reason for this was quite simple: there was nothing left to fear, for there was nothing Lilly Jenkins could do now that could make the situation any worse.

After months of surreptitious investigation, Muriel had incontrovertible proof that the housekeeper, by bringing Celia's pregnancy to Henry's attention in such a way as to enrage him beyond reason, had indirectly not only caused their daughter's banishment, but had made all the subsequent arrangements. At the same time, she had aided and abetted Henry in spreading spiteful and almost certainly untrue rumours concerning David Gillespie and the sacked housemaid, so was equally responsible for his being sent away to war, though for the life of her, Muriel could not understand why. Not only this, but as Muriel had long since worked out, she had been behind the rapid disappearance of Celia's baby, doubtless acting on Henry's instructions, but probably with relish.

The woman was in cahoots with Henry at every turn and would, it seemed, do anything at all to gain his favour, no matter what the cost to other people's lives. The very thought of the lengths to which Lilly Jenkins would go to feather her own nest made the hairs rise on the back of Muriel's neck. Well, as far as she was concerned, Henry Bryant-Smythe and Lilly Jenkins deserved each other; they were cut from the same cloth and when Henry was brought down, his former paramour and more recently, she was fairly sure, the procurer of young women to satisfy his lust, would go down with him. Muriel wrinkled her nose with distaste. For too many years she had been turning a blind eye to what went on in the household and in so doing, she was perhaps as guilty as they, but no longer. On that, she was determined.

It would not be easy to bring about their downfall. Muriel was all too well aware that what she must do would be detrimental to her heart condition, which had recently been diagnosed as angina. Any form of stress, as now, left her short of breath and sent spasms of pain into her chest. She was fatigued to the point of exhaustion, a state that was permanent these days. Looking back, she realised her health had been deteriorating from the moment she stepped foot into this bleak old Hall to be subjected to the vulgar, often violent demands of her husband. Demands that had yielded four children; they had been the one saving grace in this mockery of a marriage. And now three of them were dead and one of them banished in disgrace. Grief rising in her throat, Muriel shivered involuntarily, becoming aware that George Brand was politely clearing his throat.

George gazed at Muriel Bryant-Smythe with amazement and admiration. He had never thought she had it in her to speak to anyone as she had just done, let alone Mrs Jenkins of all people! It heartened him that the mistress was finding the strength to cope with everything and although he could see that she was shaking and struggling to control her emotions, he knew she was not afraid. There was a noticeable change in her demeanour: even though she looked as if a puff of wind would blow her over it was like she had found some inner strength. He had been impressed by her efforts to locate Miss Celia's child, even though he knew the Squire would destroy him – and likely her too – if he ever found out. He had not told a soul, not even Gladys, for although he loved and trusted her, the fact remained that she was Lilly Jenkins' sister-in-law and like the posters used to say, 'Careless talk costs lives.' What Gladys did not know, she could not give away.

It troubled him that he had accepted money from the Squire on many occasions in the past for doing things that went well beyond his job description, but particularly those concerning Miss Celia and the abduction of her baby. On the other hand, what choice did he have? The Squire controlled his very existence, threatening his welfare and that of his family if he dared step out of line. And with Henry Bryant-Smythe, as George well knew, it was no empty threat. So he took the money, sent it on to his sister and her husband, who struggled to support a large brood of children, and kept his mouth shut. He had never done anything that caused actual harm to anyone, leastways not so far as he knew. But things had changed:

now he and Gladys were to be married, he meant to get away from Satchfield Hall and out of the Squire's clutches, even if it meant them having to emigrate. He had not yet mentioned that to Gladys, but he reckoned she would agree.

It was Gladys that had brought him here today, but he now wondered if it was bad timing. The winds of imminent change were swirling all around him: the Gillespies' chauffeur had tipped him the wink about David Gillespie some days before the rumours started circulating. It was no business of his, so he had kept the information to himself. His father had once taken him aside and said, 'Never volunteer information, son, and that way you'll stay out of trouble.' It was a maxim by which George lived and it had served him well, for all it had given him a reputation for being a mite standoffish. He was not concerned about that: 'Wipe your feet and keep your nose clean,' his old ma used to say and he did, to the best of his ability. The things he knew about the Squire's nefarious activities were enough to make your hair curl, but so long as he kept it to himself then him and his family were safe, which was all he cared about - and Gladys too now, of course. He cleared his throat again then coughed for good measure and saw the mistress' eyes come back into focus.

'Forgive me, George, I was miles away, but with every reason, as I am sure you have heard. Yes, I can see that you have. We have something to celebrate at last.' She smiled, 'Tell me what I can do for you, but before you do, let me take this opportunity to thank you. Not just for all your help, but for keeping it in confidence. I realise you have risked a good deal in so doing and I hope you know how much I appreciate it.'

'Thank you, Marm, glad to have been of service.' To his surprise, George found that he meant it. He *was* glad; not, as it turned out, that he had been much help. He warmed to the mistress thinking about how she cared enough to find out if the nipper was being well cared for. He liked that in a woman. And he liked the way she called him George when there was nobody else about; made him feel like he was more important than the rest. She was a *real* lady this one.

'So what did you want to say to me?' she asked, bringing him up short.

He hesitated, shuffled his feet, gazed out of the window. Decided what he had to say could wait. 'I'm sorry, Marm, I realise this is a bad time.' He got up from his chair, but she motioned him to sit down again.

'You know I am always happy to talk to you, George, but if it is about your employment, then I'm afraid you must speak with my husband.'

George heard the implied question. It was nothing to do with his work, it was personal and the last person he wanted to discuss it with was the Squire. Of late he had become increasingly afraid of the man. Like the mistress, her husband too had changed, but the difference was, Henry Bryant-Smythe had grown evil.

Swallowing, George felt uneasy and not sure how to proceed. 'Er ... it's a personal matter, Marm.' He tried to sound more confident than he felt and seeing that Muriel Bryant-Smythe was glancing back at her letter and beginning to look just a little impatient, he said a silent prayer, because he knew that if Captain Gillespie still had his mind intact, then she was going to need all the strength she could find. He had heard all about Miss Celia's ramblings about who her baby's father was. Gladys had told him. He had also heard rumours that David Gillespie had got one of the housemaids in the family way too, but there was something a bit odd about that whole business and he was not sure he believed it. Whether or not it was true, it would only be a matter of time before more pain would befall this woman and her daughter. Whichever way it went, it was one big tangle and he didn't envy them one bit.

'It's really not important, M'am,' he said finally. 'I think it would be best if I tell you another time. I can see you have urgent things to be doing.'

'Very well, George. I hardly think you would have asked Mrs Jenkins to see if I was available were it not important. However, as it happens I need you to drive me to Rookery House and from there to Ridge View Cottage. What I suggest is that you bring the car to the main entrance and during the drive you can tell why you needed to speak with me, but just to set your mind at rest ...' she broke off and gave him a teasing smile, 'if it is a personal matter, would I be correct in thinking it might have something to do with Mrs Thrift?'

George gaped at her and then his face split in a wide grin of assent. Getting up from his chair, he gave her a half bow and said, 'I'll go and fetch the car right away then, Marm.'

Chapter NINETEEN

Celia recovered consciousness to find her mother bending over her waving smelling salts under her nose. The foul, pungent odour brought her to her senses, but her head was still spinning as she struggled into a sitting position and leaned back against the sofa, closing her eyes. Nothing, in all her wildest dreams and heartrending prayers had prepared her for the news that David was alive. On hearing it, she had passed out.

'Are you all right, Celia? Thank goodness you fainted onto the sofa! You haven't hurt yourself?'

'No, Mama, I'm not hurt, just shocked.' Opening her eyes, Celia, her head swimming, watched the rivulets of rain streaming down the window pane. It had been so wet and windy today that she had not taken her customary walk, so had been reading quietly, sitting with her book on Gladys' threadbare sofa by the window, when her mother had unexpectedly arrived, flustered and wanting to speak to her.

Judging by the noises coming from the scullery, Gladys was still busy doing the washing; Celia could hear the swish of water in the tub and the squeak of the mangle. Not a good day for it, she reflected; the place would be festooned with wet washing for days. She remembered that Lizzie had set off for the village just before the storm. The poor girl would be soaked. Through the rain she could see the black Daimler in the lane; no doubt George Brand was inside it waiting patiently for her mother – as always.

All these thoughts flitted like moths through the edges of Celia's mind as though she needed to distract herself, afraid to think about what she had just been told in case it was not real. Still reeling from the shock, she became aware of her mother's worried gaze and tried to focus.

'I'm sorry, Mama, I didn't mean to frighten you, but it was such a shock. I was so sure he must be dead. I thought and thought about what you said all that time ago when I told you I was expecting his baby. Almost I believed you, for if he had really loved me why would he have gone away without saying goodbye? At first it felt like a betrayal, but deep down I knew he wasn't like that, Mama, not David. I *knew* he loved me, which could only mean he'd had no choice but to leave me as he did. Then, when he didn't write to me, I was certain he must have been killed. It was the only explanation.' Celia's brain was teeming with so many questions she did not know what to ask first. She started with, 'How and when did you hear he is alive?'

'I received a letter from his mother this morning. I wasn't sure how to tell you because I knew it would be such a shock, but I wanted to tell you straight away, even though I am aware this news is going to bring you joy and sadness in equal measures.' Her mother paused, drew breath then spoke again, her voice husky, 'I know things have at times been awkward between us and that I have not been a good mother to you. I wish things could have been different. I should have found the strength to stand up to your father and insisted he allow you to come home. I wish I could turn the clock back ... I only hope you can find it in your heart to forgive me.'

Turning to look at her, Celia's stomach clenched with worry. Her mother's face was grey, her breath coming in short, sharp gasps as she clutched at her chest and held onto the arm of the sofa for support. She looked so ill and far older than her years, and although there was a tremulous smile on her lips, her eyes were dark with pain.

'Sit down, Mama, you look so tired,' Celia patted the sofa next to her and tried to ignore her swimming head. 'There is nothing to forgive. I know you had little choice and anyway, I had no wish to go home, so it really doesn't matter. I have grown to love it around here. This is my home now and it suits me far better than that draughty old mansion.'

That was not quite true; she loved the Hall, it was the people in it she detested: her father and Lilly Jenkins most of all. Hesitantly, she took hold of her mother's hand and gave it a squeeze. It was the closest they had ever come to a rapport. There had never been an overt show of affection between them, her mother was not demonstrative, but Celia had never doubted her love. 'I have always known that you wanted only what you thought was best for me, Mama, and that it is my own fault I landed in this predicament. I too wish things could have been different and I am sorry to have caused you so much pain and anxiety, but let us not talk about the past anymore. Now, please, tell me again what the letter said. I want to hear it over and over. I hardly dare believe it's true.'

Sinking into the lumpy sofa, Muriel took hold of her daughter's cold, clammy hand and almost she smiled: they were both trembling like the leaves on the windswept trees. It occurred to her that in these last three years, her daughter had matured; no longer was she an innocent girl, but a young woman with a mind of her own and the ability to control her emotions. Unlike me, Muriel thought, aware of the irony as she struggled to contain her tears. Even so, she was hesitant about how much information to impart and for the time being decided to settle for the barest minimum.

'David was wounded and went missing in action, but he is alive and the doctors are confident that his recovery will hasten now he is back at home with his family around him.'

'When can I see him?' Celia gasped, her eyes brimming with tears.

Muriel knew what the implications of David Gillespie's return would mean to her daughter, had she herself thought of nothing else since going to Rookery House only hours earlier? Her first appalled sight of the Gillespies' son would stay with her for a very long time. It transpired that David had been home for over a week before Zilda had written to tell her the good news. In that time he had said nothing about what had happened to him in the intervening years since he was wounded, in fact, he had said nothing about anything, Zilda had told her.

'It's like he has no memory about his life after leaving Rookery House; we are not even sure if he remembers much about the time before,' his mother had confided to Muriel, weeping as she described the moment when David had returned home. 'The news we received telling us he was alive was such a shock that it seems all of a blur now. Believe you me, Muriel, we were overcome with joy at the news, but his eventual arrival was heartbreaking ...'

At this point, Zilda had stopped to blow her nose and wipe her face before continuing. 'When he arrived home, he was wrapped in blankets and in a wheelchair and as the orderly pushed him into the house, I could see David shaking as if his whole body was unable to be still. As if that was not enough, when I looked into his eyes it was as if there was nobody there; they were just deep pools of darkness. We spoke to him, Robert and I, but although David turned towards our voices, I'm sure he didn't see us at all.' Zilda had broken into racking sobs and Muriel had reached for her friend's hand and held it, knowing perfectly well there was nothing she could say or do, except listen.

The Gillespies' joy in their son's return had, it seemed, been swamped by their desperate sorrow at what had happened to him. This was not hard for Muriel to understand when she had seen for herself what David had become. The handsome young man, who had left more than three years ago, had gone for good. In his place was a thin, palsied wreck, in a wheelchair and with a haunted expression that tore at Muriel's heartstrings. Whatever experiences he had endured had aged him; he was a shadow of his former self and she would hardly have recognised him. Shocked and saddened, she had left Rookery House, so deep in thought she had barely registered the journey to Ridge View Cottage.

Muriel did not want her daughter to have to face this tragedy; not yet. On top of everything else, it would be too much for her to bear. So she forced a smile and said, 'Not for a while yet, I'm afraid, Celia. It is wonderful news, but we must be patient. David is very weak and needs time to recover.'

'I'd like to see him,' said Celia, the colour slowly returning to her face. 'I need to talk to him.'

'As I said, I'm afraid you are going to have to be patient, he is very sick and not up to seeing anyone at the moment, not even you.'

'What are you not telling me, Mama? How sick? I thought you said he would soon get better now he is at home.'

'Yes, given time. *Time*, Celia. You have waited this long, surely, for his sake, you can wait a little longer? And wouldn't it be a good idea to ascertain first that he wants to see you?'

'Of course he will want to see me. How could it be otherwise and how would it do any harm? It might even help him to get better. He needs to know what has happened, Mama. I have to tell him about the baby. Now he is home we can be married as we planned, and we will find our son.'

This was what Muriel had most feared and her heart sank. She could feel the pressure building in her chest, the pain making her catch her breath. She held onto her daughter's hand and looked into her eyes. 'Celia, as cruel as it must seem to you, you cannot tell David anything about what has happened. Certainly not until he is well again, and as I have just told you, that is not going to be for a long time. I wanted to keep this from you because I know how you will worry, but David's wounds were very severe. He cannot yet walk and he has lost his memory. He may not even know you, so how is it going to be for him if you tell him he has fathered a child? The shock could set him back months.'

Celia cried out, 'No! No!' Covering her ears with her hands, she burst into tears.

'There, there,' Muriel murmured, awkwardly pulling her daughter's hands away and hanging onto them. 'Don't take on so. He is alive and he *is* going to get better. All I am asking is that you be patient. Celia, listen to me: he is *alive*. Isn't that enough for now?'

As she was speaking, Gladys Thrift came into the living room, drying her hands on her apron. 'I am just going to make a cup of tea, would anyone else like one?'

'Thank you, Gladys, and for this,' Muriel handed her the smelling salts then turned back to Celia who, miraculously, was smiling tremulously through her tears.

Wrinkling her nose, Gladys replaced the small, green glass bottle on the kitchen shelf then went to put the kettle on. One look at Muriel Bryant-Smythe's face when she had arrived at the cottage was enough for Gladys. She had known to keep out of the way, but she could not help but overhear what had happened. Rushing in with the smelling salts, she had seen that the mistress was coping so had gone back into the scullery to give the two women some space. With such stupendous news it was not surprising Miss Celia had fainted. Of course, the return of poor David Gillespie from the dead would alter a few things. For a start, he would likely have to be told about the baby and that was going to open a can of worms and no mistake. Whatever was going to happen in the future, Gladys knew Celia's mother would always be there for her daughter; hadn't she been visiting every week all these past years, putting up with Miss Celia's hysterics in the bad times, and never complaining. Gladys knew George had a very high opinion of Muriel Bryant-Smyth and it was one she now shared.

It seemed that no matter what she started thinking about these days, she always ended up thinking about

George. Smiling at the thought of him, Gladys lifted the net curtain to look out of the window at the car. Normally, he would come in, but he must have decided to keep out of the way today. He was a tactful man, her George, love him. She would take him a mug of tea and a piece of her shortbread, he liked that. Just as she was dropping back the curtain, to her dismay she caught sight of Lizzie propping her bicycle up against the wooden shed. Oh Lord! In all the excitement she had completely forgotten she had sent the poor girl down to the village. She would be soaked through. Rummaging for a dry towel, Gladys tapped on the window and motioned for Lizzie to come round to the back door.

Later that afternoon after her mother had gone back to Satchfield Hall, promising to return the following day, Celia, in the privacy of her room, wept for David. To know how ill he was, but to be unable to go to him was torture. She should be by his side, looking after him; he was the man she loved, the father of her baby and he didn't even know it. He might not even know her. After all this time thinking he was dead and then finding out he was alive, it was all so cruel.

For David's sake, if nothing else, Celia knew she had no choice but to comply with her mother's plea for patience. As she always did, she sought solace in her diary. In the three and a half years since the birth of her baby, she had filled hundreds of pages with thousands of words, all of them describing her life, her thoughts and her dreams. Writing everything down had helped her to survive.

Each day she thought about her son, now rising four years old, and sent him her love. In her mind she had named him David Junior and it had comforted her to know that somewhere in the world, a part of his father lived on in his son. She had never given up hope of one day finding him; it was why she had persuaded George Brand to teach her to drive. Sooner or later, she would be free to search for him and could go further with a car. She had not yet thought beyond that. She was convinced after all this time that Gladys Thrift had not been lying and really did not know where her baby had been taken. But someone must. Thinking about the unknown woman who was raising her son had given Celia an idea; it was as yet only half-formed, but because of it, her diary had become even more important than ever.

Over the years, sitting on her bed each day, when it had got too dark to write and was too soon to light the hissing Tilley lamp, Celia had gazed out at the fading sky and done a lot of thinking. She knew now that even if she did succeed in finding her son, as much as she wanted him back it was no longer possible. Too much time had already passed. She would be a stranger – how that hurt - and he, please God, loved and cared for by the people who had taken him in. How could she wrest her child away from the only life he had known and the people he loved? She could not, of course. That was not why she wanted to find him, not anymore. It was the very fact that she had no way of knowing if he was still alive, let alone loved and cared for as she hoped and prayed, that obsessed her waking thoughts. She wanted to reassure herself; be able to keep an eye on him from a distance in case he ever needed her. Thinking about it now, as she had so often in the past, Celia knew she could content herself with that.

Yet now David was alive, everything had changed. When he was better, he would be able to read everything she had written and would know how it had been for her while he had been missing and how much she had thought of him and loved him. And he would learn about their son.

These thoughts gave Celia the happiest of feelings, the first she had felt in years. Knowing that David was living and breathing and barely fifty miles away, despite her frustration at not being able to see him, made her feel so happy that for the first time since her mother had left, Celia smiled.

'David, David, my darling,' she whispered, 'one day we will be together and no matter how long I must wait for you, it will be worth it in the end.'

Chapter TWENTY

Henry Bryant-Smythe had not given much thought to the return of David Gillespie nor, having long since justified his actions to his own satisfaction, did he dwell on the fate of his disgraced daughter, who was, after all, entirely to blame for her own predicament. He had a vague niggle at the back of his mind that there was something about the Gillespie boy that ought to trouble him, but could not recall exactly what. Henry, for whom past events had with the passing years become increasingly blurred, had intended to bandy it about that the fellow had fled in the face of enemy fire, but by all accounts Gillespie had returned *non compos mentis* - or 'doolally' as they called it in the village – so whatever had occurred in the past the boy was no longer a threat; no need to blacken his name then. Reassured, Henry, having enjoyed tormenting his wife, had erased David Gillespie from his mind. He had more important things to worry about than what might or might not have happened in the past, which in any event, had little to do with him.

Strolling to the drawing room window, he saw the Daimler making its slow way down the drive, his wife's head visible in the rear window, doubtless on her way to see Celia. It continued to amuse him that she still appeared to believe he was unaware of her visits and troubled him not at all that she apparently wished to be constantly at the girl's side. Of late she had stopped pleading with him to allow their daughter home, which was a shame as he had enjoyed tormenting her with his adamant refusals. He had to admit that her heart attack had shocked him, not because he cared, indeed, he would be glad to be rid of her, but he did not want her dropping dead before his lawyer had found a loophole in her father's legacy - something else she thought he knew nothing about - so that he could get his hands on it. It was unfortunate she had drawn up her will independently. He would bet his bottom dollar she meant to leave everything she owned to their one surviving offspring, including her half of the estate. Could he only discover with whom her will was placed it would be a simple matter to have it destroyed so that her assets reverted to him. There was nothing among her papers to give him a clue; he had looked through them while she was out. Henry glowered at the departing car; much as he hated to admit it, his wife was a lot shrewder than he had anticipated. He would keep looking; something would turn up.

Frowning, he moved away from the window and hesitated by the brandy decanter. It was perhaps a little early, but God, he could do with a drink. Lately his waking moments were being taxed in more ways than one. The building project in which he was heavily investing was time-consuming and demanded all his resources. He had been forced to raise a second mortgage on the Hall, which was a tad risky, but he needed to make some money, and sooner rather than later. The push by the Government to build new homes after the war had been heaven sent; he was not about to look in the mouth of that particular gift horse!

Henry poured a large slug of brandy and raising it to the portrait of his grandfather, gulped a mouthful, enjoying the burning sensation as it shot down his throat. It always calmed him when his mind turned to failed business ventures, such as the last one, which had turned not so much sour as bitter after the British Government had devalued the pound. The consequences for him were dire: he had lost a considerable sum of money and had been a whisker away from losing Satchfield Hall. In order to save it he had been forced to part with most of his other assets, including those he would rather not have lost.

'Well not *this* time!' he muttered, swallowing the rest of his brandy. His present investment would put him back on the right foot; this time it would succeed. For a start the new venture was entirely his own idea, so how could it fail? He smirked, poured another drink, slumped in his chair and stretched out his long legs with a gratified sigh. It had been an astute move to involve Patrick Beaumont: the man had his fingers in numerous pies and a reputation for getting things done. 'Sweep aside the red tape or get in underneath it, if you know what I mean,' he had said with a sly wink, tapping the side of his nose. Henry had laughed out loud. Oh yes, he knew only too well; it was an approach to which he subscribed wholeheartedly.

Swirling his brandy, his eyes narrowed and his mind focussing on his goal, Henry thought through the various points he had raised at their last meeting. He had earmarked several parcels of land for future development, but there was one little parcel that was so ideally placed, he just knew it could not fail to bring him exactly what he needed: money; plenty of it and speedily. He intended not only to have the developers move in as soon as possible, but to get all the paperwork sorted out before anyone was aware of what he was up to. Stealth, he knew, was the key to his success and there was no better man than he when it came to furtive operations.

The country, to his annoyance, had gone mad with bureaucracy and it seemed pieces of paper in triplicate were needed for almost everything anyone wanted or needed to do. If bits of official paper were what it took to get this project moving, then one way or another he would make sure he had them, and this was where Patrick Beaumont came into his plans. 'You don't need to be worrying about such things,' Patrick had told him. 'That's what you pay me for, to do your worrying for you,' he had added, stuffing the fat brown envelope into the inside of his well cut jacket. 'You be patient and concentrate on the little meadow on your side of the boundary first, and I will ensure you get the necessary paperwork and licences to build on the rest. I'll have them ready for our next meeting.'

Checking his watch, Henry grunted, knocked back his brandy and got to his feet. It was time to set off for the meeting that should, if all went to plan, deliver those self same pieces of paper. 'Damn!' Muriel had taken the Daimler, he remembered, swaying slightly. He would have to take the other car and drive himself. Maybe it was just as well, he reflected. He didn't want anyone to know who he was going to meet, not even George Brand, who had been giving him strangely furtive looks of late. 'I'll have to rattle his cage again,' thought Henry, slamming out of the door, 'remind him who is the master around here!'

Patrick Beaumont had waited for over half an hour in the thick fug of the dingy bar in which he had insisted they meet. Beginning to think Henry Bryant-Smythe had chickened out, he downed another pint of ale, slammed the glass down on the beer-sodden mat on top of the bar and slid off the stool, just as Bryant-Smythe appeared in the doorway. Hiding a smile, Patrick watched him make his way a little unsteadily through the smoke to the bar; the man had clearly already had a few. Dressed in a fine tweed suit that had Saville Row written all over it, his hand-tooled, brown leather shoes gleaming and gold cuff links glinting at his wrists the Squire looked entirely out of place in this environment, but few of the customers looked up and his presence went unremarked. It was why Patrick had chosen the place. He wanted no reliable witnesses to this exchange.

'Afternoon, Squire, let me get you a glass of decent brandy,' he said beckoning the barman, a greasy looking individual with a grubby tea-towel flung over one shoulder, who stuck two fingers into two empty tumblers, picked up a bottle in his other hand and approached.

Looking around him, Henry grimaced in obvious disgust at his surroundings. 'I cannot imagine why you insisted we meet up in this hellhole, Patrick. I'll have a whisky, a large one, if you insist - and I hope it's to seal the deal.'

Patrick smiled, he disliked the man intensely, but he could not turn good money away and he enjoyed a challenge. He was not only good at what he did, but the best this side of the county border; Henry Bryant-Smythe would not find anyone better. The barman, paying no attention to either of them, replaced the bottle of brandy on the shelf behind him and pulled down the whisky then placed the tumblers on the bar and filled them almost to the top with the amber-coloured liquid. Patrick nodded, slithered over a ten-bob note and told him to keep the change.

Drinking half his whisky in one gulp, Henry, his eyes watering, coughed, stared at Patrick then held out his hand. 'Well, where are they then?'

With a quick look around the bar to be sure they were not being observed, Patrick opened the folded copy of *The Times* he was carrying to reveal a large manila envelope inside. Quickly re-folding the newspaper, he placed it in Henry's outstretched fingers. 'You'll find it's all there,' he said, 'licence to do whatever you want.' Henry nodded, pulled open the envelope and glanced at the contents, then tucked the newspaper under his arm.

Patrick, hoping he had covered his tracks sufficiently well, because as sure as eggs were eggs this project of Bryant-Smythe's was going to go tits up and when it did, the proverbial was going to hit the fan, masked his thoughts behind a blank smile, 'I think you'll not be disappointed.'

'I'd better not be is all I can say,' growled Henry, 'it's costing me a friggin' fortune!' Handing over yet another small, but fat envelope, he gulped down the remainder of his whisky. 'I suggest you spend some of that money on a decent place to drink in, in future.' Then he turned and walked out of the bar.

Amused, Patrick watched him leave. He had done what was necessary and had been paid well enough. Good as he was, however, it was probably wise to disappear for a while. He turned back to the bar and signalled for another large whisky. When the glass was refilled, he raised it and said under his breath, 'Thank you, Squire, we all get what we deserve in the end.'

After leaving the disgusting bar, Henry got into his car and before driving off, emptied the contents of the envelope to peruse the forged documents. He smiled: they were good; very good and exactly what he needed. Furnished with these, carefully chosen officials, given enough incentive in their back pockets, would look the other way. He could now go forward with his plan. His new venture was not only going to recoup the money he had lost, it was going to make him a considerable fortune; of that he was certain. Discretional payments had always worked for him, he reflected. Throughout his entire life he had paid for whatever he wanted; legal or otherwise. It was the only way to operate and it had made him powerful. Money was power and power was like a drug to him, he freely admitted it – if only to himself. This new venture was going to make him the wealthiest man in the county. Then perhaps he would rest on his laurels; maybe even dabble in politics. Who knows, I might even buy a title and secure a seat in the Lords, he thought.

Grinning at his reflection in the rear view mirror, Henry started the engine, put the car into gear and cut into the traffic, ignoring the honking horns. He would never lose Satchfield Hall, but he knew of a few others who were about to lose their shirts. Laughing out loud, he headed for a dubious establishment on the other side of town where he could be sure of a warm and raunchy welcome.

Chapter TWENTY-ONE

Standing in front of the French windows looking out at the terrace and the rolling expanse of lawn beyond, David Gillespie caught sight of his reflection in the glass and grimaced. 'I look like an old man; a bent, empty husk,' he thought, leaning on his stick to brush his hand over his prematurely grey hair. Could it really be six months since he had arrived home? Try as he might, he had no recollection of the first few weeks. Indeed, until recently he'd had no recollection of anything much at all. It was as though his head was a big, impenetrable ball of cotton wool. In the last month or so, hazy images of his past life had at last begun to emerge from the fog, together with an overriding sense of guilt. At first he had no idea *why* he felt so guilty. He began to work at it, picking at the tangled threads of memory until at last a woman's face had emerged. The impact had thudded into his chest as if someone had punched him, knocking all the breath out of his lungs. Celia: the woman he had loved, who had been uppermost in his mind through all the missing years. The woman he had abandoned; betrayed.

Weeks ago, the team of doctors who had pulled him through had said he could receive visitors. 'You need someone to take you out of yourself,' one of them had said. Huh! Who in his right mind would want to visit me? he had thought, shaking his head and taking refuge in silence. The last thing he wanted was to be taken out of himself and frighten people half to death when they saw him; even worse, have to witness their compassion. He shunned company, wanting neither pity nor sympathy, he just wanted time and preferably time alone. More importantly, he needed to come to terms with everything that had happened and work out how to face another day, because there were far too many days when he would have preferred not to have to open his eyes and face life as he now saw it.

David's self-pity filled him with contempt. He was painfully aware that he had got off lightly: he had not been blinded or disfigured; his limbs were intact; the scars on his body were hidden from view beneath his clothes. Good food and care had returned the strength to his legs and despite the deep, suppurating wound in his thigh that refused to heal, he had long since abandoned his wheelchair. Too many of his friends would never come back; lost in the brutal bewilderment of conflict. Their families would have paid any price for them to have returned as he had done. Racked with nightmares and guilt, he tried never to forget that he was one of the fortunate ones, but it was not always easy.

Flexing his bad leg, David turned away from his reflection and gazed back out at the terrace. Nothing had changed since his return: the terror of the missing years clung to him like a goblin on his back that he could never shake off and maybe never would. Yet despite this, and even though the thought of it filled him with acute anxiety, he at last felt ready to speak to Celia Bryant-Smythe. He could only hope she would want to speak to him. He dreaded her first sight of him; the thought of the shocked pity he would see in her eyes curled him up inside.

To his shame, he had not responded to any of her numerous letters and notes, although he had read them all carefully. She wrote of the past, much of which he could no longer remember; of her love and longing to be with him, clearly with no idea that the man she had loved no longer existed. He had wanted to reply; there was so much he wanted to say to her, but he had not been able to, convinced that time and distance had changed everything. He had even begun to hope that once she saw him, she would understand and be free to find someone special to spend her life with. Was this what he really wanted? Not for himself, perhaps, for in reality he did not know *what* he wanted, but he could not saddle her, out of some misguided sense of loyalty and memory of love, with the permanently terrified husk of the man he had become. He was scared of everything nowadays: afraid of the dark, afraid of losing his mind; any loud noise sent him into paroxysms of fear.

Celia's letters did not imply that she had met anyone else, on the contrary, she simply asked - and of late, begged - to see him: '*If only for a moment...*' David knew he could not ignore her forever. He needed to explain; he owed her that much.

His eye drawn to the flight of a solitary bird soaring over the trees that fringed the lawns, David found himself remembering the distant, beautiful, carefree days when he and Celia had watched the swallows flitting above them; had laughed, made love and talked of marriage. Even in his darkest hours, when he had lost the image of her face in his mind, he had never stopped loving her, nor had he forgotten the way she had made him feel. But that was just what they were, he reminded himself, *distant*, carefree days when they'd had everything to live for, not like now when he had nothing to offer her beyond the burden of his broken mind and feeble body.

Although he had not replied to any of her letters, on a number of occasions he had asked his mother how Celia was. To his puzzlement she had always evaded the question, quickly changing the subject. He did not press her, but drew his own conclusions: either she did not want Celia hurt or, more likely, she did not want him hurt. Sighing, David moved away from the window, sank into a chair and covered his eyes with his hand. He knew Celia would want him to tell her what had happened to him in the intervening years since he went missing. His parents often asked him; he pretended he had no memory of them. He wished that was still the case, but they had been the first images to return to him and he knew they were imprinted on his mind and would remain with him forever.

Words could not even begin to portray the horrors of the time he had spent lost in the wilderness. For that reason he knew he would never be able talk about it. Not now, not ever. The doctors had tried, they had even sedated him for a period of time in the hope that he would talk. He had resisted.

'Talking just might help you come to terms with everything, darling. Pain bottled up will only destroy you,' his mother would say in despair.

'I don't remember and even if I did, I don't want to talk about it,' he would say, like a petulant child. 'I just want to find a way to cope again. Please leave me alone.'

Each time they had this conversation he would see the hurt in her eyes. He wanted to tell her not to worry, to let her hug him, but he could not even do this small human act: he could not bear to be touched and would flinch away from her embrace. It seemed that all he was good for these days was to hurt the people who loved him. Brushing away traitor tears, he looked once more to the window, aware that his mother had entered his room. He always knew it was she by her fragrance, which reminded him of wild honeysuckle on a warm June evening. David braced himself for her reaction to what he was about to say.

As Zilda Gillespie entered her son's room, she saw that he was staring out through the French windows, his slumped, abject form silhouetted against the light. He did not stir as she moved towards him and not for the first time in all these long months, she wondered what was going through his tormented mind. It pained her that she could not even begin to guess. She had watched him every day since his return and in all that time, not for one moment had she seen a spark of the boy she had brought into this world. It seemed that the young man, who had marched out of the house years earlier, had returned a stranger. With these thoughts flashing through her mind, Zilda was totally unprepared for what David said as he turned his head to look her full in the face.

'I'd like to go to Satchfield Hall.'

'What? Whatever for?' Zilda gasped. The last thing she wanted was David reacquainting himself with Celia Bryant-Smythe. The girl's behaviour, she knew, had been a scandal. It appalled her; it would have appalled her in any event, but knowing that her son had been seeing Celia before his departure to the war effort and grown fond of her, made it even worse. Zilda had dismissed any rumours about her son's involvement with Celia - or any other girl - as spiteful gossip. Not for one minute had she believed David would behave so dishonourably and she feared his reaction should he ever find out that Celia Bryant-Smythe had simply toyed with his affections, as she had clearly done with another's – to her cost! Her son teetered enough on the brink of insanity without adding any of this knowledge to his disturbed mind.

'Because I owe it to Celia to see her again,' he said quietly. 'I've been home for months and at last I feel able to speak to her. Please, Mother, I want to see her now, today and I would appreciate your help.'

With some difficulty, Zilda recovered her composure, but was momentarily unsure how to handle this extraordinary request. Normally, she would have called on Robert for advice, but he was out. Something nasty was going on, he had said, and he needed to get to the bottom of it. She had not really been listening; something to do with one of the paddocks, she gathered, but quite what had escaped her. Without Robert here to talk to David, she must try to encourage him to change his mind. She drew breath to speak, but as she looked again at her son and saw, for the first time since he had returned home, a spark of intelligence in eyes that were normally blank of any expression but torment, she choked back the words swirling around in her head. David's request was a huge step forward. The fact that he was thinking about seeing someone – anyone at all - be it the disgraced daughter of their neighbour, then she must see it for what it was: progress.

Thinking on her feet, she said, 'I think it would be best if we ask Celia to come to visit you, there is chaos at Satchfield Hall, I understand there is some renovation work in progress. For us to go unannounced would be inconvenient. You may not even be able to see her, which would be disappointing for you. So please be patient, David, and allow me to arrange for Celia to come here instead.'

In fact she had no idea exactly what was happening at Satchfield Hall, although had heard it involved heavy machinery, but she did know that Celia no longer resided there, and why. For now, she simply wanted to give herself time to organise a proper visit for the girl to come to Rookery House, thus avoiding any further explanations. Thankfully, with David not seeing anyone he had heard no gossip so knew nothing of Celia's disgrace. Zilda wanted to keep him in ignorance for as long as possible - it was unlikely, she thought wryly, that the girl would mention it herself.

Smiling at her son, Zilda reached for his hand and was more pleased than she could express when instead of flinching away from her, he allowed this small gesture of intimacy. Looking down at his thin, wan face she said, 'I'll organise it for Celia to come to Rookery House just as soon as possible, I promise.'

David nodded and smiled, 'Thank you. Thank you for everything, Mother. I know I'm not that easy to deal with these days. I don't even like myself, which doesn't help the situation.'

'Don't be silly .... Oh, David, look!' Zilda pointed out of the French windows.

Releasing her hand he looked to where she pointed. A hedgehog had emerged from the pile of dead leaves in the corner of the terrace. It looked around blindly for a moment then scuttled away.

'It looks a bit like I feel,' David said. 'As if I have just emerged from hibernation, shaken off the dead leaves and can at last face the world and go and look for worms!'

'Oh, my darling,' Zilda laughed shakily, holding back her tears. 'I have prayed to hear you speak those words. Well, maybe not the bit about the worms! Unable to resist, she rested her hand lightly on his head and stroked his hair. 'Now, at last, perhaps you can begin to move forward. Rest now and I will go and write a note to Celia.'

Reaching the door, she turned back to see he was again staring out of the window, but his body was no longer slumped in the chair. 'He looks as though a great weight has been removed from his shoulders,' Zilda thought, overwhelmed with relief and allowing her silent tears free rein, she quietly closed the door behind her.

Chapter TWENTY-TWO

Tramping across the fields towards the fence that marked the southern boundary of his estate with that of Satchfield Hall, Robert Gillespie drew in a lungful of fresh air and attempted to still his anxiety about David. The doctors had said that all the boy needed was time, but had been singularly vague about how much time. Robert, a reconnaissance pilot in the RFC towards the end of the First World War, had seen shellshock at first hand and recognised it in his son. He knew full well that it could be years before David regained his mental health, he also knew that sometimes the damage was irreparable and the boy might never recover completely. This thought appalled Robert, but he tried to remain positive and kept his fears to himself.

Each day he observed his son, hoping to see some improvement in his condition, and each day his hopes were dashed. David refused to discuss his experiences; hardly spoke much at all in fact, just sat gazing out of the window; refused to countenance visitors and flinched at the slightest sudden noise. It hurt Robert to witness the boy's haggard features and tormented soulless eyes, so much so that it was a relief to get away from the oppressive, anxiety-ridden atmosphere in the house this morning, even if his mission was to tackle another problem, albeit one of lesser concern than that of his son's health.

He had lately been hearing a few rumours about something odd going on in the area, but never one to pay much regard to gossip, had dismissed them as unfounded. However, when some days ago it had been brought to his attention that strange men had been observed walking on his land, most particularly on the level stretch of ground that lay alongside the neighbouring estate of Satchfield Hall, Robert had determined to get to the bottom of it.

As he crested the rise and was able to look down on the far paddock, what he saw alarmed him. Two men, one bending over a theodolite, the other some distance away from him, with a folder clutched under one arm and scribbling on a clipboard, were indeed on his land and appeared to be surveying it. Robert did a double-take. What the hell was going on?

Striding briskly down the hill, he made his way over to the man with the clipboard, who was directing the other to move further down the field. Assuming him to be in charge, without preamble Robert called over, 'I can only conclude that something is wrong or why else would you be on my land without my consent?' He kept his tone firm, but non-confrontational. 'Are you aware that you are trespassing?'

'No, nothing's wrong, sir. I've been told by the Squire to come along and check up on a few things and that's why you find me here.' At this point the man shouted down the field for his companion to wait, then pulling out from his folder two documents, turned to face Robert.

'This is what I've been given and all is perfectly in order. Fully signed and stamped.' As he spoke, he handed the sheets of paper over.

Robert took them and glanced at the contents. He knew exactly what the papers represented. With over four million homes lost or damaged during the war, the need to house the nation was one that concentrated the mind of the Government, both at local and national level. Robert and other landowners had been in talks about the likely building of new homes on parts of their land. He had not been aware that Henry Bryant-Smythe had been similarly engaged, though had been warned by a business associate what the man might be up to. As much as Robert had listened, he had dismissed it thinking it could not possibly be true. Aside from not wanting to believe that his former friend and colleague would stoop so low, there was the undisputable fact that he owned the land this side of the boundary and had all the title deeds to prove it. Now, however, having seen what was happening for himself, he realised bitterly that not only should he have known better, he should have listened.

His face betraying none of these thoughts, he handed back the documents. 'I think you need to stop work until I have spoken with your company,' he said pleasantly, striving to be reasonable.

With a glare that said, *I'm only doing my job,* the man took the papers and replaced them in his folder. 'Very well, sir. Just as soon as we've finished this, we'll be gone.'

Robert gritted his teeth in an effort to hold on to his temper. 'No, you do not understand me. You will stop whatever it is you are doing. Right *now*!'

Not waiting for a reply, he spun on his heel and trudged back up the hill, stopping only once to look back. His instruction had been ignored; the two men had continued working. Seething, he hurried home, intending to make an urgent call to his solicitor, but when he marched breathless into Rookery House, Zilda was waiting for him, her face, though wet with tears, was lit up in a beaming smile. What she told him drove everything else from his head until later, by which time offices were closed, and since it was a Friday, he was forced to postpone speaking to his solicitor until after the weekend.

On Sunday afternoon, saying nothing to Zilda about what he suspected Henry Bryant-Smythe was up to, Robert returned to look again at the paddock. Far from the work being suspended, it seemed to have moved on apace. A shiny new excavator had been parked in the field and his land clearly marked out for a building project. It being Sunday, the site was deserted and for one wild moment, Robert was tempted to sabotage the machinery, but what could he do? He had no idea how to drive it and no tools. He shook his fist in the direction of Satchfield Hall, just visible in the distance, 'You bastard, Bryant-Smythe,' he muttered, 'this is outright war!'

They had once been friends; attended the same school, gone into business together on numerous occasions after the last war. It had seemed only natural to maintain the tradition of friendship between their two families. If he was honest, Robert had never quite trusted Henry and had begun to distance himself when, over the years, it became clear there was nothing the man would not do for his own gains. Refusing point blank to have anything to do with business deals that were even slightly shady, Robert had fallen out with him on more than one occasion.

After David had been summarily dispatched to the army, Robert had thought long and hard about what had happened. At the time he had been convinced that his son had been sowing wild oats, and to avoid a scandal it had seemed best that he join the war effort to remove him from the scene. The last thing Robert had wanted was to see the boy trapped in a loveless marriage with some chit of a girl who, by all accounts, had no way of knowing precisely who might have fathered her child. Fuelled by Henry Bryant-Smythe's fury that one of his housemaids had been compromised, Robert had acted quickly in securing a commission for David. Only afterwards had it occurred to him to question the apparent extremity of Henry's righteous indignation. Knowing the man as he did, it had not rung true. An awful suspicion had lodged in his mind, which had grown when he discovered that the Bryant-Smythes' housekeeper had been largely responsible for spreading the rumours about David's involvement. Why would she have done that if it were not true? Robert had drawn his own conclusions. He was under no illusions about Henry's appetite for sexual gratification, which had been obvious right from the early days when, as young men, they had together sown their own wild oats. It had been in wartime then too, Robert reflected. What he could not fathom was why Henry would have selected David - a family friend for God's sake! - as his scapegoat, and because he was not entirely sure, he had kept his suspicions to himself. Now, however, it came back to haunt him. This latest episode was evidence enough for Robert that far from being a family friend, Henry Bryant-Smythe had, for whatever reason, deliberately set out to destroy him and his son. 'Yes,' he said, picking up a clump of mud and hurling it impotently at the excavator, 'this is war.'

Wandering slowly back to the house, he thought through the documents the surveyor had shown him, which appeared to grant full licence to building on the land on either side of the boundary of their two estates. He knew that the paddock, close to an existing road, accessible and relatively flat, was an ideal spot for development. He had himself already considered it and ruled it out because of its proximity to Satchfield Hall. What a fool he was! Instead, he had engaged his solicitor to seek planning for a plot of land to the west of his estate. It was taking a long time to obtain the necessary paperwork, so how in the hell had Henry managed to secure planning consent so quickly and without any approach being made to himself, who held the title to the paddock? The whole business stank of corruption. It dawned on Robert that perhaps the documents were illegal and if so, that this time, Henry Bryant-Smythe had shot himself in the foot. Was the man so arrogant and stupid he imagined that for old times' sake and in the interest of upholding the unspoken code of landed gentry, he, Robert Gillespie, would turn a blind eye? 'Well, we'll see about *that*!' Robert muttered.

With a grim smile, his stride lengthening, Robert cut across the fields and letting himself into the house, went straight to his study to look through the Rookery House file. The land could prove to be the most effective tool in his armoury for taking ultimate revenge. And, by God, he would have his revenge!'

Chapter TWENTY-THREE

In the months since her son's return, Zilda Gillespie had been on an emotional seesaw: one minute joy because he was alive and the next sadness, because he was so damaged. She still could quite not believe he had come back to her. So grateful was she, that first thing each morning when she opened her eyes and last thing at night before she closed them again, she thanked God for granting her another day with her offspring. In the years that he was gone she had refused to believe he was dead, convinced that as his mother she would know instinctively if it were true. She had prayed constantly that the news they had been given on that darkest of days was wrong. Someone must have heard her prayers, for they had been answered, but the man who had returned was so unlike her son that in her bleakest moments it seemed to Zilda that he had been killed after all and a stranger taken his place.

Whenever she looked at David, she knew how ungrateful it was to allow such thoughts to cross her mind. She and Robert were the lucky ones, she told herself, for unlike so many thousands of other families, their son, however changed, had come home in the end and one day, please God, would get better.

As the months had crawled by, despite David being a shadow of the vigorous young man who had left home a lifetime ago, or so it seemed to Zilda, she had seen tiny improvements in his condition and was encouraged by them. It troubled her that he would not speak of the missing years: what he had been through and where he had been. Nasty scars on his upper body, and a wound to his left leg that regularly became septic and had left him with a limp, were all she and Robert knew of their son's war.

She often heard him cry out in the night, a heartrending sound that brought her to tears, but when she woke him from his nightmares he would never say anything about them. The doctor had told her to be patient: 'What your son has been through we can only begin to guess at,' he had said. 'It is apparent he has been subsisting on the barest minimum of nourishment and it is quite remarkable he came through it alive. We must hope that time, proper care and a mother's love will bring him back from wherever his mind has gone and return him to his former self. Give him time, Mrs Gillespie.'

She had tried to be patient, but David's recovery had been painfully slow. Zilda continued to believe that this was as much to do with his state of mind as his physical health. Both she and Robert had worried about their son's self-imposed isolation: in all the time he had been home, he had not once left the grounds of Rookery House. So after her initial reaction, it was with indescribable relief that she greeted his request to see Celia Bryant-Smythe. For Zilda, this was the first sign that David's mind was at last coming back. She had been so afraid that it never would. All her anxiety, which until now she had kept tightly under control for his sake, had been released, pouring out of her in a storm of weeping that left her utterly drained. She had then dried her tears, told herself to pull herself together and, true to her word, penned a brief letter inviting Celia to tea the following week. In a covering note to Muriel, she had asked her to pass the letter on to her daughter and had sent it off to Satchfield Hall. That done, and hearing Robert coming in from wherever he had been, she went to give him the joyous news of what had occurred in his absence.

Two days later, a reply was brought from Satchfield Hall by the Bryant-Smythe's driver. In it, Muriel expressed her delight that David was sufficiently recovered to receive visitors, but regretted that her daughter must decline the invitation as she had come down with influenza. Celia hoped she might call at Rookery

House as soon as she was better and all risk of passing on the infection had gone.

Zilda's first reaction was one of relief, but the affect on her son was a further cause for anxiety. Clearly it had been an effort for him to make the request and having built himself up to the point where he could face seeing someone after all this time, he was in a fever of impatience. His disappointment on learning it would be some weeks before Celia was able to visit was correspondingly acute. Fearing he would slip back into the mind-numbing despondency that had been a feature of his mental state, Zilda sought out her husband, finding him in his study.

'Robert, you have to think of something to keep David's mind occupied,' she said. 'Muriel's daughter has flu so can't visit and he is working himself up into such a state.'

Although in the circumstances Robert was none too happy about David renewing his acquaintance with Bryant-Smythe's daughter, at the same time he had been more than delighted when Zilda had told him of this apparent breakthrough. If the boy was at last finding a way to lift himself out of the pit of depression that had held him in its grip for so long, then, thought Robert, how could he do other than encourage it? The girl could not be held responsible for the actions of her father, and whatever mess she had got herself into a few years ago, he had always liked her; a pretty young thing as he recalled. Knowing Bryant-Smythe as he did, Robert felt extremely sorry for her - and her poor mother. Even so, he hoped David's affections were not going to become engaged with the girl; it could well become awkward and the last thing he wanted was for the boy to be hurt.

Now, in response to Zilda's plea, he shuffled the papers he was reading back in their file, laid his reading glasses on the desk, smiled at his wife and made his way to his son's room. David was in his usual position, standing motionless by the French windows, staring out at nothing. Deciding not to mention Bryant-Smythe's illegal incursion onto their land, Robert cleared his throat. 'It is time you picked up the reins and started managing the estate again, son. I need you to take it off my hands. I have another meeting tomorrow to discuss the development of the fields at West Point. Why not join me? There's much talk of the need for new homes. The war destroyed so much and we have what the Government is looking for; acres of it to be precise.'

He had asked more times than he could count that his son accompany him to these important meetings, but David had categorically refused. It had been a frustration to Robert, who was of the opinion that if the boy could only see what needed to be done, then maybe he would be able to release himself from his demons. Troubled by David's continued lack of interest in anything and everything that surrounded him, Robert desperately wanted him involved, but his efforts over the last few months had so far been in vain. He believed that his son, who like so many had suffered because of the war, would want to help, but each time he had said as much his request had fallen on deaf ears - or a stubborn mind more likely, Robert thought, his patience wearing thin.

Still staring out of the window, David shrugged. 'Not sure I'd be able to follow what they're all talking about. I have a job to follow my own nose these days,' he quipped, but his voice was flat. 'Another time, Father, eh?'

It was his customary response and in the past, defeated, Robert had let it go. This time, however, thinking that if David was now able to face a visit from Celia Bryant-Smythe then he was sufficiently recovered to turn his mind to other things, he persisted. 'I would have thought that you of all people would be interested in what is going on, David,' he said, more harshly than he had intended. 'So many people have lost so much – some of them everything. If getting new homes built will help them to have a better life, then shouldn't we, who have lost so little, be there to make sure it happens? Our local people have suffered too and need homes to start up again. Land like ours is what the Government is looking for and I for one want to make sure it gets considered. Involving yourself in something like this will help you get back into belonging and also get your mind thinking again. We all have to move on, son, even you.'

Robert did not want to sound unsympathetic to his son's troubled mind, but felt it high time the boy made more of an effort. There was a mountain of paper work to be done, along with numerous meetings at all levels, and despite the Government's urgency to get things moving, typical of bureaucracy, the pace at times almost ground to a halt. This frustration, added to David's ambivalence to everything and now the situation with Bryant-Smythe, made Robert feel increasingly fraught. 'Will you look at me, please David; I find it hard to talk to your back.'

His son swung round to face him and in a harsh voice that took Robert by surprise, retorted, 'Thinking is the last thing I need at the moment, Father, my mind does nothing *but* think! Can't you understand that?'

Robert grimaced at this response, but was determined not to be thrown off course. 'Yes, of course, but what you don't understand is that I need you. This national plan for building new homes is huge. Our acres of land are but a drop in the ocean in the overall scheme of things, but nonetheless, for a simple chap like me to be left to get on with it on my own ... well, I confess it is all just a bit too much for me. I don't want to beg, David, but please can I ask that you think about it, son? Believe me, I wouldn't ask if I didn't need your help.'

'I'll try, Dad. I can't make any promises, but I'll try.'

Robert raised his hand and patted David's shoulder, wincing as he felt the bones standing proud beneath the boy's shirt. 'Well then, son; I won't press you anymore. Let's just say next time, eh?'

David nodded and Robert, heartened, smiled. Maybe this time his son meant it. 'I'll leave you to it, then.'

Turning away, he left the room. There was nothing more he could do except hope that at the very least, David would think hard on what he had said.

Chapter TWENTY FOUR

Pacing the floor in his room, his agitation building by the minute, David could think of nothing beyond seeing the person whose very existence had kept him alive all these years. Three weeks ago, he had promised to think about what his father had asked, and he had tried. How he had tried. He could not begin to consider attending a meeting, the mere thought of it turned him into a gibbering wreck, but he had attempted to read through the various documents his father had passed to him. He found it impossible to concentrate for more than a few minutes at a time; he barely had the mental energy to tie his shoelaces, never mind sift through policy documents and development schemes. His mind simply refused to grapple with words that were just a meaningless jumble on the page.

This morning his mother had told him Celia was coming to see him after lunch and since then he had been unable to stay still. Would she turn away in shock at the sight of him; never want to see him again? Would she view him as an object of pity? He would not be able to bear that. What would she look like? Was she as beautiful as he remembered or was it just in his imagination that she resembled Rita Hayworth? Did she really love him as her letters implied or had she built her memory of him into a fantasy? What would he say to her and she to him? What would they talk about? He began to panic: he could not possibly talk about the missing years, but like everyone else, she was sure to want to know. Would she think him dull and stupid if he refused? His stomach knotted into an even tighter ball of anxiety.

Turning to pace back across the room, the sound of soft voices on the other side of the door stopped him in his tracks. He held his breath. In the absolute stillness he could clearly hear the timbre of her voice: she sounded just the same. He broke into a sweat and his heart pounded as he began to breathe again.

Thrusting his hands behind his back to hide their trembling, he stood stock still and with eyes that threatened to embarrass him with tears, he watched as the door slowly opened and the woman he loved - and aside from a brief period of amnesia had never stopped loving - stepped not only into his room but, he fervently hoped, back into his life.

The sight of her took his breath away. He had imagined this moment time and time again, but even in his nightmares, nothing had prepared him for how she would look. To support himself, he held onto the back of a chair, desperately trying to hide the shock at what he saw. He had thought he was the one who had suffered in these last years, but whatever had happened to Celia, it was clearly nothing short of terrible judging by her drastic loss of weight and the sadness etched on her haggard face. Seeing this devastated him and his heart lurched from elation to sorrow.

With her back to the closed door, Celia gazed across the room. She saw a pale, thin man with greying hair, slightly stooped, one hand holding a walking cane, the other gripping the back of a chair, and for a moment did not recognise him. He did not look like her David. In fact he looked like nobody she knew. Despite all the warnings from her mother and the lecture she has just received from Zilda Gillespie, his frailty and changed appearance shocked her to the core.

And then he smiled.

Even as she struggled to mask her reaction, Celia's heart skipped a beat. Beneath the prematurely aged exterior, the man in front of her was indeed her David. She looked past the ravages left by whatever horrors he had endured and saw the man she loved, and in that instant she loved him all the more. 'David,' she whispered in a voice that appeared to have withered like the rest of her.

As if rooted to the spot, he did not move.

'David, say something! I can't believe I am at last seeing you again.'

This time he propelled himself across the room to where she was standing. He stood for the briefest of seconds looking into her face then tossing aside his cane, he gently wrapped his arms around her. 'My God, Celia,' he croaked, his voice constricted with tears. 'My darling, is it you, is it really you?'

And then they were both weeping, their tears mingling together as their faces touched.

'Yes,' she drew in a sobbing breath and raising her arms to place her hands one on either side of his face, pulled down his head and looked deep into his eyes. 'It is really me.'

Covering her hands with his own he lifted them away from his face, bent forward and softly kissed her. His lips felt dry and warm and tasted salty.

'Now I know I am going to get better,' he murmured, 'but only if can hold onto you like this forever.'

Celia feeling David's heart beating against her body, whispered, 'I want you to hold me like this forever.'

'I want it too, more than anything in the world. I want to hold you and love you like I did all those years ago. I've thought of little else since I last saw you.'

Feeling herself blushing, Celia glanced away, wondering why he had remained silent all through those years and yet now was saying such beautiful things. Why, oh why could he not have written to her? 'When you didn't reply to my letters I was so afraid you didn't love me anymore. Not that I would blame you, I'm not the person you once knew.'

He looked down at her, his mouth twisting in a wry grin, 'Well that makes two of us! As for your letters, I can't tell you how grateful I was to receive them. You know, they kept me alive when …' he broke off, a haunted expression crossing his face. 'Well, anyway, I always meant to reply, I just couldn't put into words everything I wanted to say.'

'Can you now? I'd quite like to hear them.'

He laughed, 'Well I can have a go.' He drew her over to the window, sat on the arm of the chair and pulled her close to him, his arm resting lightly around her hips. 'If you watch very carefully, you might see a hedgehog. He's a bit like me, although it might be a she, I'm not really sure, but he spent the winter under a pile of leaves in the corner of the terrace, which, in a manner of speaking, is what I have been doing. You are the first person, aside from doctors and my parents, I have seen since I came home. You will have to forgive me if I have forgotten how to talk to a beautiful woman.'

Celia snorted at that, but he had still not said *I love you*, the three little words she longed to hear, and she could not help but wonder if he did or if he was just flirting with her. Not wanting to show her feelings, she quipped, 'They didn't tell me your eyes had been affected.'

'Did they not? What did they tell you?'

'That I was not to tire you.'

'Ah, Celia, I feel less tired now than I have felt in months – and I can assure you there is nothing wrong with my sight. To me you are more beautiful than the angels.'

'Hush; you are embarrassing me,' she laughed to cover her confusion. Celia knew how changed she was; the mirror did not lie. The recent bout of flu had left her pale, scrawny and hollow-cheeked. Years of sorrow had forged a web of lines around her eyes and mouth. Beautiful she was not, but to hear the man she loved say she was, brought a glow of pleasure to her pale cheeks. She could forgive him that lie.

Revelling in his closeness, the sight, sound, smell and touch of him, Celia could not believe how fast the time sped by. Zilda had asked her not to stay beyond half an hour, explaining that it was important for David not to tax his strength with this first visit. She had readily agreed, but so soon it was almost time to go. It had taken only a moment for her to realise that now was not the time to tell him about the baby. One day she would, but not yet. He was not ready for such a shock. So much had happened and so much had changed for both of them. After all these years of waiting she could wait a little longer, she knew they needed to get to know each other again first.

Celia sensed that David did not want to talk about his wartime experiences so did not ask, and he in turn did not ask her about what she had been doing in the intervening years. It was enough just to be together, with their arms around each other, looking out at the windswept lawns and talking nonsense, until a gentle tap on the door heralded Zilda's arrival, inhibiting further conversation. Promising to call again soon, Celia declined a cup of tea, thanked Zilda and with a secret smile at David that spoke volumes, said goodbye.

She could not wait to be alone, to re-live each moment of the meeting she had so longed for and yet feared. The return journey to Ridge View Cottage passed in a daze, Celia hugging to herself the feeling of David's kiss not wanting to let it go and already longing for her next visit.

Over the next few months, Robert became aware of the impression Bryant-Smythe's daughter was having on his son and welcomed it: he would have welcomed anything or anyone who would help bring David back to them. By the time his son had been home for a year, although much thinner than he used to be, the awful frailty was a thing of the past. The disturbed nights continued to plague him and he was still suffering from depression, but there were times now when David's old spark of humour shone through and reminded Robert of the boy he had been.

As far as Robert was concerned, if a young woman could calm David's anguished mind, then what harm would it do? He knew Celia's life had been turned upside down; some had suggested totally destroyed, but he was not here to pass judgement. What he did know was that these two souls had endured experiences that had changed them radically and not just in appearance, although the first time he had seen Celia at Rookery House, he had been shocked at how thin and pale she had looked. She had aged beyond recognition and this saddened him. He was wise enough to work out why she had been sent away. In the Bryant-Smythes' position he might have done the same – not that Zilda would have permitted it! – but never would he have banished a daughter of his indefinitely. He cared less than that about any scandal or gossip. Had the world not suffered enough without adding more misery? And if this young woman could help bring their son back to them as he once was, then she would always be welcomed at Rookery House.

However, as time went on it troubled Robert more and more that although his son had begun to relieve him of some of the burden of managing the estate, David still refused to accompany him to the development committee meetings. This morning, as he left on his own for yet another of these interminable sessions with local authority officials, it occurred to him that perhaps Celia's influence was not as helpful as he had at first supposed. Indeed, far from taking his place in the real world, David was being distracted by a woman as troubled as he was himself and that being so, thought Robert, he would have to seriously consider curtailing her visits.

There was another reason why this might be for the best, he reflected. His solicitor had secured a restraining order on development work going forward in the paddock, pending enquiries into title and the legality of the planning consent. Now, after weeks of painstaking investigation, Bryant-Smythe's perfidy was about to be brought to the attention of the public prosecutor. Whatever the relationship between Bryant-Smythe and his daughter, the girl could not help but be affected when her father was charged with corruption, which in turn, only naturally, would have an adverse effect on David. Yes, thought Robert, it would be wise to put some distance between his son and Celia Bryant-Smythe, at least for the time being. It was a decision he did not want to make because he had grown fond of the young woman, but all things considered, it was necessary.

With this resolved Robert got into his car and let his mind turn to the building project at West Point which, with the necessary licences signed and sealed, was at last beginning to move forward.

Chapter TWENTY FIVE

Zilda could see that Celia Bryant-Smythe's frequent visits over the past six months had brought about a transformation in her son. True, he had not once mentioned the missing years or what had happened to him, but he now seemed willing to involve himself with his family and the daily goings on in the household. Not only that, but he immersed himself in paperwork for hours each day and was getting to grips with the farm management and the building development programme, even though he still refused to leave the grounds of Rookery House. Today, she thought wryly, yet another visit from Celia had been the perfect excuse for him to once again refuse to go out on business with his father.

Loading the tea tray with crockery, Zilda, placing a few shortbread biscuits on a plate, reflected that despite David's improved mental state, she was not as happy as she ought to be. She put this down to a nagging worry about the impact Celia was having on her son. It was clear to her that he was becoming increasingly fond of the girl and as much as she appreciated the benefits of these regular visits, Zilda feared the implications. She knew exactly why Celia had been sent away from Satchfield Hall and whilst she considered Henry's treatment of his daughter overly harsh, she could not condone what had led to the young woman's disgrace. How could a girl of Celia's privileged background have allowed herself to indulge in such vulgar behaviour? It did not bear thinking about! And the war was no excuse, she thought. She and Robert had not leapt into bed simply because there was a war on when they met - the war to end all wars as they had thought then. No; she had kept her mind and body pure until the day Robert Gillespie had put a wedding band on her finger, and that was how it should be. She was not so naive as to believe her husband had not sought such pleasures outside their marriage bed – it was the way of men – but if he had, she had no knowledge of it; he had never been anything but discreet.

Confident that they had passed their values on to their son, his upbringing guided by a strict moral code that included treating women, particularly those of his own social standing, with respect, Zilda dreaded David finding out about Celia. He was far too well bred to forgive such misconduct; he would be both shocked and disappointed. Not only that, but in his fragile state she feared he would be terribly hurt. Zilda had known, of course, that David had become acquainted with Celia before he left; taken her to a ball once, as she recalled, but she was quite certain that nothing untoward could possibly have taken place between them, nor could he have known the girl had been messing about with someone else or he would have had nothing more to do with her.

Seven years ago, when rumours had emerged about David and a girl from the village, who happened to work at Satchfield Hall and whom he had met on occasion when he was there on business with his father, Zilda had been appalled and outraged. It was quite obvious to her the girl's father had seized on his daughter's predicament as a way of extorting money from them. That David had been the victim of some malicious little slut who had set her cap at him and had her nose put out of joint when he quite rightly ignored her, was to Zilda the only possible explanation. But the rumours had persisted and eventually had led to a heated argument between Robert and the detestable Henry Bryant-Smythe. Normally a very tolerant person - Zilda knew her loathing of the man had always surprised her husband - on that occasion, however, she'd had some sympathy for him, reluctantly admitting that although her son was not to blame, something must be done to extricate David from the situation.

Robert had agreed: 'The safest thing to do is to send him off to do some good for his country. Aside from averting a scandal, it will get Henry off my back and take away some of the boy's restlessness at the same time.'

Now, thinking about what had happened to her son as a direct result of that unfortunate episode, Zilda slammed the teapot onto the tea tray and carried it grimly to the drawing room where her son was ensconced with Bryant-Smythe's daughter. Fixing a smile on her face, she balanced the tray on one hand and reaching out with the other pushed the door ajar.

Zilda did not mean to eavesdrop, but inadvertently overheard a snippet of conversation that shocked her so much she almost dropped the tray. Milk slopped onto the biscuits; the crockery rattled and a teacup slid off its saucer to smash on the parquet floor. Her mind in a whirl, she leaned for a moment against the wall and tried to calm her rapid breathing.

'Mother? Are you all right,' David called out.

'I'm fine, just a little accident, don't concern yourself.' With her thoughts turning somersaults, Zilda pushed the door wide and walked into the room. Attempting to speak normally, she put the tea tray down on the occasional table in front of where they sat side by side on the sofa, 'I'll clear it up directly. I've brought you some tea. You can have my cup, David; I don't really feel like tea anyway.'

In those briefest of moments Zilda wanted desperately to believe she had been mistaken in what she had overheard, but her hopes were dashed by what she saw: her son was sheet white, his body taut with shock that mirrored her own. Celia's face was wet with tears and she was clinging to David's hand, but her expression was one of such utter relief that it made the hairs rise on the back of Zilda's neck. Neither of them appeared to have noticed anything untoward in her manner as she lifted the teapot to pour.

Looking up at her, David cleared his throat, 'Thank you, Mother, that is kind of you. Please would you just leave it, we can manage.' His tone was clipped, his voice husky with emotion as he smiled at her; a smile that did not reach his eyes.

Zilda wanted to say something, but what could she say? She had caught only the tail end of their conversation and could not be absolutely certain she had not made a false assumption. Yet, looking at their stricken faces she did not think she had and if that were true, she had been completely wrong about her son's previous relationship with Celia Bryant-Smythe. Dear God; that poor, poor girl!

With these frightening thoughts chasing each other around in her head, Zilda instinctively wanted to wrap her arms around these two young people and find a way to help them, but even as she struggled to control her emotions, she knew there was nothing she could do. She had to wait for them to tell her what was hurting them. So, with tears stinging her eyes, she nodded, turned away and left the room, closing the door behind her. Shuffling the pieces of broken teacup to the skirting board out of harm's way until later, Zilda fled to the privacy of her room and collapsed into a chair to recall what she had overheard.

'Oh God, Celia, I'm so sorry, I had no idea. Why did you not tell me? I would never have left you, whatever happened.'

'How could I? By the time I knew, I was told you had already gone away and then I was banished in disgrace. I thought I would never see you again ...'

It was clear to Zilda that David had fathered Celia's illegitimate child; what else could those tormented words mean? It appeared that she had made a grave error of judgement about Celia Bryant-Smythe and her son. 'Oh my God,' she murmured, 'what have we all done?'

David barely heard his mother leave the room; his heart was breaking, not for his lost son, though that was bad enough, but for the pain, anguish and humiliation that Celia had been forced to endure alone. Now, after all these months of looking into her sad, beautiful face he understood why she was so painfully thin and frighteningly fragile. Holding her tight and listening to her sobbing, he wondered who had known about all of this. Had his parents known? Was that why his mother was always so frosty towards Celia? Even as his mind posed the question, he found it hard to imagine; but then, so much of what he had witnessed in recent years was unimaginable. Listening to Celia's sobs, he wanted to speak, he wanted to say a few words of comfort, but he could not find the right ones to convey even a fraction of his thinking. What she had told him was unbelievable, horrifying, and he ached for her pain.

Trying to piece together the last few days before he had been sent off to war, it came to David like a body blow that it was not coincidence he had been called up so suddenly and unexpectedly at that crucial time. There were other factors too, he realised. In the days before he left Rookery House, he had repeatedly telephoned Satchfield Hall and asked to speak to Celia, but had been told she was indisposed. Worried, he had left messages for her to call him, but had not heard back. Swept into the harsh regime of officers' training camp, he had made two further attempts to contact her before he was shipped out to North Africa, only to be told by her father that she had no wish to speak to him. As hurt as he was, he had assumed she believed the ridiculous rumour about him and the housemaid. Now, thinking it through, to his despair it was becoming clear that he and Celia had both been lied to and kept apart deliberately, but why?

As these thoughts vied for space in his head, the pain that always returned when he became agitated or emotional was sparking throughout his body. Every nerve end was throbbing. Despite this, he pushed himself to remember more, but as the agony began to take over he could no longer put the events together. It was like everything these days; it all jumbled itself into one big muddle. He squeezed his eyes shut as if to help him concentrate, but nothing else came back to him: his mind simply could not dredge out those memories.

Squeezing Celia's hand, he kissed away her tears, his lips searching for hers. 'I love you so much. I never stopped loving you. I just *wish* I had known. I would never have left as I did. I tried to call you, but I was not allowed to speak to you and then it was too late. Everything was done in such a frightful rush.'

Celia, fresh tears spilling silently down her cheeks, kissed his hand. 'I wanted so much to tell you, I begged to be allowed to see you, but I was told you'd been called up and gone to war. Everything was such a shock, the realisation that I was going to have your baby and then learning that you had already gone away without even saying goodbye. I couldn't believe it, but even in my most desperate moments, I knew I could live with it all, because I knew you would come back to me. When they told me you were dead, killed in action, I thought I was going to die. I certainly didn't want to live and by then, of course, our baby had been born and they'd taken him away from me too.'

Listening to the terrible tale of betrayal inflicted on the woman he loved by the very people she trusted, David's head throbbed more than ever. He was numb with the shock. But what pained him beyond anything he had hitherto endured was that he could have prevented all of this, if only he had known; if only he had not been sent away. The questions now ringing through his head demanded answers: why did all of this have to happen? Who had sent him to his hell? He was filled with anger, both for himself and for Celia. A spike of hot rage rose in his throat and almost choked him. Not only did he want to know who was responsible; he wanted vengeance.

Celia, her heart rent in two at the sight of David's distraught face, wished she had not told him. She had not intended to, not today, but he had said he wanted to make his first excursion from Rookery House and had insisted on accompanying her back to Satchfield Hall. Unable to put him off, she had been forced to explain that she no longer lived there and then it had all come pouring out: everything that had happened once her father had learnt of her condition; her banishment; the baby; the years of despair at Ridge View Cottage, all of which she had meticulously recorded in her diary in the hope that one day he would read what she had written and understand what she had been through.

Angry with herself, Celia bit her lip; she had not meant to tell him about wanting to die, on top of hearing about the baby, it was too much for David's fragile state of mind. It was too much for hers too. She had tried to suppress the memory of that dreadful time, because it had almost destroyed her. Ever since hearing the worst news of her life, Celia had repeatedly told herself that she must learn to live without the two beings who mattered most to her, but as much as she had worked at trying to convince herself she could, she had known it was hopeless; she never would. Now, listening to David's harsh, sobbing breath, Celia wished with all her heart she had not mentioned any of it. Her mother had advised her not to tell him and it seemed she had been right.

'As painful as it is,' she had said, 'you will eventually get over it, Celia, but we must prepare for the fact that David may never fully recover. Telling him about what happened after he had gone to war could turn him completely. I say this, not to hurt you, but as a kindness.' Celia had known this was true: they had grown close in recent months, ever since her mother had come to Ridge View Cottage with the news that David was alive.

The tea sat in the china teapot going cold, the biscuits soggy with spilt milk, untouched. Celia, her throat sore with all the emotions she had released, was frightened. She could feel the tension in David's body as he stared at her, a vein throbbing at his temple; his pain-filled eyes sunk into dark hollows. 'Oh, David,' she whispered, 'What have I done?'

Chapter TWENTY-SIX

Muriel disliked using the telephone and rarely made a call. She had heard it ringing and had imagined it would be for Henry, so was startled when a moment later Lilly Jenkins announced from the doorway of the drawing room, 'Mrs Gillespie is on the telephone for you, Marm.'

Hurrying to the half-moon side table in the hallway where the instrument was kept, Muriel grasped the receiver, wishing Henry would arrange to have an extension put in the drawing room. He had often said he would, but had never got around to it. She disliked having to speak on the phone in the hall, it was too public.

'Hello Zilda, Muriel here. Is something wrong?'

David's mother sounded breathless and anxious and Muriel's first thought was that something awful had happened to Celia, but as she listened to what Zilda had to say, her knees began to tremble and her hands to sweat. Her first reaction was one of relief: at last she no longer had to keep this dreadful secret to herself. Her second reaction was panic: should she admit she had known all along? I can't, she thought, I simply can't. And so she said very little, implying that she had suspected, but allowing Zilda to think she was overcome with shock, which indeed she was, if for a different reason.

Putting the phone down, Muriel gazed unseeing at her reflection in the gilt-edged mirror that hung above the table. Now that Zilda knew the secret, the burden of guilt and betrayal that Muriel had carried alone all these years, which at times had threatened to crush her, seemed suddenly lighter. Dabbing at her eyes in a vain attempt to stem the flow of tears, it seemed to her that for the first time since that dreadful day when Celia had told her she was pregnant, they could at last begin to move forward.

She had been shocked and horrified that such a thing could happen to her daughter – it was unforgiveable - but Celia had paid for her indiscretion; paid far more than she should have done. Ever since that terrible day, Muriel had lived with regret for not having had the courage to stand up to her husband and stop their daughter's banishment. Staring down at the phone receiver she had only moments earlier replaced on its cradle, Muriel once again castigated herself for being so weak. Had she herself not brought four children into the world? It was not difficult to understand what her poor daughter had gone through, was still going through, under a shroud of disgrace and shame.

What truly bothered Muriel after what Zilda had told her, was that it need not have happened at all. It seemed that Celia had not been mistaken; David really *had* loved her and according to his mother, still did. It did not excuse their behaviour, of course, but it did mitigate it. There was no question that had David known Celia was pregnant he would have done right by her, so why did Robert Gillespie orchestrate his son's dash to the war? Surely the Gillespies had not truly believed the fabricated rumours about the housemaid that had preceded the young man's sudden departure? Rumours which, Muriel knew had been spread by Lilly Jenkins almost certainly at Henry's instigation. But why? Had it been because he was so outraged and wanted to punish David for seducing their daughter? He had certainly been very angry. The most pragmatic response would have been to discuss the problem with the Gillespies, who had been their friends back then, and get David and Celia married straight away. She would not have been the first young woman to be hurried to the altar in such circumstances. The locals would doubtless have whispered 'shotgun wedding' behind their hands, but it would have been a nine-day wonder. The Gillespies and Bryant-Smythes could surely have risen above that. So why had everything gone so wrong?

Even as Muriel tormented herself with these questions, she knew there was more to this whole business than met the eye, and much as she did not want to travel down a road that would only bring her more pain, she could not help but fear that her husband had been far more involved than she had dared to imagine. Putting two and two together, although she found it hard to believe that even Henry could be so unbelievably, so ruthlessly, cruel, it came to Muriel that he had used David as a scapegoat. Whether or not the sacked housemaid had actually been pregnant was never discovered, but her unlikely claim that the Squire had raped her had not been believed. Of course not: Lilly Jenkins had made sure of that! Spreading the rumour that David Gillespie was responsible had been Henry's fail-safe and by leaning on Robert to pack the boy off to war, he had ensured the truth did not emerge.

The truth? As Muriel came to the inescapable conclusion, she felt physically ill. With her hand to her mouth, she rushed to the bathroom and vomited. Her husband, without thought or care, had got their housemaid pregnant and then, to cover his indiscretion, had callously ruined two other young people's lives - one of them his own daughter's. In the midst of all this pain Celia's innocent baby had been born into a confused and prejudiced world. Thankfully, Muriel told herself, the one saving grace of this entire debacle was that the child would not suffer, for he would never know who his true family was - at least, not until he was an adult and by then she would not be alive to witness it. In a moment of such extreme poignancy that it stole her breath, it came to her that she would never know her own grandson.

Making her way slowly to her room, Muriel contemplated the consequences of the Gillespie family knowing their son had fathered a child on her daughter, but instead of fearing what would happen, she welcomed it. Not that the baby could be brought back – no longer a baby, of course, but a small boy of almost seven - that would be impossible, but more that Celia might find some peace at last with the man she loved. Wiping her eyes, Muriel wondered how poor David had taken the news. She had seen little of him since his return, but what she had seen was a broken man. Celia had told her he was getting better, but he was not the man he used to be. Knowing what had happened, would he now remember the days leading up to his departure? The false rumours concerning the housemaid? Would he, as she had done, work out the part her husband had played in it all? Where once Muriel would have been appalled by people knowing the level of Henry's depravity, she now found she did not care. The man was beyond redemption and she could only hope that he would get what he deserved.

As she digested the implications of Zilda's call, Muriel was startled when Lilly Jenkins once more tapped on the door to inform her there was another telephone call for her. The caller had not given his name. Oh God, thought Muriel, what now? Walking briskly to the hall, she looked pointedly at Lilly Jenkins and waited until the housekeeper had gone into the kitchen and closed the door, before picking up the receiver.

'Hello, Muriel Bryant-Smythe speaking.'

'I'm sorry to trouble you, Mrs Bryant-Smythe, your late father's solicitor asked me to call you. He would have done so himself, but he is in court all day today. I hope this is not an inconvenient time, but there is something we feel should be brought to your attention.'

Muriel said nothing more for the next few minutes, she simply listened until the caller had finished. Managing somehow to maintain her composure, she said, 'Thank you, I appreciate all you have told me,' and replaced the received back in its cradle. In so short a space of time her world had twice been turned upside down. 'Good God,' she cried out into the stillness of the hall, 'how much more must I and my daughter suffer because of that man?'

Even as she let out her appeal, Muriel knew that now, as at no other time, she must find the fortitude to sort it all out. If she did not, then everything would be lost. She shivered involuntarily, because she knew it would indeed mean *everything*. Where to start, she asked herself, because she really had no idea, but she now realised just how much the events of the last few years had changed her. She was constantly fatigued, anxious and emotional and she was still afraid of her husband, but she had discovered in herself a core of inner strength that until the birth of her grandson she had not suspected: she had learned how to cope.

Chapter TWENTY-SEVEN

Swirling the cut-glass brandy balloon, releasing the rich bouquet from the cognac as it warmed in his cupped palm, Robert Gillespie thought ruefully that there was a time when a glass of this expensive fiery liquid helped him to relax of an evening. Not lately! He had so much on his mind it was impossible to stop thinking. Mostly it concerned the West Point development, which was a little behind schedule. Then there was the matter of bringing Bryant-Smythe to justice. The man was a slippery customer; it was proving difficult for the Gillespie family's solicitor to find evidence of corruption. Too many people were held in thrall to the Squire of Satchfield Hall. Last, but by no means least was his son, in particular the boy's persistent refusal to join him in the housing business on which he was embarked. Robert had not yet said anything to curtail Celia's visits. It was tricky. The boy was clearly smitten and the last thing he wanted was to upset David when he was doing so well. Under his renewed management, the estate farm was again beginning to prosper.

Hearing Zilda enter his study, which was unusual at this time of day; normally she respected his need to wind down when he had just got in from work, Robert, expecting to hear about some domestic trivia, looked up and frowned. 'Whatever is the matter, my dear? You look as though you've lost a pound and found a sixpence.'

Attempting to focus enough of his attention to satisfy her, his mind continued to probe all the other issues jostling for space in his mind, so at first he found it a little difficult to comprehend what she was saying. He was raising his glass to his lips just as her words impinged on his consciousness.

'*What?*' Almost immobile with shock, brandy forgotten midway to his mouth, Robert sat bolt upright in his chair. Seeing his wife flinch brought him to his senses. Not wanting to alarm her further, he attempted to sound reasonable, 'I'm not questioning what you are saying, Zilda, but David is far from himself and as much as I am pleased that Celia has been able to help lift his depression, I am just a little surprised at what you have told me.'

The implications of David having fathered Celia's child, if true, were more than disturbing and Robert was determined to play devil's advocate. 'Is it not possible that you leapt to the wrong conclusion and let your imagination run away with you, my dear? After all, you say you heard only the briefest snippet of their conversation. We know the girl had an illegitimate child, but surely she would not now try to foist it onto our son! I assume the child has long ago been adopted. What would be the point?'

Zilda's lips tightened, her annoyance at his response obvious from her tone, 'Saddened as I am to admit that I did not warm to the Bryant-Smythe girl, whatever my personal feelings, I am quite certain that nobody could feign the depth of emotion she was displaying when I walked into that room - and if you could have seen David: the look of appalled shock and love on his face as he said he was sorry ... Oh, Robert, it was awful. Why would he say that if there was no good reason?'

To Robert's discomfort, Zilda burst into tears. 'Now, now, my dear,' he said awkwardly. 'If you are right, we will find a way to sort this out.'

'*If I'm right*? she screeched, flushing with anger. 'You still believe I don't know my own son? Those two young people are suffering and we have to find a way to help them.'

'Forgive me, I do not wish to doubt you, Zilda, I just find it so hard to believe.'

Zilda closed her eyes for a moment as if by doing so it would make the situation easier. More calmly she said, 'For your information, Robert, I have already spoken with Muriel Bryant-Smythe.'

He frowned, surprised by this admission. 'You *told* her? What did she have to say about it?'

'As it happened, she did not seem particularly surprised. Apparently, when Celia informed her she was pregnant she also told her that David loved her and they intended to get married. Unfortunately, by then our son had gone off to some battlefield and Muriel, assuming her daughter had mistaken his intentions, elected not to mention it to us. Indeed, what would have been the point? In the circumstances there was nothing we could have done. Then, as you know, shortly afterwards that odious man banished Celia from Satchfield Hall to stop any further embarrassment to her family – and for once I can't say I blame him. Or at least, I didn't then.'

Zilda sniffed. 'I wish it *was* my imagination running wild, Robert, really I do. I keep thinking that if our son went away before anyone knew anything about Celia Bryant-Smythe's condition then how *could* it have been David's baby? He would never have left her in the lurch like that. And then there was all that nasty business with the Bryant-Smythes' housemaid, which was a blatant lie ...' Her voice faltered to a stop and pulling a lace handkerchief from her sleeve, Zilda dabbed at her eyes.

His mind working overtime, Robert looked up at his wife. If all this was true - and much as he wanted not to believe it, his instincts told him it was - then all the suffering that had been caused should never have happened. Despite his preoccupation with everything else that was spinning in his head and threatening to spin out of control unless he got a handle on it, Robert realised there was something very disturbing about his wife's revelations, which not only had him shuddering, but boiling with rage.

With a hand, surprisingly steady, he lifted the warmed brandy balloon to his lips and took another mouthful of cognac. This time, just a tad too much. It burnt his throat as the liquid made its way down into his stomach. But the burning sensation had the effect of bringing everything into sharp focus and Zilda's reference to that miserable affair brought back the conversation he'd had with Henry Bryant-Smythe at the time. He remembered it almost word for word, so shocked and distressed had he been.

It had been a man to man talk, or so he had been led to believe back then. Robert snorted with disgust as the conversation began to play back in his mind. 'I'll be discreet,' Bryant-Smythe had said, 'but there's much talk of your son being involved with a girl from the village, she's a housemaid at Satchfield Hall and she is telling anyone who will listen that she is pregnant and David is responsible.'

Before Robert had been able to utter a single word, Bryant-Smythe, clearly working himself up into a state of outraged indignation, had continued. 'I know boys will be boys, Robert, but I'm appalled that David could not have kept his trousers buttoned up and sown his wild oats further away from home! It is causing me no end of trouble. I have dismissed the girl, of course, but it gets worse. Her father means to extort money from you if your son refuses to marry the slut, and further, he wants compensation from me for not ensuring his daughter was kept safe while in my care as her employer. It is preposterous! I feel you should send David away for a while. Get him into the army; he can go and fight for his country, it would be the best place for him!'

Robert remembered tackling David as soon as Bryant-Smythe had gone. The boy had insisted he barely knew the girl, but there had been something in his manner that had unsettled Robert. Now, of course, he realised to his despair why his son had looked so guilty. It had not been anything to do with the servant girl, but because he had seduced Celia Bryant-Smythe. David, too well-bred to say anything that would bring Celia into disrepute, had kept silent, taking the accusation on the chin. He could have had no idea she was pregnant.

Convinced at the time that what Henry Bryant-Smythe had suggested was indeed the best way out and believing that a spot of time in uniform would do the boy no harm and might be the making of him, Robert had organised his son's speedy exit from Rookery House. Not as he had hoped, to pushing a pen at some paper-littered desk in the War Office, but straight into the jaws of the brutal conflict in North Africa.

Putting all the pieces together, Robert now realised what Bryant-Smythe had orchestrated and the likely reason why. The man was evil personified. His anger mounting, Robert took another deep drink from his brandy glass in an attempt to swallow the rage that threatened to consume him. The business he had been dealing with over the last few weeks was turning nasty – the scale of corruption even worse than he had envisaged - and now, what Zilda had just told him added more than enough fuel to ignite his wrath. In a rare spasm of violence, he clenched his fist, punched the arm of his chair and hurled his brandy glass at the wall where it shattered, leaving a yellow stain on the flocked wallpaper.

'Robert, please! Control yourself,' Zilda snapped. 'I am beginning to wonder if you are in the room with me at all!'

'I'm sorry,' he turned his mouth down in a look of abject apology for his unforgiveable display of bad temper, 'but it is all such a shock.' Glancing up at his wife, Robert registered her agitation, recognised her deep pain and knew he had to do something sooner rather than later. Alarm bells were ringing loudly in his head, but fortunately, Zilda knew nothing of them. Simply knowing about David and Celia was more than enough for her to cope with, without adding to her distress by voicing his thoughts about Bryant-Smythe. Nor had he told her anything about the impending writ to be served on the man, which did nothing to help the situation. How would

David feel about his father-in-law – for Robert had no doubt that his son and Celia would now be married – being hauled through the courts on a charge that would most likely see him serving time at Her Majesty's pleasure! Clamping down on the seething anger, which was beginning to upset his digestion, Robert cleared his throat.

'Zilda, I need you to look after David and help him come to terms with what Celia has told him. I would also beg you to speak to the girl and help her to understand that we had no knowledge of any of this. Sadly, I believe there is nothing we can do to bring the child back, even assuming that is what would be wanted, which I doubt after all this time. Most importantly, we must look after those who are here with us. I fear this will set David's recovery back by months, if not make it ...' he could not finish the sentence, gripped by the awful possibility that this revelation might have damaged their son's mental state beyond repair.

'The child you are talking about is our *grandchild*, Robert,' Zilda sobbed.

'I know; I know.' Struggling to maintain his composure, Robert stood up and pulled his wife into his embrace, holding her tight. 'I will sort this out, I promise. Please give your time and patience to our son and Celia and we will see what can be done.'

Overcome, Zilda wept in his arms and he, murmuring words of comfort into her hair, held close until her tears abated. 'Thank you,' she sobbed, her voice choked with emotion, 'I know you will do what is best.'

This was exactly what Robert had hoped. He needed Zilda to think he was in full agreement with her, and of course he was, but not in the way she believed. For now, he wanted her to worry about nothing more than nursing their son back to health. He would deal with the rest - and there was a frightening amount to deal with, he reflected. What he did not tell her was that he intended to utterly destroy Henry Bryant-Smythe for what he had done.

Chapter TWENTY-EIGHT

'What's this?' Standing on the top step just outside his front door, Henry looked down at the sealed envelope Robert Gillespie was thrusting towards him.

Without the courtesy of a 'Good day,' Gillespie looked him up and down and stuck the envelope in his hand with the ominous words, 'A writ of summons. My solicitor would have given it to you, but I needed to see you receive it for myself.' With that he turned away, ran down the steps and climbed back into his car, calling out, 'He will be sending you a copy in the post, so there is little point in denying you've received it!'

Rendered speechless, Henry watched the car roar into life, his former business partner, and at one time his friend, speeding off down the drive so fast the tyres spat gravel. Very deliberately he tore the envelope, still sealed, across and across, ripping it to shreds then opening his hands and letting the torn fragments catch the wind and scatter, watching in amusement as they were deposited like confetti all over the garden. 'You fool, Gillespie. Do you really think you can hurt me?' Henry laughed out loud, the sound of his laughter, like the paper, disappearing into the wind.

During the war years, the business deals he and Robert Gillespie had both been involved in had dwindled to none, their differences of opinion leading them in opposite directions until eventually they had gone their separate ways. It still rankled Henry that while he had lost out on a dollar deal - almost lost his shirt in fact - Gillespie had come out of it not only squeaky clean, but considerably richer.

'I'll show you, you bastard!' he yelled, shaking his fist at the departing vehicle. He had said as much back then too, and by God he had shown him; shown them all; all those pompous gits who questioned his methods. He had not lost in the end. He would never lose; he was the victor, the Squire of Satchfield Hall, no less. Henry laughed again, but was uncomfortably aware that the sound was bitter in his ears.

Over the next few days his mood turned and as he always did when he felt threatened, Henry sought solace in physical intimacy. He was less than amused, therefore, when the young maid in his room, who stood deliciously naked in front of him, announced, 'I ain't able to do this no more, Squire. Get yer dirty 'ands off of me. I wants me money or else I'll tell.'

Feeling he had more than enough to contend with, without some cheeky little tart telling him what he could or couldn't do with her, Henry swore. He knew she was neither shy, nor afraid of him, in fact she was the best little trollop he had bedded and he had sampled a good few: usually the young ones who came desperately seeking employment at the Hall. Work for women was hard to come by these days, not only because all the men had come home and back to their old jobs, but a shortage of staff in the war years and increasing taxation had put the nail in the coffin of the old way of life. Henry had seen it coming. Country landowners were being forced to sell up or downsize their houses such that domestic work for women was becoming hard to find. There was consequently a seemingly endless supply of girls finding their way to Satchfield Hall, which was still operating in the old way, albeit on a shoestring and with mounting debts. This young woman had been more than willing: she was a tease, which he enjoyed, and here she was close enough to touch saying he must keep his hands off her! The audacity of the little slut! With his mind on more pressing worries, he reached out and grabbed her.

She struggled and squealed, fuelling both his lust and his anger. He flung her onto the bed and slapped her face. She cried out, but he ignored her. Trapping her arms with one hand and sealing her mouth with the other he moved himself on top of her and thrust into her. 'I'll remind you who is master here,' he gasped, thrusting harder. How dared she give him backchat! This was what she needed, to be shown who was boss; he had bedded her enough times for her to know what it was all about, stupid little cow. Inflamed with lust by her struggles, it was over in moments.

'You're right about one thing,' he said coldly, removing himself from her now supine body and pushing her off the bed. 'I won't be having you in my bed anymore and that's a fact.' Reaching over to the bedside cabinet, he pulled a handful of coins off the top and without looking at her, flung them onto the floor. 'Take this and get out of my sight and out of my house. If I ever see you again, you will know exactly what trouble will mean. Now get out!'

'What about Mrs Jenkins?' She cried out in fear, ''er'll 'ave me guts fer garters!'

'What about her? I said get out and that means get *out*!'

Weeping, the maid pulled on her clothes, picked up the money with trembling hands and fled.

As soon as he heard the door slam shut, Henry rolled off the bed and got dressed. The girl had not improved his frame of mind. In fact, if anything, he was even angrier. What was really disturbing was not what had taken place in his bed, but that the servant's audacity in speaking to him as she had was not an isolated incident. Others with whom he had found himself having to deal of late had the same disrespectful attitude. Everyone, it seemed, wanted to tell him what he could and could not do. Well he would soon put paid to that. He had sorted out that little whore; others would be dealt with too - and not so lightly.

With these thoughts at the forefront of his mind, Henry pulled open the top drawer of his tallboy and pulled out the letter he had received two days earlier from his solicitor.

Reading it again, he swore. Then he laughed, but despite himself, his laughter was tinged with panic. He had ignored the restraining order in regard to Gillespie's paddock, which was now a quagmire. There were white markings and several wooden pegs hammered into the earth, their tops no more than a foot above the ground. Wrapped around the pegs string had been tied creating something resembling a child's game of cat's cradle. Then suddenly the work had stopped. Henry had received a call from his solicitor, who had explained that for now it could not continue and he ignored the restraining order at his peril.

That had been several weeks ago and despite frantic talks with his so-called partners, things were not moving at all. The schedule was slipping by the minute and the cost was escalating. He needed to get it sorted and the contractors back on site. If not he would face ruin. It was an alarming possibility that set his pulses racing with anxiety.

Flinging the letter on top of the chest, Henry wandered over to the washbasin in the corner of his room and looked blearily into the mirror. Rubbing his hand around his chin and feeling the prick of stubble he sluiced his face with cold water, thought about calling for his valet to shave him, decided he could not be bothered and dried his face and hands.

A copy of the writ of summons that he had torn up had duly arrived in the post, giving him thirty days to appear in court to respond to the complaint lodged against him by Robert Gillespie, who claimed title to the land on the southern border between their two estates. Huh! Well he would show the arrogant fool just who the land really belonged to. The documents he had purchased from Patrick Beaumont were clever forgeries and Henry was confident not a court in the land would see them as anything but genuine, but just in case, he had ensured that several backhanders had found their way into the right people's pockets. As far as he was concerned, the land was his and the work was authorised; bought and paid for.

Even though he believed that nothing or no one could touch him, what really alarmed Henry was that if he could not deliver the project on time, he would lose everything, and that meant *everything*, including Satchfield Hall.

It was this possibility that frightened him more than anything.

Chapter TWENTY-NINE

Muriel could trace the change in herself back to the day she had learned of David Gillespie's return from the dead. Somehow, hearing that news had stiffened her resolve to build a stronger shell and while the frightened woman that she was continued to linger beneath it, there were times, as now, when her resilience surprised her. Of course, her husband, his bullying and bombastic manner, still had the ability to fill her with dread, but when she was away from him she felt like a new woman. It was this change that enabled her to view his behaviour with far greater objectivity than ever before, and the more she discovered, the more terrified she became. Not only for her own future, which given her deteriorating health was limited, but most importantly, for her daughter's.

It appeared there was *nothing* Henry would not do to get what he wanted and from whispers Muriel had heard from certain quarters, he was consistently getting his own way, riding roughshod by fair means or foul – usually the latter - over anyone who threatened to curtail his activities. She realised it was not in her power to stop his madness, but was aware that should he take one more step towards their financial ruin, there was something she might do to put an end to his scheming. What she had in mind would not only stop him in his tracks, it would ultimately protect the one person she worried about constantly.

Before she could be certain the plan she had in mind for her daughter was possible, she had to deal with another issue. It concerned the letter she had received from her father's solicitor about something that troubled her greatly, so much so that she had taken immediate action, which is how she came to be sitting in the solicitor's oak-panelled office on this grey Wednesday morning.

'Mrs Bryant-Smythe, please rest assured that our business is strictly between the two of us,' Iain Chamberlain repeated for the third time as he sipped a cup of coffee, sitting behind his desk and looking at her, a pleasant smile hovering above his neatly barbered grey beard. 'It was hardly necessary for me to look at these documents again, but I have done so for your peace of mind. I can reassure you that they are genuine, clear and precise. Your late father made certain that nothing could be misinterpreted in any way.'

Iain Chamberlain took a further sip of coffee, propped his elbows on the desk and clasping his long fingers, gazed at Muriel over his gold-rimmed spectacles as though she were a confused child. 'All the papers are in order, nothing has changed and nothing *can* change without your witnessed signature.' Picking up the sheaf of documents, he slid then back into the large brown folder and re-tied the pink ribbon that bound them. 'However, should you amend your last will and testament, it alone would have the power after your death to override the provision in these documents,' he tapped the folder with his index finger as he spoke.

Her eyes drawn to the movement of his hand, Muriel thought about what he had said. His voice conveyed reassurance and she so wanted to believe him, but her husband's controlling depravity preyed on her mind to the extent that she wondered if she was being paranoid. Yet it seemed to her that Henry was able at best to avoid the law and at worst, manipulate it to his advantage. It was the latter that worried her greatly. Preoccupied by these anxious thoughts, she asked a further question.

'Forgive me for labouring the point, Mr Chamberlain, but can you confirm that if someone were to produce false papers and initiate bribes they would not be able to change what is written here?' She pointed to the pink-ribbon bound file on the desk in front of her. In her own ears her question sounded faintly ridiculous, like that of a foolish, anxiety-ridden woman. Anxious she may be, she thought, but she was far from foolish. Her terror at what she had been informed about her husband's more recent activities had prompted her to seek legal advice and however irrational she may seem, she needed reassurance from this man who had been her father's most trusted solicitor. Wondering how much she should confide to him, Muriel was about to re-word her question more explicitly when Iain Chamberlain made it clear he knew exactly what and to whom she was referring.

'Absolutely not and should anything materialise, there is no question in my mind that whatever false documents your husband or anyone else might produce, any court in the land will view them as illegal.' He smiled, 'As your solicitor I am duty bound to protect you and I have every reason to share your concern. Your late father was not unaware of ... er,' he coughed, 'shall we say, the potential risk to your inheritance. It is why he took great pains to have these documents made watertight.' Again he tapped the folder, 'Rest assured they are perfectly in order and legally sealed, and I will personally endorse their authenticity.'

'In that case, Mr Chamberlain, I would like to amend my will as you suggest and to have it lodged with all my papers in your care. I want everything possible done to ensure nothing or no one can take away what is mine, either from me or my daughter.'

He nodded, 'After you had contacted me for an appointment, Mrs Bryant-Smythe, I anticipated your request and took the liberty of drawing up a new draft will for your consideration.' Reaching again for the folder, he untied the ribbon, flicked through the file and pulled out a thick sheet of paper, handing it to her. 'Can I get you another cup of coffee?'

She took the document, said automatically, 'That is kind, thank you.'

Lifting the phone, the solicitor made the request to his secretary and then sat back in his chair, steepling his fingers. Muriel, aware of his avuncular gaze on her, read and re-read the new will. She was vaguely aware of a woman entering the room, placing a cup of fresh coffee on the desk at her elbow and as quietly leaving. Her brow wrinkled, Muriel focused on the words her solicitor had drafted. She read them one more time to satisfy herself they covered all her worries, they did - and several she had not thought of.

After a few minutes, she placed the paper down on the desk and for the first time since she had entered the office, she smiled. 'This seems to be perfectly in order, Mr Chamberlain. 'It is as I would have hoped and I want it formalised as soon as possible. This, along with all the other documents, must serve and protect me whilst I am alive and more importantly, those I leave behind after my death.'

Muriel cleared her throat, 'In that respect, there is just one more thing I wish to add to my will in respect of my heirs.'

'Yes, of course,' the solicitor reached for his notepad and with pencil poised waited for her to speak.

She looked across at him, choosing her words with care. 'I would like to make some further provision for any child of my daughter's body. The sum that would have gone to my late sons is to be placed in trust, to be shared equally between my grandchildren as they attain their majority. '*Any* and *every* child of my daughter's body,' she repeated. 'Can you so word this that it cannot possibly be misunderstood? It is to be made perfectly clear.'

Looking slightly startled and somewhat mystified, Iain Chamberlain nodded. 'Yes, of course. That should not be a problem. And if your daughter does not have a child?'

'There is no question of that, Mr Chamberlain.'

'Ah,' he considered her for a moment then gave her a kindly smile. 'Very well. I will have your new will typed up ready for your signature by the end of the week. Are you able to come in again on Friday morning at, say, eleven?'

'Yes, eleven will be fine, thank you.' Satisfied that all that could be done had been done, Muriel stood up. 'And thank you again for your help, Mr Chamberlain. I know this must all seem like a wife's disloyalty to you, but I sincerely believe that what we have discussed will be tried and tested to breaking point and I have to know it will not snap.'

Standing, he moved around the desk and held out his hand to her. 'I do not see it as disloyalty, Mrs Bryant-Smythe, I see it as a necessary safeguard. Rest assured that everything that is yours is safe and will remain that way for you and for your heirs. Your father was a personal friend of mine as well as a treasured client. He often spoke of you and of his fears for your future. I hope you will not mind my saying that he would be both pleased and proud of your fortitude in seeking to secure his legacy in what, I know, must be trying circumstances.'

With tears springing to her eyes, Muriel, not trusting herself to speak, nodded, shook the solicitor's hand and left his office. Only as she walked past his secretary in the outer office did she remember she had forgotten to drink the fresh cup of coffee.

Chapter THIRTY

David found it hard to believe that two months had passed since Celia had sobbed out the terrible tale of family betrayal and he learned he had a son. At the time, holding her tightly in his arms, he had done his best to control his emotional reaction to everything she told him, not allowing her to see the extent of his devastation, but as soon as she had gone the shock had taken its toll and he became very ill.

For days following Celia's heartrending visit, the doctor, a specialist in psychological disorders, had spent anxious hours trying to calm him, eventually prescribing barbiturates to still David's troubled thoughts and restore his fragile state of mind. Within days of taking his new medication, he was not only feeling much better, but according to his relieved mother, had begun visibly to improve.

During those anxious weeks, when everyone fussed around him, David came to the realisation that he could not and would not spend the rest of his life as an invalid. He knew only too well that many other people, including Celia, had suffered as much if not more than he. Confident that over time a decent diet and physical exercise would strengthen his body, it was the other side of his illness that was his chief concern. Unlike his physical wellbeing, it was impossible for anyone else to see the terrible things going on in his head and help him to put right what was wrong. David knew that if he was ever to be rid of his nightmares it was down to him alone. He had to fight his demons and learn to cage them, for no one could do it for him.

In the first few weeks after Celia had told him of the child, he had continued to allow his family and his doctor to run his life, letting them tell him what he could do and when he could do it, but as his mind began to settle and his body to grow stronger, he knew it had to stop. Now, more than at any other time, David knew he must take control of his body, his mind and most importantly, his life. Because if he did not, he was in danger of losing the only woman he had ever loved, whose beautiful face and gentle voice had always been there in his head and in his heart throughout all the horrors he had somehow survived. The time he had spent in the wilderness, perhaps mercifully, was still largely a blank. He knew that someone must have treated his wounds and he had vague recollections of being held in some kind of transit camp and then escaping, but even when everything became blurred and deafening, he had always managed to cling to mental images of Celia's face and it was these that had saved him and brought him back home, alive. And he *was* alive; it was down to him now to look after her and try to make up for what had happened and for which he felt responsible. She needed him and he needed her; more than that, he wanted her with him forever, because as long as he had Celia by his side he would be a man again instead of the snivelling wreck he had become.

These thoughts propelled David into action: he was determined to prove to the doctors and his family, but most importantly, to the one person he loved more than anything else, that he was the David Gillespie she had known in those wonderful days before their lives had been split asunder. Hiding away in Rookery House would solve nothing, he told himself. And so, with this resolve he began immediately to put his plan into action, starting by accompanying his father to planning meetings. The strain of it had exhausted him, but after the first two outings, he found he was able to cope.

'David,' his father had said, in a voice conveying concern as well as exasperation, 'there is no need to overdo it. You have to accept that you've had a serious setback and as much as I want you to be a part of the project, I think you should take it a little more slowly. You have to learn to pace yourself.'

David refused to listen. He had spent enough time living in a world of fear and dread. Medication helped, but there was only so much it could do. Reluctantly, he accepted he would, very likely, be taking drugs for the foreseeable future, but his family had rallied round him for long enough and it was time to show them he was capable of coping again.

On this Monday morning he had awoken early; he slept poorly at best, but last night had been even more fitful than usual. To keep his anxiety to a minimum, he had once again accompanied his father to an early morning meeting, this time with the architects. Having been stuck in the realms of red tape and officialdom for months, plans for the new houses were suddenly moving at an alarming rate. Knowing they must if life was to improve for people not only locally, but all over Britain, David was glad. He began to feel that he was making a difference; it was a good feeling.

Now, with the meeting behind him, he was alone in the drawing room. His father had gone off to yet another meeting and his mother was fretting in some other part of the house. It was just after noon and, as was his habit, he paced back and forth across the front of the French windows. Today his gaze was fixed on the driveway, his state of anxiety building almost to breaking point as he thought about what he was going to say that afternoon.

He had not seen Celia for weeks, his mother having written to explain he was ill and unable to receive visitors. Last week, he had prevailed upon her to write again, to say he was now well enough to see Celia should she wish to call. For some reason that he did not understand, his mother's attitude to the woman he loved seemed to have softened. Now, instead of frowning and changing the subject as in the past, she listened when he spoke of Celia, as if interested in what he had to say. So much so he had been encouraged to talk about when they had first met at Satchfield Hall and the days they had enjoyed in each other's company before he went off to war. He did not, of course, mention just how close they had become – his mother would be horrified! He supposed that eventually he would have to tell his parents about the child. Their probable reaction was another factor that added to the ever constant ball of anxiety in his stomach and kept him awake at night.

Expecting at any moment to see the Bryant-Smythes' car wending its way up the drive, David stopped pacing to stare out of the window for a moment, before recommencing his pacing. He could hardly contain his thoughts as he waited. He had rehearsed what he was going to say a million times, saying the words over and over in his head. Today he was going to say them for real.

Celia sat in the front passenger seat of the Daimler as George Brand drove her to Rookery House. Looking ahead through the windscreen, she could not stop shivering with excitement and trepidation. She had begun to believe she would never see David again; a thought impossible to bear. The day after her last visit, a note from Zilda Gillespie, delivered to her mother at Satchfield Hall and brought post-haste to Ridge View Cottage, had confirmed Celia's worst fears: *'I must beg you, Muriel, to keep Celia away for the time being. The news has come as a great shock to us all and I fear David is ill and may not recover from it.'*

'Oh, Celia,' her mother had burst out in exasperation, 'why oh why did you have to tell him? I warned you it would be too much for him. And what on *earth* possessed you to tell his mother?'

'I didn't,' Celia had protested, but then remembered the mishap with the tea tray and the expression on Zilda's face. 'Oh God! She must have overheard me telling David. I didn't mean to, but he wanted to come home with me to

Satchfield Hall and I panicked,' she had explained, feeling sick because David was ill again and it was her fault. All she had wanted at that moment was to rush to David's side, to be with him, to nurse him; but for his sake she had to be patient. In frustration she had screamed at herself and her mother, at poor Lizzie and Gladys Thrift too.

The *time being* had turned into two interminable months and Celia, overwhelmed by grief and guilt because she knew David's relapse was down to her selfishness, had never felt so desperate. How many times had her mother begged her not to mention the baby? 'It will cause more pain if you do,' she had said, and, 'Put it behind you, Celia. For your own sanity and the sake of that poor man's mind, please try to forget.'

Why hadn't she listened? *'Because David was so much stronger and he ought to know about his son,'* a little voice in her head told her, making her painfully aware that deep down she had believed her mother was wrong. Now her selfishness came back to haunt her: her mother was the wise one, it was she who had been wrong. She should have kept what had happened buried deep in her heart, that way nobody would have been hurt except herself. Now, because of her foolishness, everyone else was hurting too and she was once again alone.

As always, Celia had turned to her diary for solace, writing until her hand cramped and her fingers were sore from holding the pen too tightly, and as before, it had helped. The days had slid into weeks and the weeks to months, until at last a visit from her mother had brought good news.

With the note that would bring a smile back to her daughter's face clasped in her gloved hand, Muriel Bryant-Smythe smiled as she sat in the back seat of the Daimler behind George Brand's solid outline, reflecting on the past two months since that desperate telephone call from Zilda. The revelation that they shared a grandchild and all the tragedy it entailed had brought them together again.

Renewing their friendship, they had spent many hours discussing how best to help their children and once David's mother had come to terms with what she now knew about her son and Celia, Muriel had derived considerable comfort from her friend's pragmatic approach. 'We must encourage them to put the past behind them,' Zilda had said, 'their future is what is important now.'

If only it were that simple, Muriel sighed to herself, for of course there were other issues, which she had kept from Zilda. She was not entirely sure why, unless to prevent further pain. Being Henry Bryant-Smythe's wife did not make her responsible for his actions, did it? Yet she dreaded the Gillespies finding out about the part her husband had played in their son's plight. There was enough misery concerning this affair without that coming to light, and she would deal – was dealing - with Henry; he would get his comeuppance eventually.

Both she and Zilda had agreed that nothing should be done to find the child: 'Who knows where in the world he might be or even if he is still alive?' Zilda had said, her eyes glistening with tears.

I do, thought Muriel, but her knowledge that the infant had been adopted by a caring couple named Hargreaves and lived in the Pendleham area was her secret and would remain that way. Her priority was to help those two troubled souls, Celia and David, find happiness. Attempting to reunite them with their unknown child could only cause pain and grief to everyone concerned. It was best to keep what she knew to herself.

Yesterday morning, Zilda had telephoned to suggest they meet in town for a cup of coffee. They had met at the station cafe, which smelt of fresh paint and fried onions, but was convenient and off their husbands' radar, neither of them wishing to involve Robert – and especially not Henry – in their fragile renewed relationship, both wanting instinctively to wait until they had agreed what to do for the best before presenting a united front to their respective families.

Listening to the trains steaming through the station and feeling a bit like Celia Johnson in the crowded cafe, imagining that at any moment Trevor Howard would come to remove a speck of dirt from her eye – that she should be so lucky! - Muriel was brought up short by Zilda tapping her hand.

'You look miles away,' she had said.

'Sorry, I was thinking of *Brief Encounter*.'

'Ah, yes, lovely film, but so sad.' Wrinkling her nose as she sipped her coffee, which at least was hot and wet, Zilda had handed her a folded piece of paper. 'David is so much better and he is desperate to see Celia. Would you give her this? I have added my own wish for her to come to Rookery House. I so want her to feel welcome again.'

Muriel, delighted, had taken the note. She had wanted to rush with it straight to Ridge View Cottage, but Henry had commandeered the car and its driver for the afternoon, so she had been forced to wait until this morning. The note was in her pocket now and she could not wait to see her daughter's face when she read it.

Some minutes later, as they sat comfortably at the long kitchen table sampling Gladys Thrift's delicious fruit cake, Muriel slipped the note across the scrubbed table top, trying to keep the excitement out of her voice as Celia gingerly took the fold of paper. 'I think this is what you have been waiting for,' Muriel smiled.

Now on her way to Rookery House, Celia agonised about how David would feel when he saw her again, praying he would still want her. He had said he loved her, but that seemed so long ago and since then, as in all those years before, there had been no word from him. Had he asked to see her again in order to tell her it was all over between them? She would not blame him, but the thought of it was torture.

She looked across at George Brand's profile. He exuded happiness and despite her trepidation, Celia felt a sudden surge of gladness for him. With all of her own worries she had given barely a thought to the recent news that Gladys had at last accepted his proposal of marriage. Delighted for them both, Celia wondered how life was now going to change. In the absence of Gladys, would she continue to live at Ridge View Cottage with Lizzie Rainbow and if not, where would she go? Her father had never forgiven her and her return to Satchfield Hall was still forbidden. But she could not think about that just now. Nor did it matter. She did not care what happened to her if her future was not to be with David. In fact, Celia thought, her eyes welling with tears, she was not sure she could face life without him; just the thought of it made her want to die.

As George drove the car through the gates of Rookery House, Celia caught her breath. David was standing on the steps in front of the open door. The sight of him coupled with her fear at what he was going to say to her, curled her up inside.

Chapter THIRTY-ONE

Moments earlier, David had glimpsed the Bryant-Smythes' limousine coming along the lane that would bring it to the gates of Rookery House. Rushing from the room, he limped quickly to the front door and flung it wide open. Standing on the top step of the imposing entrance, he waited impatiently as the car approached the wide gravelled area in front of the house then slowed to a crawl before drawing to a halt a few feet from the steps. With his heart beating a tattoo, he watched George Brand get out, walk round to the front passenger door and open it. For those brief moments, it seemed to David that everything had slipped into slow motion, but when Celia stepped gracefully out of the car he could wait no longer.

At risk of falling flat on his face, he leapt down the steps two at a time, threw down his walking cane and collected her into his arms. In that moment he never wanted to let her go and when, after a brief hesitation, she wrapped her arms around him and lifted her face for his kiss, his joy knew no bounds. Brushing her lips with his own, he thanked God for letting him live and bringing Celia back to him. As he breathed in her exquisite fragrance, David knew he would never let her out of his life again. He loved this woman beyond words and life itself, and whatever demons tormented his head in the future he would be able to deal with them so long as she was with him. Nothing and nobody would ever stand in his way again to prevent him making this wonderful woman happy.

As he held her in his tight embrace he heard her gasp as if he had squeezed the very breath out of her. Relaxing his grip a little, he looked down at her face and saw that she was weeping, her cheeks were wet with tears, her lips curved in a tremulous smile. Feeling the faint flutter of her heart as it beat a little faster against his chest, his heart turned over. Struggling to control his voice, he said, 'I have counted the hours to this moment. Please never leave me again, I love you. I love you, I love you.'

'Oh, David, I love you too. You have no idea how much. I have been so afraid that you ...'

He stopped her words with his kiss, hardly able to believe she had uttered those beautiful words after all these weeks of separation. Words he had not dared to believe he would hear again. During his darkest days he had convinced himself that he did not deserve her and had lost her forever. Now, feeling the velvety texture of her skin against his face and tasting the salty essence of her tears, he fought against his own tears that threatened to unman him.

Looking into her beautiful eyes, with all the dignity he could muster, he said, 'Marry me, Celia. Please will you be my wife and marry me, soon - *now*?' The words did not come out as he had rehearsed them and his voice was strained with emotion, but he had waited far too long to ask this question and even though the lump in his throat threatened to choke him, he could delay no longer. He was so afraid it was already too late.

'Yes, oh yes,' Celia whispered, her voice breaking, 'I will.'

Overcome, David, unable to believe it was possible to be this happy, smiled. 'Thank you. You will never know how happy you have just made me. God, Celia, I love you so much.'

As if from a great distance, he heard George Brand awkwardly clearing his throat and looking up broke into sudden laughter. Oblivious to everything but Celia, he had completely forgotten the man was still there.

The driver stood by the Daimler, shuffling his feet, his face split in a wide, embarrassed grin, 'Sorry, sir, but will Miss Celia be wanting the car?'

'Not just now, thank you, George. Would you take it round the back and then go in for a cup of tea. You'll probably find Mrs Fitch in the kitchen; I think she's baking today. Tell her I sent you.'

George nodded, 'Thank you, sir.' Touching his cap and getting into the car, he added, 'Good to see you up and about again, Captain Gillespie.'

David smiled an acknowledgement, but barely heard him. Part of his mind registered the leaves falling slowly from the trees and birds fluttering around in the garden as, with a crunch of gravel, the Daimler disappeared round the side of the house. He felt Celia shivering and held her close against him. 'You're cold,' he whispered, 'we should go in.'

'No, I'm not cold,' she smiled, tilting her face to look up at him. 'I could never be cold when you are holding me. Please never stop.'

He gazed into her eyes then bent and kissed her soft, beautiful lips and as their passion mounted, time stopped.

In that moment, they were the only two people in the world.

Watching from her dressing room window, Zilda felt as if her heart would burst with happiness. She had not intended to spy on her son, but when she heard him rush out of the house, something he had not done, nor been capable of doing since his return, she had peeked out to see the Bryant-Smythes' car pull up outside and Celia alight to step onto the driveway. What followed next took her breath away and was a scene she would cherish forever.

She had not witnessed her son move with such agility in years as he raced down the steps towards Celia. It was as if the very sight of her had transformed him. Then, when he had taken her in his arms, even from the distance of her upstairs window, Zilda had seen from their faces that theirs was a love that could never be extinguished.

Looking down on them as they stood outside in the driveway, their arms entwined, their heads close together,

Zilda knew that no matter what had been inflicted on her son and Celia Bryant-Smythe during these last few years, nothing had stopped them fighting for what they both wanted: to be together. She also knew instinctively that no matter what the future held, her son would recover fully just so long as he had Celia by his side. In accepting that the woman her son now held in his arms was the only person who could bring him the peace he needed, Zilda let go of her anxiety and wept tears of joy.

It had taken a long time for her to believe Celia truly cared for her son. In discouraging the girl's visits, she had wanted only to protect him. He had been and still was very disturbed and vulnerable, but when she had learned that the child to which Celia had given birth, hidden away at Ridge View Cottage as Muriel had now told her, was David's, then everything had changed. Zilda had felt as if her heart would break at this news and although David's relapse had dominated her thoughts, she knew it was her responsibility to accept Celia Bryant-Smythe into their lives if that was what he wanted, and watching them together, she knew there was no question that he did.

Zilda was painfully aware that had she only known the true state of affairs between them, Celia's further suffering over the last couple of months could have been avoided. She sighed. It was pointless torturing herself with these thoughts: the clock could not be turned back. If it could, she would make sure every clock in the land was changed and that all those years of misery would never have occurred.

When David had begged her to invite Celia to visit him again, Zilda's intuition had told her that marriage was very likely on his mind. She had also assumed that he would propose as soon as he was well enough. She had been terrified that he was only doing what he thought was right and would be trapped in a loveless marriage. How wrong she was! Once upon a time she would have done everything in her power to stop such a union, but not anymore. She was only too aware of just how much sadness and destruction had affected all of their lives. There was nothing she could do about what had gone before, but she could help change the future and this, she promised herself, she would do no matter what. These two young people deserved all the help and support they could get and she would be there to give it. Silently, she vowed she would do whatever it took to make their lives happy ones.

As David and Celia make their way back inside the house and were lost from her view, she dried her eyes, re-applied her lipstick and waited for them to come and tell her the glad news.

She would, of course, appear to be surprised, and very happy – which she was.

Chapter THIRTY-TWO

Having imparted their glad news to Zilda, who had greeted it with delighted surprise and gone off to find something suitable to toast the occasion, David and Celia were sitting in the drawing room, cuddled up together on the sofa by the log fire.

'I'd prefer a small, private ceremony, just the two of us and of course my parents and your mother,' David said, 'but only if that's what you want too.'

'Absolutely ... I suppose it couldn't be *just* the two of us?'

Celia's wistful comment made him laugh. 'Can you imagine what my mother would have to say about *that*?'

Laughing with him, she said, 'Oh well, mustn't be selfish I suppose. Yes, darling, as small a ceremony as you like is all right by me, just so long as I am Mrs David Gillespie at the end of it.'

They were silent for a moment then, in a small voice, Celia asked him, 'Have you said anything to your mother about ... about ...'

'Our baby?' he finished for her.

'Yes,' she whispered.

He nodded, 'I told them both the other day. Perhaps I should not have been surprised to find that they already knew, though I'm not sure how, but anyway, how doesn't matter. The point is they knew and all my worrying about how they were going to react was for nothing. They both seem to have accepted what happened and their distress was more about you and what you have suffered than anything else - Mother was appalled at what you've been through, but said we must try to put it behind us.'

Seeing Celia's taut little face and the tears springing to her eyes, David hugged her. 'I know that is easy for others to say and must be especially hard for you, my darling, but I think it is probably the best way to deal with it. We cannot change the past, much as I would like to.' He kissed away her tears and held her close.

'I wrote about it in my diary,' she said suddenly. 'Every single day we were apart I described my thoughts and fears and dreams. I would like you to read it. It will help you to understand what it was like for me ... and about our son.'

'I would like that too,' he kissed her.

Springing apart as Zilda returned, brandishing a bottle and three glasses, David covered his embarrassment by telling her of their plans for the wedding. As he had anticipated, she was mortified.

'David, we simply cannot allow that! Surely we must make it a big celebration? We have so *much* to celebrate: not just your marriage, but your coming home to us alive and getting yourself well again. You are our only son. We simply have to mark such an important occasion as a Gillespie wedding! Lots of local people will expect an invitation, and then there are your father's business associates and others, as well as our two families, of course ...'

Holding up his hand to stop his mother in mid-flow before she really got the bit between her teeth, David shuddered. Knowing he was about to upset her, but determined not to let her rollercoaster his wedding into a circus, he frowned. He felt Celia tense beside him and squeezed her hand.

'There is little to celebrate with others, Mother. The way I see it, it is those very people who conspired to destroy our lives. Celia was banished for loving me, I was slandered, disbelieved, summarily dispatched and then left for dead, and as a result, the child we made that I knew nothing about, is lost to all of us. I can think of no reason to include others in what will be Celia's special day. The past cannot be changed or retrieved to start all over again, and as brutal as this may sound, I do not wish to discuss our wedding with you any further unless you are prepared to accept our plans. If necessary, we will go away. Celia and I are both of an age where we can make our own decisions and our decision is that our wedding is to be a private one. I am sorry if I've hurt you, it is the last thing I want to do, but I will not be persuaded to have the jamboree *you* envisage instead of the quiet, intimate ceremony that Celia and I would both prefer.'

Never had he spoken to his mother like this. It made David realise just how much the war had changed him. Looking at her stricken face, he softened his tone. 'I'm sorry if I sound harsh, I really don't mean to, but Celia and I need to look to the future, we must try and leave what has happened behind us. We can only do it by being ourselves. I love Celia, I always have and I owe her so much. I want to make the horrors of the past years fade for her if I possibly can. I am no longer a little boy, Mother, you *have* to let me go and please, allow me to do this my way.' Expecting a tirade, David was amazed when his mother took the wind right out of his sails.

'Of course, forgive me. You are right to chastise me, David. In my heart you will always be my little boy, you must allow me that as your mother, but I know full well that you are a man too and I must learn to accept that. You have been through so much and I am just so very proud of you.' She smiled, 'Hearing you stand up for what you believe in makes me love you all the more. Whatever you decide it's what your father and I want too, we just love you and want you to be happy. So let's say no more about it. Now then, are you going to open this bottle so I can toast you and your adorable bride to be? It'd be a shame to let it get warm!'

Laughing with relief, he stood and took the chilled bottle from her. Skilfully releasing the cork with a muted 'pop' and pouring three foaming glasses, he handed one each to his mother and Celia.

'To us,' he said, raising his glass to Celia and then to his lips.

'To you both,' his mother said, 'a long and happy life.'

As they sat together, companionably sipping champagne in front of the blazing logs in the drawing room at Rookery House, David, feeling as though a great weight had lifted from his shoulders, sighed with contentment. His mother had handed him the reins and it felt like a new beginning.

When Muriel called at Ridge View Cottage the day after Celia's visit to Rookery House, she had hardly got in the door before her daughter was flinging herself into her arms. 'Mama, Mama, we are to be married!'

'Oh Celia, I am so glad, that's wonderful.' Delighted, Muriel hugged her, 'Let me get my coat off and then we'll sit down and you can tell me all about it.'

A short while later, plied with cups of tea and cake by a smiling Gladys Thrift, they sat at the kitchen table and Muriel listened to Celia's ecstatic news.

'It was so unexpected. He rushed out of the house, whisked me in his arms and proposed to me as soon as I had stepped out of the car. Oh Mama, I am so happy. I had hoped and prayed, but I'd never dared to dream he'd still want me after all these years and everything that happened to us. He loves me, Mama, *really* loves me. I can hardly believe it. Why are you crying? You *are* pleased for me aren't you?'

Smiling at her daughter's anxious plea, Muriel dabbed at her eyes and nodded, 'More pleased than you will ever know, and I am crying with happiness, can't you tell?'

With that, they both dissolved into tears, crying and laughing at the same time as Celia described the afternoon she had spent at Rookery House and the plans for her wedding.

When Henry Bryant-Smythe learned that his only daughter was to marry David Gillespie, he smiled, not out of happiness for the pending nuptials of his offspring, but because he believed that he was saved. In fact, the more he thought about it, the more he realised he needed to change the dialogue running through his head: the word *believed* should be amended to *absolute certainty*. The change created a positive mood in Henry and made him feel very good indeed. The union between the successful, wealthy Gillespies and the Bryant-Smythes would, without a shadow of doubt, answer all his prayers. The fact that the future father-in-law of his daughter had served a writ on him and was determined to ruin him made him laugh out loud. 'It will be me doing the ruining,' he sneered out loud as he pulled on his fat cigar and let the aromatic fumes drift around his library.

Henry cared not one jot for what had gone before. His sole purpose was to ensure not just that he survived the financial mess he was in, but without loss. The only losses that counted for anything in his view were his reputation and his capital assets. These he calculated to be of equivalent value in the stakes of importance and he had no intention of losing either. Contemplating the extraordinary news that his daughter, despite her shameful disgrace, had pulled off such a coup, Henry devised another plan.

He had done plenty of thinking in the last few days and had arrived at several conclusions. One of them was: how on earth did his daughter think she could marry without his consent? With this question in his mind, he rang the servant's bell. Within seconds, the housekeeper appeared in the room.

'Mrs Jenkins, tell your mistress that I need to speak to her urgently. I assume she is in the Hall somewhere?'

With a courtesy that was blatantly false, the housekeeper answered, 'Yes, Squire, she is, I'll go and fetch her directly.' That said, she left the library and went in search of his wife.

Lilly Jenkins had grown thin over the past few weeks: the sudden disappearance of the most recent young maid to be the object of her employer's lustful attentions had added a huge burden to her daily routine. She had complained of course, but it had got her nowhere.

'I'm sorry, Mrs Jenkins, I have no idea why she left us,' Muriel Bryant-Smythe had told her. 'However, it is all to the good as we intend reducing the staff. She is not to be replaced.'

Lilly Jenkins had stood, hands on hips and glared at her mistress. 'That's not fair! You can't expect me to do *everything*. I can't cope and it's not right.'

'How dare you question my authority! It is quite simple, Mrs Jenkins, you either cope or you leave. The decision is yours. Now if you don't mind, I have things to do.'

Dropping her hands to her sides in shock at this unheard of response from her mistress, Lilly, fuming, had watched her turn away, one thought uppermost in her mind. *You just wait, Muriel Bryant-Smythe; I will get my revenge!* She would bide her time and then give the mistress the shock of her life. She would tell her everything she knew about the Squire. Only then would she leave this terrible place and take what she rightly deserved, a handsome wad of cash for all the years of drudgery and indignity she had received at the hands of this stuck up woman and her degenerate husband. But for now, she would play their game.

'Right then, I'd best get on, but you can be sure, very little extra will be done; I can't cut myself into two people,' she had snapped.

The Squire's wife had looked back over her shoulder and retorted, 'Is that so?' before walking away to leave Lilly standing alone in the room.

Now, as she went to fetch her mistress, she wondered what Henry Bryant-Smythe was up to. She had heard all the gossip about Miss Celia being proposed to by the Gillespie boy. A pure scandal, in her view what with the baby and everything. Like as not it would all end in tears, just what they deserved as far as she was concerned.

Muriel knew something was amiss with her husband. On the few occasions she'd had the misfortune to encounter him in the hall this last week, his tone had been almost polite. She was not fooled: the contempt in his eyes and his secretive manner told her he was scheming again. Increasingly, however, she found she was no longer afraid of him. Her sole purpose for the next few weeks was to see their daughter happily married. By then, she would have enough rope to hang him!

As she entered the library she sensed immediately that whatever Henry was planning she was about to learn what it was. She did not need to be standing in front of him or hear him speak, she had learnt over the years to use her instincts and as she walked towards him, each one was on full alert. There were several tell-tale signs to heighten her senses. The enormous cigar he was puffing away at was always an omen that something was about to happen. Her husband had always smoked cigars, but never a big Havana unless he was plotting. Then, of course, there was the way his wide, dark eyebrows managed to meet and create a V-shape above his eyes, which to Muriel looked satanic.

Without preamble or a pleasant greeting, he spoke. 'And when am I expected to give consent to the marriage of my daughter? I presume young Gillespie is going to talk to me before he does anything foolish again? Gossip has it that he has a lot of repaying to do and this time I mean to make sure that he does. Repay that is!'

Muriel had walked to a chair, but the words that came from her husband's mouth kept her on her feet.

Moving to stand barely a foot away from her, he leered, took another pull on his cigar and blew the smoke full into her face. Coughing, she cringed back, flapping her hand in an attempt to waft the smoke away.

A sneer plastered on his handsome features, he gave her no chance to reply. 'There can be no talk of matrimony until I know exactly what good old Robert Gillespie is prepared to pay for my daughter's hand,' he said. 'A hand that will no doubt please the heart of his cowardly, whoring offspring. I assume they are happy that the prodigal son has come back to the family fold at last - be he somewhat half-witted by all accounts.' Henry sniggered as he added these words.

Muriel was aghast. Had her husband finally taken leave of his senses? She could feel the blood rushing around her body, it felt as cold as ice. As well as she knew him, it seemed that nothing could prepare her for her husband's callous, calculating mind. Instead of replying, she felt herself recoil and for a moment the old fear of him snapped back at her as she gazed at him in horror.

With total disregard for anyone but himself, a sardonic smile crossed his lips. 'I'll teach them to remember that I'm the Squire of Satchfield Hall. I'm the Master around here and you'd all do well to remember that. And when I say all, I include you, my weakling wife, and your slut of a daughter. You will all pay for the shame you have brought to the name of Bryant-Smythe. And when I say '*pay*', that is exactly what I mean!'

Staring up at her husband, it took Muriel a few seconds to compose herself. Inwardly she was shaking, but somehow she managed to maintain a blank facial expression, one lifted eyebrow the only sign of her horrified contempt. 'Do you really think that after all you have done to Celia whom, I would remind you, you long ago denied was any daughter of yours, that she would think to ask your *permission*? She is over the age of twenty-one and no longer needs your consent. Or have you forgotten that too?'

'There are times, Muriel, when you surprise me. I find myself almost admiring your insolence. Almost! I called you in to have a civil conversation and to sort out the best way for *our* daughter. But I see I have wasted my time. That girl will not marry anyone without my permission and until I have a response from Robert Gillespie, there will be no marriage. Believe me, Muriel, go against me and you will find out just how much you have to lose. For your information, Robert Gillespie is aware that a sum is expected from him, so until we hear from him on what is not only right and proper, but expected, then you can forget about buying a new hat, because there will be no wedding.'

For a moment, Muriel gazed at the deluded reptile she had innocently and naively married, and realised that nothing could be done to stop him believing he was being reasonable and would have his way. Very soon he would be brought to book, this she knew. So without anything more to be said, she turned and walked out of the room. Hearing her husband's mocking laughter as she closed the door, she almost tripped over Lilly Jenkins, who had clearly been eavesdropping. The woman's face was wreathed in smiles at what she had overheard.

'Ah, yes, Mrs Jenkins. I am glad to find you here. I wished to speak with you. I have reached a decision concerning your employment at Satchfield Hall. In the circumstances, I feel it would be best if you leave us. You may have a week's notice, but I regret that I am unable to give you a reference. Never mind, I am sure you will be sufficiently compensated by my ... *husband*,' she snapped.

Lilly Jenkins almost leapt out of her skin. 'Sack, you can't sack me,' she said, nastily, 'the Squire would never allow it.'

'You think not?' Muriel turned to her, looked her up and down, registered the woman's vengeful glower and shrugged, 'But I can, Mrs Jenkins. I can!'

Chapter THIRTY-THREE

Had he not been up to his ears in documents, plans and endless meetings, Robert Gillespie would have laughed at Bryant-Smythe's audacity, but his mind was too overloaded with the concerns of his project and instead he exploded with rage.

'Does he seriously believe that he can stop the marriage of our son to the daughter he so callously had removed from his home and at the same time, expect us to quiver at his threats?' Robert fumed as he re-read the letter they had earlier received from Satchfield Hall.

Filled with incredulity he shook his head as if that would help bring about a change to the meaning of the words he had just read, even though he knew Bryant-Smythe meant every word he had written on his expensively embossed headed notepaper. To Robert, reading carefully between the lines, the position was clear. Despite the arrogant tone, there was no mistaking that this letter had been penned in a flurry of anxiety by the hand of a very desperate man.

As the words raced around in his head, he slammed the palm of his hand down on to his desk and took a deep breath as the implications of the letter became evident. It was a blatant attempt at blackmail without a care for the two young people it concerned. Incensed, but not wishing to cause offense either to his wife or Muriel Bryant-Smythe, both of whom were looking at him with mounting anxiety, Robert bit back the stream of bad language he had been about to utter and flung the letter away from him with a muttered, 'Damn the man!'

Muriel watched as Zilda's husband tossed the sheet of notepaper onto his desk, which was cluttered with correspondence, invoices and architects' drawings. The letter had not come as a total shock to her and she had come to Rookery House to warn them about what she suspected it contained, beating the postman by a whisker. Even so, she could see that the viciousness of Henry's words and the size of the demand had more than taken their breath away.

The disturbing facts Muriel had earlier learned from Iain Chamberlain about Satchfield Hall appeared to be true. Not that she had doubted him. It was clear to her now that her husband was going to use Celia's and David's marriage as the only way left open to him to sort out the financial mess he found himself in.

Looking up at Robert and Zilda, she grimaced. 'I'm so sorry. Not just sorry, but desperately ashamed. I don't know what to say.'

'Hush, my dear,' Zilda reached across from where she was sitting and patted Muriel's hand. 'You don't have to say anything. We know it has nothing whatever to do with you.'

Frowning, Robert gazed at her for a moment as though choosing his words. 'I heard rumours that your husband had got himself into financial difficulties; it must be a lot worse than I'd imagined. Although I find it hard to believe, I assume he is looking for a way out and in the belief that he can hold my son's happiness to ransom, he expects me to put his doomed venture back on an even footing. I'm sorry to say this, Muriel, but your husband is seriously deluded. There is nothing he can do to prevent David and Celia from marrying. At worst he can create ugly rumours, but it would not be the first time and much as I regret the implications for you, I feel the man's credibility has sunk so low that nobody would believe him. Not this time.'

Muriel nodded, wondering how much Robert knew. From his choice of words and the expression of concern in his eyes as he met her gaze, it was apparent he had guessed Henry was behind the rumours that had sent David off to war. She was fairly certain Zilda did not know, so made no comment. Instead, she said, 'I appreciate your concern, Robert, but you do not need to worry about me. I have taken steps to minimise the damage Henry may do, but let me explain. Without my knowledge or consent he mortgaged Satchfield Hall to the hilt to finance his latest project and recover his earlier debts. Now he has fallen so far behind on interest payments that the bank is threatening to foreclose. If he does not meet certain amounts by a given time all will be taken from him - and that will mean every capital asset he owns.'

Robert's eyebrows rose. 'Dear God, Muriel! Are you telling me that you may lose Satchfield Hall? Forgive me, but how could your husband be so stupid as to offer your home as security for such a risky scheme? Words fail me!'

A small smile crossed Muriel's lips, 'Do not apologise. I feel no sense of loyalty whatsoever to my husband. Not any more. What he does not know is that as soon as I was informed about what was going on, I sought legal advice. You see, I have owned fifty percent of Satchfield Hall for many years. This knowledge is shared only by Henry and my father's lawyer – well, he's my lawyer now - although my husband appears to have conveniently forgotten that ownership of the estate is divided equally between us.'

Aware that both the Gillespies were staring at her in amazement and hanging onto her every word, Muriel continued. 'It is not the first time Henry has found himself in trouble. Two weeks before our wedding, he lost heavily at a game of cards. By heavily, I mean many thousands of pounds. In those days he appeared to be so ashamed of his actions that my father, believing him repentant, gave him a large sum of money to clear his debt on the condition that half the Satchfield Hall estate was transferred to my name. My dear father did this to ensure I would always have a home. At the time he believed Henry had made a mistake, but was essentially a decent man and having learned his lesson would make me a good husband. When the same thing happened again within a year of our marriage, he changed his opinion. Despite this, for my sake he once again cleared Henry's debts. At the same time, he had the foresight to set up a trust fund for me so that I would have independent means my husband would not be able to touch.'

Her eyes narrowing, Muriel looked across at Robert and then at Zilda. 'It is clear from Henry's actions that he has forgotten he does not own the Hall outright. Either that or he has deliberately misled others in order to manipulate whatever was required to provide enough information for the bank in order to secure the funds he needed. But I can tell you now that he will never get his hands on my share of Satchfield Hall. Over the years, he has systematically destroyed our lives and it is time to put a stop to it once and for all. As far as I am concerned, my marriage to Henry Bryant-Smythe is over; indeed, it has been for a very long time, but until recently I have not had the courage to do anything about it. My only regret about it all is that poor Celia and David are once again the stick that Henry intends to wield in order to beat whatever it is he wants from you or me ...' Muriel gasped as a pain knifed across her chest. She bent over in her chair, tried to calm her breathing.

Zilda leapt up, 'Muriel, my dear, are you all right? What can I get you?'

'Forgive me; please don't worry. It's my angina. I have some pills in my handbag ... some water ...?'

'Yes, of course,' Zilda went rushing out of the room and came back in seconds with a glass of water.

Reaching for her pill case, Muriel swallowed the tablets then sat back until the pain and palpitations began to ease. 'They work quite quickly; I will be all right in a moment,' she said breathlessly.

Robert, who had risen in his chair, sat down again. Listening to everything Muriel had told them, for the first time in all the years he had known her he felt a huge admiration for her. She had lived all her married life in the shadow of the man who had once been his friend and business partner, but who had turned into a ruthless degenerate who cared nothing for anyone but himself. Robert knew from Zilda that when Celia had been forced out of Satchfield Hall, Muriel had begun to change. There was no question that her health had suffered, but even so, it was clear to him the woman sitting before him, despite her obvious frailty, had over the years learnt to deal with Henry Bryant-Smythe and intellectually, was more than a match for him. Whether she had the physical strength was another matter. This knowledge added the extra weight Robert needed, stiffening his resolve to bring down the man who was set on destroying them all for his own ends and would if he got his way.

When Muriel was sufficiently recovered, they repaired to the drawing room for afternoon tea before George Brand was summoned to take his mistress back to Satchfield Hall. Robert then went back to his study to think. The price Bryant-Smythe was demanding for his daughter was high, very high, but Robert had not succeeded so far in business without thinking on his feet and as he contemplated the enormity of the man's ludicrous demand, he also saw an advantage that would sort the bastard out once and for all. Knowing that Muriel had washed her hands of the man made it easier than it might otherwise have been.

Pacing backwards and forwards, he knew what he had to do. The question was what was the best way to do it? It was clear from the letter lying on his desk that Bryant-Smythe had taken leave of his senses, but until today Robert had not realised just how low the man had sunk. To what lengths would he go to make sure he received his payment in full? With a qualm of fear, Robert wondered if Muriel's husband was capable of physical violence to get his own way if all else failed.

It was paramount to keep such thoughts to himself. Zilda would panic at any mention that Celia or David might be in danger. Robert looked up as she came to find him, having waved goodbye to her friend. Not allowing his anxiety to show, he smiled. 'Let us not worry about what that fool believes he can blackmail out of us, I promise you it will be sorted out. We both know his permission is not required for Celia to marry our son; they are both of an age where they are free to make their own decisions.'

Robert took hold of his wife's hand and pulled her towards him, he could smell her scent as he held her to him, the same delicate fragrance she always wore: everything about Zilda was understated and elegant. He was filled with a strong desire to protect her and knew she could not face any more harm coming to their family. So much damage had already been done. His job was to stop that bastard from doing any more. Stroking his wife's hair, he planted a kiss on her cheek. 'Zilda, just leave all of this with me, I think I know how to deal with Henry Bryant-Smythe for good and all.'

She leaned back to look up into his face, 'Please don't let him hurt them, Robert, they've been through so much already. I couldn't bear it.'

'I promise you he will never again hurt our son or our family – and Celia is part of our family now.' Meaning every word, Robert held Zilda tighter. 'I suggest you speak with David and it might be a good idea to ask Celia to come and stay at Rookery House until the wedding. It will most certainly give David an added boost.'

Zilda, who understood her husband far better than she suspected he ever imagined, had never loved him more than she did at this moment. She knew instinctively that he was far more concerned than he was letting on, but for some reason, despite the terrible letter and its implications, she was confident he would sort this mess out and that everything would be fine in the end. As so often in the past, she silently thanked God for giving her such a strong and caring man.

Keeping her voice calm and refusing to worry about what underlay his unexpected suggestion, she smiled up at him. 'What a splendid idea, darling. I will do it straight away. The house will be a little brighter for having Celia around and I will enjoy her company.'

It was on the tip of her tongue to ask what her husband had in mind to sort out Muriel's husband, but then she changed her mind. What she did not know too much about would save her from further worry and also from telling David, who would be sure to ask.

Chapter THIRTY-FOUR

David arrived at Ridge View Cottage in Robert's runabout Morris Minor to find the place a hive of activity. Gladys Thrift was in the middle of cleaning the outside of the windows, Lizzie was hanging out the laundry on the long washing line at the side of the cottage and he could see Celia, her back to him, busy in the vegetable patch.

'Oh my goodness,' cried Gladys as soon as she saw him limping down the path towards her. 'We weren't expecting you. You have found us all up to our elbows.' Splashing water from her pail as she threw her cleaning rags into the water, she stumbled down from the little two-step folding stepladder she always used for window cleaning, wiped her hands on her apron and beamed at him.

'It's a surprise visit,' he said in a cheerful undertone, pointing at Celia and placing his index finger to his lips.

'You can say that again,' Gladys said in a loud whisper, looking over to where Celia was kneeling between a row of cabbages, her hair swept back in a headscarf knotted on top of her head. 'Best you go and surprise that young lady of yours and I'll put the kettle on.'

David smiled. It was Gladys Thrift's answer to any situation: make tea. Celia had introduced him to her on his first visit here a few days ago and he had liked her on sight. She was a stout, homely woman, who had looked after Celia tirelessly over the years, for which he was extremely grateful, all the more so when he discovered her wages from Celia's father had ceased abruptly a long time ago. Anyone else might have packed her bags and left, but Gladys had stayed and with Lizzie Rainbow's help, turned the cottage into a comfortable haven for Celia, getting by on her own meagre savings until Muriel Bryant-Smythe had found out and reimbursed her. To show their appreciation, he and Celia had planned a surprise for Gladys and he had been looking forward to seeing her face when they told her about it, but it would have to wait. His visit to Ridge View Cottage this morning was urgent and he did not want to linger. He had no intention of sharing this information with Gladys, however, and forcing a smile to his lips he winked at her.

As Gladys bustled into the cottage, David stood and looked across to where Celia, oblivious to his presence, was busy working in the garden. Intoxicated by the sight of her, he wanted to soak in the scene right to the very marrow of his bones. He could not believe that after so much pain and hurt, she still loved him. Not a moment passed when he did not realise just how lucky he was, and as he watched the most precious person in his life absorbed in her weeding, he knew he would never allow anyone ever to hurt her again, most particularly her father.

Earlier that morning his mother had come to his room and asked to talk to him. 'I've got an idea and I am sure you will like it,' she had said, sitting herself down in the chair next to the window. In the process of completing the double knot to his tie, having dressed in his smart suit prior to accompanying his father to an important meeting at the Town Hall, he had not noticed if she was smiling, only that her voice had a false cheerfulness to it that set his nerves jangling.

'What idea is that?' he had asked warily.

His mother had watched him fiddling with his tie. 'I've been thinking that it's high time Celia left that poky cottage and came to live with us at Rookery House,' she announced.

'Well yes, of course, she will as soon as we are married.' Puzzled, he had swung round from the mirror to stare at her, adding, 'but only until we find a place of our own.'

'I mean today, David; now; immediately. I've arranged for her room to be made ready. It will make organising the wedding so much easier with her being at hand. Muriel is in total agreement with me. And of course, it will give Celia an opportunity to settle into her new surroundings before the big day, which will be much less stressful for her. So you see, it's simply perfect for all of us,' his mother had gushed out the words, her smile forced and a small furrow of anxiety creasing her brow.

Under different circumstances, David would have been delighted at the idea of Celia coming to Rookery House as soon as possible, but his mother's burst of words and her forced smile had betrayed that there was more to this than she was saying. He was only too pleased that she had at last warmed to the woman he was going to marry, but something about her demeanour had disturbed him greatly. 'Why the urgency Mother? What are you not telling me?'

She had sighed, 'You will have to ask you father. He's in the study.'

His anxiety building, without another word David had limped to the door and gone straight downstairs to his father's inner sanctum.

'Ah, David, I see your mother has told you.'

The look on his father's face told David that something was wrong; worse, it concerned Celia. 'She's told me very little. What's this all about?'

'It's nothing for you to worry about, son. We just feel that Celia would be safer here with us. Please believe me that everything will be sorted out, just do as your mother has asked and bring Celia to Rookery House as soon as you can.'

'You are both talking in riddles! What do you mean *safer*? Is Celia in some sort of danger?'

'It's unlikely, but better safe than sorry, eh? I would be happier if she came to live here with us from now on.' He had spoken in a flat tone, still not volunteering any information.

Trying with only limited success to hold down his panic, David had planted himself squarely in front of his father. 'For God's sake tell me what is going on. I am not a child, Father. Level with me, please. What are we up against?'

To his surprise, his father had smiled. 'Son, you are up against nothing and if you will permit me to deal with this, I promise you nothing will stop your marriage to Celia or cause either of you any harm.'

With a tight grip of fear squeezing his heart at the very idea of losing Celia again, David, fists clenched at his side, had struggled not to lose his temper. 'I do not doubt what you say, Father, but I have to know what is causing such an urgent necessity to bring Celia to Rookery House. We are talking about my future wife. As grateful I am to you, it is *my* duty and responsibility to protect her, not yours. So you will tell me *exactly* what is going on and *right now*!'

His father had viewed him with narrowed eyes, clearly nettled by his tone then, as if reaching a decision, had nodded. 'Very well. I had hoped to keep this from you and I would prefer it if you did not tell your mother you have seen it.' He had picked up a letter from his desk and handed it over.

Standing rooted to the spot, David had read the words that spelled out Henry Bryant-Smythe's demands, then had broken into surprised and relieved laughter. 'For goodness sake, Father, this must be a joke. Admittedly the man's sense of humour is warped, but you can't believe he's serious. It's preposterous. He must know he can't stop us marrying. Celia's over the age of consent.'

'It's no joke, David. The man is unhinged and perfectly serious. I realise he cannot stop you from marrying his daughter, but he might do untold damage if he is thwarted. Although we have never spoken of it – nor do I wish to since we cannot undo the past and there is no point in raking over old wounds - but you must by now have worked out that Bryant-Smythe was responsible for the scandal that sent you off to war? Everything both you and

Celia have suffered can be laid at his door. Who knows what he is capable of? For God's sake don't tell your mother this, but the man is in dire straits and I am prepared to believe he might even resort to threatening Celia with violence to get his own way. *Now* do you understand why it would be best for her to come here?'

'We have to do something ...' David had spluttered, the smile wiped from his face, further speech impossible as the implications of what his father had said sank home and roiled him with rage.

'Rest assured that I am taking steps to sort the bastard out, David, and he will soon be in no position to harm you or Celia – or anyone else, come to that. And before you ask, I do not wish to say more on that for now,' his father had smiled, 'but suffice it to say that you and your bride will be the beneficiaries of all that is achieved.' He had tapped his chest just above his heart, 'On my life, son. Trust me. Now go and bring home your fiancée. Take the Morris,' he had reached into the desk drawer, rummaged for the car keys and handed them over.

Grabbing them, David had nodded and was quickly on the road, driving at reckless speed to Ridge View Cottage. It was the first time he had driven himself since his army days and it brought back a whole plethora of black memories, but he kept them at bay, his chief concern to get to Celia as fast as possible.

Now, watching her in the garden, his emotion caught in his throat and made it hard to breathe, he crept up behind her, but his foot scuffed against the bundle of canes she had piled to one side of the path ready for the runner beans. Looking round she caught sight of him and her face lit up. It was as if the sun had just come out: God, he loved this woman!

'Hello,' she cried, 'what are *you* doing here?'

He smiled, 'I thought I'd come and pay my fiancée a visit and also give her a little surprise.'

Getting to her feet, her face glowing from the fresh air, but also from the sight of him, she ran towards him.

'Where's your driver,' she asked, looking around and peeling off her gardening gloves.

'Solo today, my darling,' and as he spoke the words, he dangled the car keys over her head. Celia looked up amazed, but as she opened her mouth to speak, David took her in his arms.

In a voice that was lighter than he felt, he said, 'I've come to take you back to Rookery House. Mother thought it would be better if you were closer at hand to sort out the wedding. I think she fancies some feminine company – but I daresay I can put up with having you around. So how's about it?'

Celia was about to laugh, because the quiet wedding they had planned hardly needed sorting out. There would be only a handful of people and she did not intend to wear white nor he a morning suit. But as she looked up into David's face she caught something in his expression. She did not know what it was; perhaps a shadow behind his eyes, but it was enough to alert all her senses.

'So why do you *really* want me to come to Rookery House today of all days. What's wrong, David?'

As the words left her lips, a shiver ran through Celia's body. Instinctively she knew her father was somewhere behind this sudden turn of events. She had been half expecting it. She might be banished and ignored, but in his eyes she was still an asset and at worse a pawn to be used in his game of life. She was no fool: she had guessed David's proposal of marriage would provoke her father into some kind of reaction and he would be considering what benefit their marriage could be to him.

Even as these frightening thoughts entered Celia's head, she could think of nothing that would be of use to him anymore, but then, she hardly knew what his business was about these days. In truth, apart from occasional words from her mother, she knew nothing about him at all. Despite this ignorance, she was quite sure that if her father believed he could gain from her marriage to David Gillespie, he would take steps to ensure that he did.

'Why should anything be wrong?' David kissed her, regardless of who might be watching. 'So what is your answer, my muddy girl?'

She pushed him gently away, 'Don't try to fob me off, David. I can guess why you are here. My father is behind it isn't he? He may have long ago excommunicated me, but that won't stop him scheming to take advantage of me if he can. Stop trying to protect me, David. I take it you see him as a threat?'

With a twinkle in his eye, David turned his mouth down, 'I can see there is never going to be any point in my trying to keep things from you.'

'David, be serious: tell me what has happened.'

'I won't lie to you, my darling. Your father is demanding that unless my father stumps up a large sum of money, he will withhold his consent to our marriage. There is nothing we need to worry about. You are far too old to need his permission, I think he must have forgotten you are no longer a teenager!' He smiled, 'I just wanted you with me and this seemed like a good excuse. Seriously, though, I can't bear even the thought of anything coming between us again and I'd be a lot happier if you would come back with me today. Come home to Rookery House with me, please say you will.'

Celia looked into David's eyes and knew he was hiding something. The concern in his face betrayed him and she knew he was worried about her. He had no need to be, she was past caring about anything her father might want to do to her. He had almost destroyed her once, but she would not let him destroy the man she loved. If it would bring peace to David, then she would go and at least she might learn what was going on at Satchfield Hall.

While her heart skipped with the joy to be going back with David to Rookery House, at the same time the thought of leaving Ridge View Cottage brought an unexpected surge of sorrow. It had been her home for the best part of eight years; she had borne her son here and found solace in the environment; the garden; the stunning panoramic scenery and, eventually, in the company of Gladys and Lizzie, who had become her friends. How was it possible to feel both joy and sorrow at the same time, she asked herself? She forced a smile, 'Of course, I will, but does it have to be today?'

'I'm afraid it must, but we can always pop back to collect anything you forget to take with you.'

The relief in his voice was palpable, reinforcing her belief that he was hiding something from her. 'Oh my goodness, *Mama*! I need to get a message to Mama,' Celia suddenly cried.

'There is no need, your mother knows. It was she and my mother who came up with the idea, so stop fretting,' he cupped her face in his hands and kissed her.

Celia could not help fretting, everything was happening too fast. She had wanted to talk to David about the surprise they had in store for Gladys, but supposed that would have to wait now. Letting David's arms slip from her, she turned and looked across at the beautiful view. It had taken her a long time to accept this place 'on the top of the world' as her home, but she had and once the pain had eased, she had felt secure and at peace here. She experienced a sudden feeling of panic to be leaving it, but a little voice in her head laughed at her. *'You're much too young to have left the world behind,'* it said.

'Before I am whisked away from what has been my home for all these years, I want to take a walk around the gardens. I need to find a few words to say to Gladys and Lizzie.' What she did not say was that she needed to thank the place that had not only been a safe haven, but had given her hope again; she wanted to say goodbye, but she could only do this alone.

David turned her round to face him and looked deep into her eyes. 'I understand,' he said. 'You go ahead; I will wait. Take all the time you need.'

Loving him for his sensitivity, she reached up and kissed him then watched as he retraced his steps back to the cottage leaving her alone.

She took fifteen minutes, wandering to her favourite place in the garden and sitting on an upturned tree stump to gaze down at the sheep-dotted valley. At peace, she returned to the cottage to find David, Gladys and Lizzie drinking tea, seated at the table, which was piled high with homemade goodies.

Taking her place beside them, Celia, a lump in her throat, broke the news to Gladys and Lizzie, explaining the real purpose of David's unexpected visit. 'I know it is a shock to you, it most certainly is a shock to me, but it seems my father is behaving badly again and Mr and Mrs Gillespie want me to move to Rookery House where they can keep an eye on me.'

Celia did not want to say any more, but neither Gladys nor Lizzie were fools and would know what she was not saying: that her father had threatened her marriage to David. Long after she had first come to the cottage and she and Lizzie had become friends, the maid had told her why she had been sent away from Satchfield Hall. Celia had been appalled and horrified; even knowing of her father's cruelty, she had been unprepared to learn he was a rapist. The man was evil and they all knew it, none more so than Lizzie, who now, to everyone's surprise, burst into tears.

'Oh my, Miss Celia,' she sobbed, 'I will miss you more than you will ever know. I knew one day you would be leaving us, but not today.' She lifted her pinny to her face, huge tears splashing from her eyes.

Celia sprang up from her chair and wrapped her arms around Lizzie. 'My dear, dear friend, please don't cry. I'll be visiting you so much you'll want to lock the door to keep me away.' Lizzie shook her head, smiling through her tears and Celia, choking back the lump in her throat, said lightly, 'I'd best go and pack.'

Escaping to the privacy of her room, she pulled garments from drawers and cupboards and threw them onto the bed, all the while the tears she had managed to contain until now spilling uncontrollably down her face.

'Let me help you. I did it before when you left Satchfield Hall, I can do it again.'

Celia swung round to see Lizzie standing in the doorway. 'Oh, Lizzie, thank you. What will I do without you?'

'Now don't take on so you two girls,' said Gladys, coming up behind Lizzie, her eyes suspiciously moist belying her cheerful tone. 'Anyone would think you were planning a funeral instead of a wedding. Whatever next? Come along Lizzie, help me get the trunk out from under the bed. Miss Celia, you should go and talk to that young man of yours, the poor chap looks like he doesn't know where to put himself with all this weeping and wailing going on.'

'Oh Gladys!' Celia was forced to laugh, but she stayed where she was and in the end it was Gladys who packed the trunk. Lizzie and Celia just hugged each other and sobbed.

Chapter THIRTY-FIVE

Ten days after Celia had been welcomed into the Gillespies' family home she was waiting eagerly for her mother, who had been invited to Rookery House for tea. 'We have something we want to tell you,' David had said earlier to his parents, 'but we'll wait for Celia's mother to arrive and then we can tell you all at the same time.'

Mystified, his parents had exchanged glances, but Celia and David, grinning like Cheshire cats, refused to say more until both families were ensconced in the drawling room by the fire, sipping tea from delicate porcelain cups – a far cry from Gladys' mugs, thought Celia with a sudden pang of homesickness for the cottage.

When there was a lull in the conversation, all of them studiously avoiding the subject that was uppermost in their minds: Henry Bryant-Smythe's demands, Celia, unable to keep the surprise plan to herself any longer, burst out, 'We have decided to offer Gladys Thrift and George Brand a double wedding.'

There was a stunned silence broken eventually by Zilda, 'But my dear, it simply isn't the done thing!'

'Don't be so old-fashioned, Mother, what is the *done thing* these days?' David said. 'The world has changed or hadn't you noticed?'

'Let's face it, we are rather unconventional,' Celia chipped in with a smile to soften David's outburst.

'Well I can't argue with that!' Muriel agreed.

Raising an eyebrow, Robert helped himself to a biscuit and sat back in his chair, smiling as he looked from one to the other, but saying nothing.

'The thing is,' Celia said, 'for one reason and another they have waited years to tie the knot and we wanted to give them a wedding present to say thank you to Gladys for all she's done for me. David came up with the idea of a double wedding and I think it is a perfectly lovely plan. The only other person we have told is Lizzie, who is sworn to secrecy. I have asked her to be our joint maid of honour.'

'Well, whatever next! I've never heard of such a thing.' Zilda looked thoughtfully at David then added, 'but what does it matter if it is what you both want? And besides, I will be so relieved to see you safely married that I am not going to argue.'

'Thank goodness for small mercies!' Robert teased. Laughing at the disgruntled look Zilda shot in his direction, he pushed himself out of his chair. 'Well that's that settled then. And now, if you'll excuse me, I have one or two things I must do and I am sure you ladies can manage to discuss the paraphernalia of weddings without my contribution.' He gave David a conspiratorial grin, 'Care to join me in the study, son?'

David laughed and got up to go, bending over Celia to plant a chaste kiss on her cheek before he followed Robert from the room.

After the men had gone, Muriel pursed her lips and looked across at Celia. 'I think it's lovely of you both and I agree that Gladys has been a treasure, but I think you might find she will take some persuading. I know you have never been particularly conscious of your social standing, Celia, but it is not the same for Gladys – or George, come to that. I can imagine they will both be hugely embarrassed by the very idea of sharing such an important occasion with you.'

'Don't worry Mama, David could charm the birds out of the trees; he'll persuade them, especially since it is to be such a small affair and now we've decided on the private chapel, it isn't as if there will be hordes of people to see.'

'Mm, well I only hope you're right,' said Muriel.

A few days later, when David drove Celia back to Ridge View Cottage ostensibly to pick up a box of books she had left behind it was to find that, as always, her mother had been right.

'Goodness me, Miss Celia, Mr Gillespie, we cannot entertain such an idea. Good grief, what is the world coming to?' Gladys protested in shock.

'I owe you so much and what better way of trying to repay just a little bit back,' Celia pleaded.

'But that's what I've been doing,' Gladys said, her eyes springing with unshed tears, 'trying to repay you for what I did ... you know, back then ...'

'Did you have a choice, Gladys?'

Gladys sniffed, pulling out a handkerchief from her sleeve and dabbing at her nose. 'Well, no, not really, except I could have said no and walked away.'

'And then where would I have been?' Celia smiled. 'You only ever did what you thought was for the best, I know that. We may have had our differences at the time, but I stopped blaming you years ago.'

'Thank you, Miss Celia, it gladdens me heart to hear it. Even so, I don't see how me and George can share your special day, it isn't right.'

'Ah,' said David, 'you've misunderstood us, Mrs Thrift. We are not asking you to share our special day.'

'I thought I must've got it wrong, Mr Gillespie,' Gladys smiled with relief.

David beamed at her, 'You did. What we are asking is if *we* can share *yours*.'

Gladys' mouth dropped open and she stared at him.

'I'll be honest, Gladys ... er, you don't mind if I call you Gladys?' She shook her head. 'Thank you. Well, as I was saying, Gladys, we were going to talk to you about it last time I came to Ridge View Cottage, but as you know, events took over on that day. Speaking for myself, I owe you so much. You have looked after my girl and given her back to me even more beautiful than before, when I was forced into the terrible war. All we are asking is that you and George share your wedding with us. It will be an honour for us: a double wedding, the end of one chapter and the beginning of a new life for all four of us. Please say you will; it would make us both very happy.'

Nonplussed, Gladys turned to look at Celia, 'He could sell sand to the Arabs, that one!'

Celia burst into laughter, 'I should have warned you. Seriously, though, Gladys, will you?'

'I don't deserve this,' Gladys cried, 'but if you insist then I'd be honoured, but I don't know what George will say and what about the banns?'

'George knows,' Celia confessed. 'My mother has already asked him and he said he would be happy to do whatever you wanted.'

'And I've got us a special licence and spoken to the Vicar,' said David, 'we don't need banns and it's a private chapel anyway. So you see, you don't have to worry about a thing except getting yourself down the aisle.'

'And keeping our maid of honour calm,' Celia murmured with a smile at Lizzie.

Gladys turned her mouth down in a small grimace, 'You don't think folks will talk?'

'Of course they will,' David grinned. 'Haven't they been talking about us all for years? Now they have something very real and important to talk about. And, also, it's David from now on.' He smiled and then hugged Gladys and for first time they could recall, she openly wept.

Since their contretemps concerning the proposed marriage of his daughter, Henry Bryant-Smythe had barely spoken to his wife. He was fully aware how important it was to her that Celia's wedding to the halfwit Gillespie boy went ahead without a hitch. Indeed, he had been banking on it – quite literally! He laughed to himself. It had given him the deepest of pleasures that it could only have been at her intervention Robert Gillespie had finally agreed to his demands. Muriel must have orchestrated the whole thing.

Quite how she had managed it, he could not imagine. Had she made the Gillespies believe he would do something dreadful to Celia? Yes, that was probably it. Would he have done? Damn right he would! Quite what he wasn't sure, but happily he didn't have to think of what; the implied threat had been enough it seemed. He had signed Gillespie's stupid contract to say it had been paid; as if it mattered. What a fool the man was.

Pouring himself another glass of cognac, he raised it high, 'Well done, my little weakling wife, well done indeed! You had to make sure your precious daughter's wedding went to plan, didn't you. I wonder how you persuaded the halfwit's father to part with his cash. Did you tell him about the baby, eh? Goddamn! I wish I'd been a fly on the wall.'

He laughed out loud; not a penny did he owe anyone now. 'By God, Henry,' he roared, 'what a clever fellow you are.' Tossing the contents of the glass down his gullet, he poured another and raised it again. 'To my precious daughter,' he slurred, 'what a priceless thing she has turned out to be.'

Falling back into his chair, he hiccupped, drained the glass again then, still laughing, slammed it down onto the table. He had not thought for one moment that Robert Gillespie would meet his demands in full – what an idiot. He had set the price for his daughter's hand deliberately high to allow for negotiation. Now he only wished he had demanded more for the little slut.

'Lilly?' he yelled at the top of his voice. 'Where are you woman? Get in here; I want you to do something for me.'

As Henry Bryant-Smythe drank himself into a stupour, a quiet double wedding was taking place in the little chapel on the other side of the Satchfield Hall estate.

With the coins she had been paid still jingling in her purse, Lilly Jenkins slipped into one of the pews at the back and kept her head down. The combined wedding had got a few tongues wagging, she had enjoyed stirring it up in the village, raking up old scandals and rumours. The Squire had paid her to keep a close eye on the proceedings, telling her in an inebriated tone, 'I want you to report back to me on the wedding of my daughter.' It had been on the tip of her tongue to ask why he would not be there to see it for himself, but she already knew the answer. He simply couldn't. The girl was a disgrace to him and a threat to his privileged standing in society. His wife would be there, of course, but then, she was clearly strange in the head when it came to her trollop of a daughter. Strange in the head altogether putting up with me and the Squire all these years, she thought. I'm blessed if I would have done. What a weak, stupid woman she is to be sure.

Lilly smiled inwardly at her own importance in the Squire's household, but then, she told herself, she had been the number one woman there from the moment she arrived as a twenty-five-year old, until he'd worn her to a frazzle with his demands then tossed her aside like a worn out shoe. Even then she had known how to hang on to her position and had stayed number one - and he darn well knew it too. He had flared into a huge rage about her getting the sack and promptly reinstated her. She had not been surprised; she knew far too much for him to risk her blabbing about what had been going on in that house for years. When earlier he had handed her three guineas and told her to be discreet, Lilly could have laughed out loud. Me discreet? She had laughed smugly to herself, oh yes, Mr High and Mighty, she thought, I'll be discreet for as long as you pay me, and not a day longer. She knew he hated her; it worried her not one jot. She was an asset to him and had demonstrated it on many occasions all down the years. Right now was another one of those occasions. Eyeing the blushing bride, she smirked. Fat chance they'd make it work with the Squire keeping his tabs on them.

Muriel had spotted Lilly Jenkins the moment the odious woman had sneaked into the little chapel, but she did not care. Nothing was going to spoil this wonderful day. Celia, wearing a cream costume and carrying a small bouquet of pink rosebuds, had looked stunningly beautiful as she walked down the aisle. Muriel had prevailed upon Iain Chamberlain to give her away; he had needed little persuading, only too delighted to be invited. Robert had done the same for Gladys, and George Brand's brother-in-law had been best man for both grooms. A jolly man, he had made them all smile as he joked about having two rings to look after. Everything had gone to plan so perfectly. Muriel had nothing more to worry about. The ceremony was over, the marriage witnessed. Her beautiful daughter was now Mrs David Gillespie and was safe at last, and her father was about to get his just desserts.

While the two couples were signing the register, Muriel caught sight of her husband's spy, Lilly Jenkins, clearly believing she had not been seen, slipping out from the pew and away through the slightly open door of the chapel. Muriel's attention was then distracted by Gladys and George Brand, who had left the vestry and were walking towards her, their faces wreathed in smiles.

'Thank you from the bottom of my heart, Marm,' Gladys said, holding out her hand. 'You have made this day one that we will never forget.'

Smiling with gratitude for all this woman had done for her daughter, Muriel shook Gladys' hand. 'You have nothing to thank me for, Mrs Brand. I owe you a debt that is too high for me ever to be able to repay.'

Gladys blushed to hear her new name and glanced quickly up at George, who stepped forward, a faint flush staining his cheeks. 'I'd like to add my thanks as well, Marm. It's been such an honour to share our wedding with Miss Celia and Mr David.'

'Well, as you know, George, the idea of the double wedding was theirs not mine, but please believe me when I say I think it was absolutely splendid. I am the happiest mother alive to witness such special people being joined together here today.'

At the same time as the newly married couples were walking down the aisle to have their photographs taken, there was a thunderous banging on the main entrance door of Satchfield Hall.

'What the hell ...?' Remembering he had sent the housekeeper off to spy, Henry swore roundly and struggled out of his chair.

Stumbling to his feet, he got no further than the door to the drawing room. The visitors, having found the front door unlocked, had let themselves into the Hall and were standing on the threshold of the room.

Swaying, Henry attempted to focus. 'Who are you and what do you mean by barging in here like this?' he slurred, outraged. 'How dare you ...'

'Henry Bryant-Smythe?' asked one, stepping forward.

Chapter THIRTY-SIX

When the news reached Robert Gillespie that Bryant-Smythe had been arrested and that his housekeeper was 'helping police with their enquiries', he felt lightheaded with relief. He had thought it would make him laugh or at least smile, but it did not. His overriding feeling was one of disgust, but also of regret that a man who had once been his friend and business partner could have sunk so low. A man who, with his abundance of privileges and advantages could have done so much good, had instead chosen to destroy others in his deluded, twisted belief that it would give him wealth, status and power.

When Bryant-Smythe had turned his attention on the Gillespie family, he had come very close to shattering their lives. Too close, thought Robert, grimly. Because of him they had almost lost their son and nearly lost a large portion of their land. The threat to David's and Celia's happiness had been the final straw. Robert had known it was imperative to deal with the man who, if he did not, would have no compunction in destroying them all.

Following Muriel's disclosure concerning her part-ownership of Satchfield Hall, Robert, with his wife and Muriel, had put together a plan that was not, as it might appear to Henry Bryant-Smythe, to acquiesce to his demand and help him out of his current financial predicament, but to save David, Celia and their children, should they have any, from any future threat and pain.

Before executing their plan, Robert had made one final attempt to persuade Bryant-Smythe to withdraw his demand, at first through his lawyers and then in person, in the faint hope that somewhere beneath the man's blustering arrogance there still lurked a shred of the friend he had once been, but Celia's father was beyond redemption. Much as Robert might have expected, his hopes had been dashed: he had been abused and threatened.

'Fine words, Gillespie, but it will change nothing. It is pay-back time for all the help I have given you to my cost in the past. My daughter belongs to me and I will not have you steal her away. I have asked a fair price and if you want her to marry your witless son, you will meet my demand and nothing more will be said. If you do not, then I will not answer for the consequences. And that is all I have to say.'

Had Robert been just a step closer, he might have hit the man. As it was, he neither uttered a word nor flinched, but turned and walked away. Only then did it truly come home to him that Bryant-Smythe was dangerously deranged and that no amount of talk or threats of legal action would stop him. He had crossed the line and walked too far from reason and responsibility to be able to return.

Driving home to Rookery House, Robert had thought through the plan he, Muriel and Zilda had conceived to stop Bryant-Smythe from hurting his family ever again. It involved a hefty financial outlay, but that had seemed a small price to pay to rid themselves of any future threat. They had agreed that Robert would meet the man's demands, but only on condition that he sign a contract ostensibly to relinquish any further demands on his daughter once she was married. Doubtless Bryant-Smythe would be both incredulous and incensed should he ever learn that his wife had been the one who arranged to have the contract drawn up by her lawyer!

Robert had expected Bryant-Smythe to refuse to sign or at least to argue, but Muriel, who knew her husband all too well, had said he would not even trouble to read it. It was just this bombastic, careless approach to business that had got him into trouble in the first place. Aside from which, she had said, he would believe he could break any contract with impunity.

Robert had been relieved and surprised to discover she was right. Henry Bryant-Smythe, so in fear of the consequences of his financial crisis, had paid little heed to the documents that had been placed before him for his approval and signature. Carelessly assuming that his daughter had been a good sale having yielded him the means to avoid bankruptcy, he had taken up the pen and sneered, 'Show me the money and I will sign. I don't need or want to read concocted words. I trust you have ensured the full amount will be paid? Anything else, will amount to nothing,' and with a flourish, under the eagle eyes of Iain Chamberlain who witnessed his signature, he had signed.

'The money will be transferred to your bank account as soon as your daughter and my son have formally legalised their marriage by signing the register,' Robert had told him, thinking that it would take more than a good lawyer for Bryant-Smythe to overturn this contract when he eventually realised the true price of his blackmail.

'Good. Then we will hear no more on the matter. I wish your son joy of her. Judging by her past performance, he will have no complaints in the conjugal rights department.' Bellowing with coarse laughter, Celia's father had walked away, a satisfied sneer on his full lips.

Only after the wedding, in the knowledge that his son was married and at last safe, had Robert divulged to the newly married couple what had happened and what the consequences of Henry Bryant-Smythe's actions now meant to them.

Had he troubled to read the contract, Celia's father would have discovered that his signature was not just the means to obtain the money he was so desperate to have, but would wipe away his home, his estate and most importantly his power. In fact, he had blithely signed away all the privileges that went with ownership of Satchfield Hall.

Now, with the news of the arrest on charges of conspiracy, corruption, rape and attempting to pervert the course of justice, Robert knew it was the final nail in

Bryant-Smythe's coffin. It had taken far too many years, but at last - to use the man's own words - it was indeed pay-back time!

Celia's father was where he needed to be: homeless, penniless and in the hands of the justice system. And there he would remain for many years to come.

Chapter THIRTY-SEVEN

After the quiet ceremony in the chapel, the small wedding party returned to Rookery House for a special meal of smoked salmon, caviar and roast pheasant, accompanied by a delicious selection of vegetables. Zilda's cook, with the help of the housekeeper, Mrs Fitch, had excelled herself.

With the celebrations drawing to a close, Iain Chamberlain and George's brother-in-law having taken their leave, David led everyone out onto the front steps to wave George and Gladys on their way. Parked at the bottom of the steps was his Morris Minor, polished until it shone like a brand new car and decorated with white silk ribbons.

'Oh my!' Gladys cried, pulling her hand from George's arm, adjusting her hat and clasping her gloved hands to her face. 'Will this lovely day ever end?'

'Not just yet,' replied David. Squeezing Celia's hand and delighting in the sight of the evening light reflecting in her beautiful eyes, he removed a set of car keys from his trouser pocket and jingled them in his fingers. With a broad smile, he handed the keys to George, 'Your wedding car awaits you, Mr and Mrs Brand.' He noted the look of surprise and embarrassment cross George's face. David had led the couple to believe a taxi had been organised to take them to the station where they were to catch a train to Brighton. To avoid making George any more embarrassed, David turned his attention to Gladys and winked at her. 'Now why else would we decorate a car with such beautiful ribbons unless it was for the bride and groom, eh?'

Still holding Celia's hand and without the aid of his cane, David led her down the steps and across the gravel drive until they stood beside the car. Not wanting to let go of her, he twisted his body so he could pull open the passenger door with his other hand, whispering as he did so, 'I do so love you, Mrs Gillespie.' Celia smiled up at him and his heart skipped a beat. He simply could not wait until they were alone together he had so much to make up to his beautiful bride. 'Come on, Mr and Mrs Brand,' he called, trying not to let his impatience show, 'it is high time you were away to your honeymoon.'

Gladys slipped her hand through George's arm and he, covering her small hand with his large one, escorted her down the steps to the car, with Lizzie, sniffling and wiping tears from her face, looking as pretty as a picture in the new frock Gladys had insisted on buying for her, following along behind.

Letting go of Gladys as he reached the car, George stuck out his hand to David, 'I don't know where to start to thank you, sir ...'

Hearing George's voice was tight with emotion, David shook his hand and grinning, slapped him on the back, 'The best start I'd say is to begin your new life.' Turning to Celia and resisting the almost overwhelming temptation to kiss her, he said, 'Come, my darling, let us step back so these two lovebirds can be on their way.'

Pulling her hand away from his grasp, Celia rushed over to Gladys and wrapped her arms around her. 'Have a wonderful honeymoon, Gladys, and thank you. Not just for this lovely day, but for *everything*.' Tears slipped down Celia's face and as she stepped back, she added softly, 'I would not be here if it were not for you.'

'Oh, Miss Celia, who would have thought all those years ago it would turn out so well and happy? You have nothing to thank *me* for.' Smoothing out the little creases that had begun to appear on her new costume, so many times had she been hugged, Gladys smiled. 'What a day we all have had. A day I'll never forget and I know my

George won't either. So come on, Miss Celia, let's not spoil your lovely day with tears.'

Listening to this exchange and aware it had been an emotional day for everyone and they were all tired, David again took possession of Celia's hand. 'Come on, sweetheart, let's join the others at the top of the steps and wave this happy couple on their way, shall we?' Catching sight of Lizzie hopping from one foot to the other behind them, he added, 'And Lizzie needs to say goodbye too.'

Turning, he looked up at the steps to see his parents and Muriel standing at the top, the two women dabbing their eyes with white handkerchiefs and Robert looking on with a wide smile, a glass of champagne in his hand. Feeling an unexpected rush of joy and love for his family, David knew he had been blessed all those years ago and today's ceremony had sealed every blessing.

As he and Celia moved back to wait for Lizzie, he watched Gladys thrust out her arms to the maid, who was unashamedly sobbing, 'Oh, Mrs Thrift ... I mean, Mrs Brand, be happy and have a wonderful life. I shall miss you so much.'

Hugging Lizzie tight Gladys let her go, her own eyes suspiciously moist. 'I'll be back in less than a fortnight, silly goose. You'll be able to keep an eye on my wonderful life and will hardly have time to miss me, so dry those tears.'

With the back of her gloved hand, she surreptitiously wiped away a tear of her own, but seeing it, David grinned. Gladys was no less tired and emotional than everyone else it seemed. Even George looked close to tears, but David was even more amazed when in front of everybody the driver leaned forward and kissed Gladys full on the lips. Flushing bright pink and clearly flustered, she allowed her new husband to take her by the hand and help her into the car.

'Brighton here we come,' George said to her as she settled herself into the front seat. 'I think it's high time we made new memories there, don't you? The old ones, we'll store away for posterity. What do you say Mrs Brand?'

'I couldn't agree more, Mr Brand. What are you waiting for?'

Laughing at this exchange, David pulled Celia away and up the steps to stand beside his father, watching as the car slowly disappeared from view down the drive.

'Right, now for some more champagne,' Robert said, 'and then it is time for you, my son, and your beautiful bride, to receive our wedding gift. I'm afraid it's a bit too big to wrap.' He said no more, but grinning at David's mystified expression, made his way back into Rookery House.

'What's he talking about?' Celia asked.

'No idea.' David glanced at Muriel, his eyebrow raised in query, but shaking her head, she simply smiled and beckoning for Lizzie to join her, followed Robert into the house.

'What have you two been up to?' he then asked his mother, who waited for them just inside the front door.

'Not just us, Muriel too,' she smiled. 'Have patience; all will be revealed. It is your father who wishes to make the announcement. So come, my married son, and let us hear what he has to say.'

Anxious to have everyone settled before he revealed what had been occupying much of his time for almost a month, but was now, thankfully, organised to his satisfaction, Robert, ignoring his son's intense curiosity, opened another bottle of champagne and filled their glasses. He was fully aware that the wedding gift was one of unusual proportion and by any measure a very, very expensive gift indeed, but had it been twice the cost, he would never regret what it had taken to finance what, with Muriel's help, he had ultimately acquired for David and his bride.

As everyone sat in the drawing room looking up at him, including Lizzie Rainbow, who looked decidedly uncomfortable - like the proverbial fish out of water, he thought, hiding a grin - Robert stood, leaning one elbow on the mantelpiece and waited. Enjoying the moment, he let the anticipation build until he saw his wife twitch with impatience and knowing she was about to steal his thunder, he lightly tapped a silver spoon on the side of his glass. As the resonance rang out in the room, each set of eyes focused on him.

'Please may I have your attention,' he asked, a twist to his lips, a lightness in his voice, knowing he already had it. His gaze fell onto each face in turn, their happiness adding to his own elation at what he was about to reveal, almost it stopped him from speaking. Taking a deep breath to steady his voice, he began.

'Today is not a day for dwelling on what has gone before. It is, however, a day to celebrate that our son and daughter have joined together as man and wife.' He paused, turning his gaze to Muriel, a woman he knew as a wonderful mother and loyal friend, to smile at her. Transferring his gaze to the glass in his hand, for a moment his mind replayed the events of the last month, then coughing to fill the embarrassing pause, he lifted his head and focused on his daughter-in-law. In a strong voice and with a smile that stretched his face, he said, 'With the help of your mother, Celia, I have purchased fifty percent of Satchfield Hall.'

David frowned, clearly puzzled. Celia stood up and ran over to kneel on the floor at her mother's feet. 'But, Mama ...'

Taking hold of Celia's hand, Muriel, gently pulled her daughter to sit beside her on the sofa. 'Please, Celia, do sit and hear what your father-in-law has to tell you.'

Robert knew what he had said had shocked the newlyweds, but he hoped the shock would quickly turn to happiness. He had planned this moment carefully: he too wanted to savour the spoils of what he had achieved, aided by the devoted dedication of both his wife and Muriel. Each of them had worked hard to ensure this day arrived.

Clearing his throat, his voice rising in excitement with the news he was about to impart, Robert continued. 'I just want to add, that apart from my wife and Muriel,' he nodded towards her and caught the look of satisfaction in her eyes, 'and of course our lawyers, it was impossible to divulge this information to anyone at all until the matter was signed and sealed. But, my dear son and daughter-in-law, I can now tell you that you are joint owners of half of Satchfield Hall. It has been transferred to your names as of this day; *that* is our wedding gift to you.'

Into the stunned silence, David murmured, 'I can see why you decided not to wrap it!' His comment broke the tension and everyone laughed.

'Your generosity is boundless, Father, what can I say?' David added.

'Yes, thank you; all of you,' Celia echoed. 'I cannot find words ...'

Robert smiled, 'There is no need. Your mother, of course, owns the other half, Celia; a share that has been in her name since her marriage. It is down to her perspicacity and courage that I was enabled to purchase the half that was formerly in the possession of your father. I would add that with this gift comes an assurance that he will harm neither you nor David again. Indeed, I have to inform you all – and I am sorry if this casts a brief shadow over our mood, but is best that you learn it from me before the tittle-tattle starts tomorrow - that Henry Bryant-Smythe was today taken into custody on numerous criminal charges, which I will not go into just now, but suffice it to say he will never again be in a position to hurt this family. Muriel has refused to put up bail and nobody else has come forward, so he will be held in custody until his trial. I do not doubt he will be found guilty and it will be some years before he is released.'

Celia gasped in shock and with tears cascading down her face, wrapped her arms around her mother.

Giving them time to recover, Robert placed his glass down on the mantelpiece and walked across the room to where Lizzie, her eyes wide as an owl's, was perched on the edge of her seat, her glass of champagne untouched on the occasional table at her side. Robert had only recently learned what Bryant-Smythe had done to the poor girl and was appalled, though not totally surprised. Bending to take her hand, he said, 'My dear girl, this will also protect you. Rest assured, that man will never come anywhere near you again, although it is possible you may be asked to be a witness for the prosecution, but if so, there is no need to worry. We will all help and support you.'

Lizzie, embarrassed, nodded her head and whispered, 'Thank you kindly, Mr Gillespie, thank you. I'd be 'appy if it 'elps lock 'im away.'

'That's the spirit.' Noting the pink flush on her checks, Robert smiled down at her, let go of her hand and walked to the ornate chest-of-drawers on the other side of the room. Opening the top drawer, he took out a set of keys then strode over to where his son had risen to his feet, an expression of incredulity at this news stamped on his features.

'We can talk about it later, now is not the time,' Robert cautioned softly as he read the questions forming in his son's eyes. Turning, he beckoned to Celia, 'Come over here and stand by David, Celia, this is a day for many celebrations, so please, both of you, raise your glasses to your future as husband and wife, and with all our love and wishes for your happiness, take the keys to your new home: Satchfield Hall.

Chapter THIRTY-EIGHT

Once they had settled into Satchfield Hall, life had very slowly begun to return to some form of normality, but not long after they had moved in, Celia, deliriously happy, had found she was pregnant. Nine months after their wedding day, almost to the day, she gave birth to a son.

Not for a single moment did she forget he was their second son, but she did not allow this to mar her joy. She could not believe how different the experience was to the one she had endured nine years earlier. For a start a doctor and midwife were in attendance, but more importantly, as soon as her baby was born and had made his first cries, the squalling infant was handed to her. As his cries quietened, she held his tiny body as close to her heart as was physically possible and this time no one took him away from her. Tears of joy splashed from her face onto her new born as she took in the fragrance of his newness: it was a scent she knew that for as long as she lived, she would never forget. Her heart bursting with love, Celia kissed his silky soft skin, 'You are so very beautiful and so very precious,' she whispered. Looking down on the son she had conceived on her wedding night, Celia, for the first time since the birth of her lost baby, felt truly at peace. 'Please,' she said to the midwife, 'can David be allowed to come in now?'

'Just as soon as we have tidied you up, dear,' the midwife smiled as Celia winced and with another contraction delivered the afterbirth. 'There now, that's better. I'll just make you comfortable. He'll be with you in a jiffy and then you can have a nice cup of tea.'

Bounding into the bedroom as the midwife, a wide smile on her lips, beckoned him in with the words he had longed to hear, 'Congratulations, sir, you have a healthy son,' David approached the bed.

'Oh David, he is so beautiful,' Celia smiled up at him through her tears.

Looking down in awe at the bundle in her arms, David, so overwhelmed with emotion at seeing his new born child and relief that his beloved wife was all right, found it hard to constrain his own tears. For the last ten hours, pacing backwards and forwards in the hall and trying not to hear what was happening behind the closed door of their bedroom, it had truly come home to David what Celia had gone through without him all those years ago at Ridge View Cottage. He had read her diary from cover to cover, but only now, in the extremity of his anxiety, had he really understood how it had been for her. Gazing at her, speechless, his mouth working, he tried to express the mix of joy and anguish he was feeling, and failed.

'Take him, David, he is your son and needs your arms around him too.'

Forcing down his emotion, he leaned forward and let Celia place the baby into his arms. Holding the tiny bundle awkwardly against his chest, he dared not sit and so remained standing, peering down at the red, wrinkled face of his son. 'Welcome, Ashton, David, Robert Gillespie,' he whispered. 'I just want you to know that I love you so much it hurts.' Looking back at Celia, he said, 'Thank you my darling, darling wife for giving me a beautiful son. He is perfect.'

He saw from the sudden shadow in Celia's eyes that he should have said 'another beautiful son', but it was not something he could bring himself to say. Much as David hoped with all his heart that the other child was as happy as he himself felt right now, he needed to focus on the present. There was no going back; their first son was lost to them, but now they had another, conceived and born in love and security; Ashton was their future now. David laughed as his son squirmed, a small fist escaping from the towel as the baby quested with his tiny rosebud mouth. 'He looks like a little bird! I think he wants his mother.' Afraid of dropping him, David handed him gently back to Celia, 'I'm terrified I might crush him, he's so tiny and fragile.'

'Nonsense,' the midwife said, coming forward with a smile, 'babies are a lot tougher than you think. I will leave you for a moment to get to know each other while I go and make Miss Celia a cup of tea, but don't tarry too long, Mr Gillespie, your wife needs to rest.' With that she bustled away with an armful of soiled linen, closing the door quietly behind her.

With the baby safely back in his mother's arms, David perched on the side of the bed and kissed Celia gently on the lips. Then standing, he strode over to the window and looked down the tree-lined drive that led to the entrance gates of Satchfield Hall. Keeping his back to Celia so she would not see his face, he released his unshed tears. *'Wherever you are, my son,'* he thought, *'I love you. You are just as much my son as your new born brother. Maybe one day, when everyone is much older, we can talk of you again and who knows what might happen? But not for now; no, not for now.'*

Dashing a hand across his face, he moulded his features into a smile and turned back to the bed. 'I think I had better leave you to rest, my clever girl, while I go and tell the parents they have a grandson, don't you?'

PART TWO
1952 - 1986

Chapter ONE

Muriel Bryant-Smythe was laid to rest on a chilly October day when the leaves were whirling red and gold from the trees and the Vicar's surplice, caught by the wind, flapped against his legs at the graveside as he intoned the sombre words of interment.

Her death had not been unexpected. The stresses and strains of her life at the hands of her unspeakable husband had, in the end, proved too much for her weak heart. Celia, devastated by her loss, could only thank God that her mother had lived for long enough to experience a year of happiness after she and David were married, and had been able to hold her baby grandson in her arms.

Shortly after the funeral, Celia received a call from her mother's old friend and lawyer, Iain Chamberlain, asking if he could see her with regard to her late mother's will. David had offered to take her, but having in the last year passed her driving test, Celia, insisting she was perfectly capable of dealing with it on her own, had left their infant son in his care and driven herself into town.

The contents of the will were much as Celia had expected, apart from the provision her mother had made for her grandchildren. When Iain Chamberlain read out the strangely worded phrase, 'Any and every child of my daughter's body,' he had paused and raised his eyebrow, looking at Celia across the desk, but when she made no comment, he had continued reading.

It was as much as Celia could do not to burst into tears, for she understood only too well the message her mother had sent her from beyond the grave. Ever since the first few dreadful weeks after her baby had been taken from her, they had never spoken of him. It was as though her mother had denied the very existence of her first grandchild. 'We must forget him and move on, Celia,' she had said. The fact that she had not after all forgotten him, made Celia want to howl. Not that the trust fund would be of any use if she could not find him, but perhaps her mother had thought that one day she might and this was balm to Celia's soul.

Before she left, the elderly lawyer with a kindly smile handed to her an envelope. 'Your mother wished me to give you this,' he explained. She looked down at it, the words written in her mother's hand blurring in her sudden rush of tears, '*To be delivered to Celia Bryant-Smythe in the event of my death.*'

'I have no idea what it contains, Mrs Gillespie,' Iain Chamberlain said, 'but I have been looking after it since she gave it to me some years ago. I regarded your mother as a personal friend. She was a remarkable and very courageous woman and I am more sorry than I can express for your loss.'

Numbed, she had thanked him and left the office, barely aware of her surroundings as she made her way back to the car: a green Austin Countryman that David had purchased in readiness for their expanding family. Sitting in the driver's seat, she released her pent up sorrow in deep, racking sobs. 'Oh, Mama, I miss you so much,' she whispered as with trembling fingers she opened the envelope, took out a single folded sheet of paper and read what was written in her mother's neat hand.

June, 1945

My dear Celia,
If you are reading this, it can only mean that I have gone from this life into the next. The doctors have told me that I have a weak heart and cannot expect to make old bones, but as I write, I hope I may continue to survive long enough to see you settled and happy, with all the

distress you have suffered in the past three years behind you.

I know I have never been one to show my love and affection for you, but you must believe that ever since the day they handed you to me, my own little girl, I have always loved you and wanted only what is best for you. Lately I have come to understand that what I thought was best was not necessarily the best for you, but while I will never forgive your father for dealing with you so harshly, I continue to believe that the adoption of your son was in the best interests of both you and, perhaps more importantly, your child, even though I took no part in it.

I beg you to forgive me for choosing to write in a letter to be opened after my death, what I have today discovered. My justification for not telling you straight away is that at last you appear to have accepted your loss and to be regaining your health. There seems little point in re-opening the wound now, and more than anything, I do not want you to have to face the anguish of finding your son then losing him all over again, because I know that you, who love him as I love you - as any mother loves her child - would not be able to take him away from the life into which he will by now be settled.

After your baby was taken from you, I endeavored to discover his whereabouts so that I could ascertain for my own peace of mind that he - my grandson - was being properly cared for. It took me many months to discover where he had been taken and by the time I did, the couple who adopted him had moved away. However, by talking to those who know them, I was able to set my mind at rest that they are good, honest, caring people who were childless and desperate for a baby of their own. There is no question that your son is being well cared for and loved. Rest assured had that not been the case, I would have taken steps to find them and remove him from their care.

However, although that is not the case, I do not want to go to my grave without giving you the information I have found. Thus, I can tell you that your baby was adopted by a Mr and Mrs Hargreaves and at the time of writing, they are living somewhere near Pendleham. Beyond this I was unable to discover, but it should be enough if, at some time in the future, you should have a need to seek your son, for we none of us can know where our lives will lead us.

I beg your forgiveness that I was never strong enough to be the kind of mother I had hoped to be. Have a good life, my darling girl and strive to be happy. One day, this nightmare will all be behind you. They do say that time heals and I have to believe that.

Your loving mother,
Muriel Bryant-Smythe

When she had recovered sufficiently to drive, Celia started the car and drove straight to Ridge View Cottage, knowing that at this time of day she was unlikely to find anyone at home. She needed desperately to be alone and in a place that had always brought her peace. Wandering blindly to the old tree stump beyond the orchard at the end of the garden, she re-read her mother's letter, her tears falling unheeded onto the page. She sat there for over an hour until chilled to the bone, she slowly made her way home. Celia could hardly believe it: at last, at long, long last, she had the means to find her son.

From time to time she and David had talked about the possibility of tracing him, however hopeless a task it had seemed, but her husband was dead set against doing anything at all that might so easily lead her into more pain. 'You must let him go, my darling. We have another child now, and more to follow, God willing. Wherever he is, our little boy has his own life now. Almost certainly he is not even aware we exist. Would you risk his happiness for the sake of your own?'

But Celia did not see things that way. She had no intention of risking her firstborn's happiness: she just needed to know he was alive and well - or so she told herself.

The last time she had raised the subject with David, it had led to their first real quarrel and so she had not spoken of it again. If she was to find their son it would have to be without her husband's knowledge. Celia argued with herself that this was wrong; she loved David more than anything or anyone else, with the possible exception of her babies, the one she had and the one she had lost. Certainly she had no wish to be deceitful, but the yearning in her to know if their son was indeed happy was too strong. If she could just find him, see him, hear his voice, she would not reveal herself to him.

The intensity of her need was not something she could deny and so, by the time she arrived back at Satchfield Hall, her mind was made up. David did not need to know and what he did not know could not hurt him.

Chapter TWO

Throughout all the years of Jack's life, Jean Hargreaves had never quite been able to dispel the fear that someone would turn up, announce they had given birth to her boy and take him away. Nobody around here knew that Jack wasn't their real son, but despite this, Jean still kept a lookout and worried. Even after all this time, she still found herself tensing up whenever someone came unexpectedly to the door. Tom called her a daft old biddy, and she probably was, but she just could not help herself.

Heavens, she thought, Jack will be eleven soon. Had they really been here for eleven years? She found it hard to believe. 'Wherever does the time go?' she asked herself, wringing out another bowl of rinsed sheets and piling them into the laundry basket. For once it was a fine day. She had taken advantage of the weather and spent the best part of the morning washing. They had not had many good days so far this summer. It was good to be able to hang it out on the line for once instead of on the clothes horse in front of the range. Things never smelt as good as when they had dried outside in the sunshine.

Jean liked their home in Top Farm Cottage, they'd had good years here: Tom had quickly settled into his new job and got on so well that he had soon been promoted to farm foreman, which meant he brought home a decent wage. He still worked all hours God sent, of course, but that was her Tom; always on the go. Jack was just the same. He liked to help his dad on the farm at weekends and in the school holidays; he was going to be a farmer and drive a tractor when he grew up, he had announced the other day. He enjoyed his school in the village too and with his sunny disposition made friends easily. When he was little she used to walk him there each day and then walk back to meet him in the afternoon, but Tom had given him a bicycle for his ninth birthday – not new, of course, but a good bike even so. Jack had been over the moon with it and had cycled to school ever since. It would be different when he went to big school in Pendleham; he'd have to catch the bus from the village then, but there was another year before she had to start worrying about that.

She heard a car in the lane as she was pegging out the last basket of linen on the long line that ran down the length of their garden. She could hear a tractor chugging away in the distance: Tom had said if it was fine they'd be cutting hay today. Just as she was reaching down into the basket to pick up another towel, a soft voice called out, 'Excuse me.'

At the sound of the cultured tones, Jean spun round, her heart racing. Panicking, she looked quickly around for Jack then remembered he was off helping his dad.

'I'm sorry, I didn't mean to startle you, but I'm looking for someone,' continued the stranger. 'I saw the gate was open, so I ...'

Icy fingers clutched at Jean's spine, so shocked at seeing this smartly dressed young woman walking up the garden path behind her that she dropped the wet towel onto the grass.

'Oh dear, please let me help.' Before Jean could stop her, the stranger had bent down and picked it up. 'Here, I don't think it will need rewashing,' the young woman smiled and handed it back. 'Such a lovely day today, it'll be dry in no time.'

As Jean with shaking fingers took the towel from the woman's gloved hand, she knew her worst fears had come true. Bracing herself for the blow that was about to fall, she heard the cultured voice say, 'I'm actually looking for the school. I think I must have taken a wrong turning.'

Jean opened her mouth to answer but no sound came out. With a mixture of relief and confusion that made her knees wobble, she cleared her throat and in a voice that didn't sound like her own, replied in a rush of words. 'Oh, it's that way,' she pointed, 'the other side of the village, just past the new houses they're building. It used to be all part of Top Farm, but they sold off some land back along and now they're making lovely new places for people to live. But the little cottages are still there, at the far end of the village, only you won't find anyone there, the school's closed for the summer holidays.' Jean knew she was babbling, hardly stopping to draw breath, but the relief that this woman was not here to take her son away had her talking too much.

'Oh yes, of course, how stupid of me, I had forgotten they'd be closed just now. Ah well, never mind. I can come back another time. I'm sorry to have disturbed you. Thank you any way.'

Jean watched her retrace her steps to the gate, where she turned to smile and wave. Lifting a hand in response, Jean had the weirdest feeling she had seen the young woman somewhere before, but for the life of her could not think where. She was clearly a stranger to these parts. You could always tell country folk and whoever she was and whatever her business at the school, she was no country woman. And yet, as Jean juggled with her pegs and the last of her washing, she could not help the unsettling feeling that there was something familiar about the woman's features, particularly when she had smiled.

A few moments later, when she saw a green shooting brake driving off down the lane, Jean breathed a huge sigh of relief, but her knees were still wobbling. Stop being so silly Jean Hargreaves, she told herself. Her son was safe; no one was going to come looking for them to take away their boy, not after all this time. Finishing pegging out the washing she picked up the empty laundry basket and went back into the cottage to make herself a cup of tea.

Waiting for the kettle to boil, Jean continued chiding herself. Whatever happened from now on, nothing could take away the years of love and happiness they'd had with Jack. She looked over to the sideboard at the framed photograph of the three of them, taken on his seventh birthday, and smiled knowing she had been blessed.

In a nostalgic mood, she fetched the photograph album out of the chest of drawers and sitting down with her cuppa at the kitchen table, opened the book at the page that showed Jack's first school photograph. A big, gappy smile grinned up at her: he had just turned six and had lost one of his front teeth. It had been the first year the school had taken individual photographs, before that it had been just one big photograph of the entire school and in the sea of other faces, Jack's was hard to spot.

Two weeks after the photograph had been taken, he had come down with chicken pox. Jack still had the scar on his forehead from one of the spots he had picked. Smiling, Jean could almost smell the calamine lotion. Looking through the pages of photographs, each one bringing back memories, Jean recalled the evening, just after they had finished their tea, when Jack had suddenly asked, 'What does adopted mean?'

'What on earth makes you ask such a question?' Shocked, she had turned to Tom for help. She had not meant to sound so defensive, but she couldn't help it.

Tom had come to her rescue. 'It depends, son, on what you mean? It could be a few things.'

'Oh, only it's just that Jimmy Smith said something about his sister having her baby adopted and I was wondering where she got a baby from.'

Tom and Jean had looked at each other and smiled, 'Well the stork brought it,' said Jean. 'When people get married and want a baby, the stork brings them one.'

The answer had seemed to satisfy Jack at the time, but afterwards, Jean and Tom had agreed it was probably time they thought about telling their son he was adopted.

They had not got around to it before the subject had come up again some weeks later. 'What *does* adopted mean, Dad? Jimmy said adopted was when babies go and live with someone else. Why would they do that, Dad?'

'Well, as to the right way to describe the word, I'm no scholar, son - school was not my best time - but what I do know is that it means you bring up a baby that someone else had and it becomes your son or daughter, like you did for us when we adopted you.' With a quick look at Jean, Tom had added, 'And that's what makes you so very special to us.'

'I'm adopted?'

'Yes,' his dad had said, 'and you came to live with us.'

'And we have never stopped thanking God that you did,' Jean had added.

They had seen Jack was thinking about what had been said. They always knew when he was seriously thinking because he puckered his lips and it had always reminded Jean of a little pink rosebud, though she would never tell Jack this. As his lips had straightened out from his pucker, he had smiled a knowing smile because he had already thought through his next question.

'So does that mean the stork made a mistake and should've brought me to you first, is that it?' Jack seemed quite pleased with himself at having worked out the procreation of the human species.

Stifling a chuckle, Jean said, 'Not quite, but something like that.'

'So who was my mum before you then?'

Jean had smiled at his logic that there had to be someone before her. 'I don't know, Jack, all we were told was that there was a special little baby who needed a new mummy and daddy.'

Jack had listened, but he had frowned. 'So does that mean she'll come to take me away again?'

'Good heavens, no!' Jean had gasped, 'Whatever next?'

Calmly ruffling the boy's hair, Tom had smiled, 'I shouldn't think so, son, and even if she did, we'd never part with you, so you don't need to go worrying about that.'

Nothing more was said on the adoption subject, until some months later, when Jack arrived home from school and in a matter of fact tone had explained to Jean all that he knew about adoption.

'It's simple really, if people can't make their own babies they have to go and get one. I suppose if you make too many babies, then you can't look after them all, so then those who can't get a baby take the ones left over. The teacher told me this, said the war had changed things. I suppose the stork sorts it all out in the end.'

Relieved that Jack's teacher had explained it all so well, Jean had hidden a smile as Jack, the subject finally laid to rest, had run off to the biscuit tin and helped himself to a piece of homemade shortcake.

'Naughty boy, your tea will be ready soon,' Jean had sighed.

'I know, but I'm starving, Mum.' With a cheeky grin on his face as he bit into the biscuit, he had looked back at her, his cheeks bulging. As well he knew, she could refuse him nothing.

Now, working her way through the album, Jean dwelt a few moments on each school photograph, seeing the changes in Jack year on year. He was growing up so fast and there was no denying the fact that he was developing into a very handsome young man. It would be girls next, she supposed with a sigh, thinking, *'Please don't let the years pass too quickly.'*

Closing the album and replacing it in the drawer she washed up her teacup then decided to do some dusting. That was the trouble with the sunshine, it showed up all the dust!

Chapter THREE

As she always did on a Wednesday morning, as soon as Jack and his dad had gone off to work carrying their lunch boxes, Tom to oversee the new cowman and Jack to drive the tractor – he was ploughing today, he had told her - Jean took the early bus into Pendleham. Jack had been working at Top Farm ever since he left school – almost eleven years now - and just like his dad, he loved the work. 'It's not a job, Mum, it's a way of life,' he had said to her only the other day, strapping great lad that he was, she thought fondly.

Putting on her coat, a headscarf and hand-knitted gloves against the early morning chill, worrying about Tom's persistent cough in this cold weather and wishing he would go and see the doctor; it was past time he retired, but would he ever listen? - Jean left the cottage and hurried down to the village, catching the bus by the skin of her teeth. It was always full on Wednesdays, but she found a seat near the back and still out of breath, sat back with a smile of relief.

Once a quiet market town, Pendleham had become such a bustling place since the early fifties when the new housing estate was built at Craven Edge on the outskirts. Designed to give the people of post-war Britain, many of whom had been bombed out of their homes, a better place to live, the houses had seemed very modern when they were first built. With homes for over two thousand families, the population of Pendleham had swelled rapidly and now, in the late sixties, the town was barely recognisable as the place she and Tom had known when they first came to live near here with their baby nearly twenty-five years ago. The picturesque town centre had not changed though, with its quaint old cottages and shops surrounding the market square. Wednesday had been market day in Pendleham for as long as anyone could remember and it was to the market that Jean came each week.

Unlike the housing estate, where the buses ran every twenty minutes, the bus service to the remote village where she lived with Tom and Jack was still infrequent. There was a school bus now, but aside from that there were only two buses out of the village and two back each day. So to make sure she was back home by mid-afternoon, Jean always left her cottage early and walked to the village to catch the first bus of the day. Her shopping list was the same each week and she knew the best choice of fresh fruit and vegetables was when the market first opened.

As she walked around the stalls checking out the quality and prices, Jean noticed a crowd gathering on the pavement opposite the market. Curious, she stared across the road and to her surprise saw they were all waiting outside the little bookshop on the corner. It was not a shop she visited very often; not because she did not read, but she simply could not afford to buy the expensive novels into which she loved to escape. Instead, once a week she visited the library, a welcome addition to Pendleham five years ago. At one time she had borrowed books from Boots the chemist, but they had closed their library once the new one opened in the town. Jean's passion was to immerse herself in the murky waters of murder and detective novels, in particular the unflappable Miss Marple and the fussy detective, Poirot. She just loved Agatha Christie's books.

Looking up at the clock tower, which stood in the middle of the market square and was surrounded by stalls selling fruit, vegetables, hot teas, pies and peas, meat, pastries, clothes and crockery, and all manner of other things that attracted people into Pendleham on a Wednesday, Jean saw that she had plenty of time before she had to catch the bus. She could buy what was on her list, visit the library and still have time to take a look at what was going on over the road.

Forty-five minutes later, with her shopping bags full and her library books changed, Jean made her way over to the bookshop with its yellow striped canopy, which today was fully opened out. The little throng of people she had seen earlier had grown in number and was now spilling out all over the pavement where a haphazard queue had formed. Instead of joining it, she walked around to the front to see what all the fuss was about. 'Oi,' someone shouted, 'there's a queue, love. Join it; you'll get your turn soon enough.' Flushing, Jean did not look to see who had yelled at her, but ignoring the grumbles gazed into the shop.

The sight that met her eyes took her breath away: seated at a small table, signing the books that were piled up around her, a smartly dressed woman was chatting and smiling to people as she handed out the signed copies. Even though Jean's last sight of her had been fifteen years ago and then only briefly, she recognised her instantly; she had hardly changed at all. Jean guessed she was in her early to mid-forties, but she had one of those faces that made it difficult to judge. Much as they had done before, the woman's vaguely familiar features unsettled Jean, though she could not have said why. Wondering who she was, Jean heard someone in the queue behind her saying, 'That's the author, Margaret Made; she's signing her new book.'

Turning to see who had spoken, Jean spotted a middle-aged woman wearing a silk headscarf. She smiled at Jean and pointed to a large poster hanging in the bookshop window. It showed a picture of the author and underneath in bold lettering: MARGARET MADE WILL BE SIGNING HER NEW BOOK '*TOMORROW WE CAN TELL*' HERE ON WEDNESDAY.

'I read about it in the Gazette,' the woman went on. 'Evidently it's a true story and a sad one too. Mind you,' she grimaced, 'folk our age could all tell a sad story what with the war and everything and that's a fact. Still, I thought I'd treat myself; I've never had a book signed before. To tell the truth, I've never even seen an author before,' she laughed, 'it's quite exciting, isn't it.'

Jean nodded and was just about to say thank you, when the queue moved along and the woman, quickly grabbing up her shopping bags from the pavement, shuffled out of earshot. Turning back to peer once more through the bookshop window, Jean frowned: what it was about the author that gave her these qualms of anxiety? For reasons she could not understand, she felt she would always know that face when she saw it. Deciding not to join the queue but head straight for the bus stop, Jean, still puzzling, turned to walk away. As she did so she felt a light touch on her arm.

'I can see you're undecided,' said a voice in her ear. 'From what I've heard I think it's worth getting a copy. Someone said it's a bit unusual, all about a family in the war years but written like a diary.' The voice belonged to an elderly woman leaning on a walking stick, who peered short-sightedly at Jean and said conspiratorially, 'The author is signing each copy sold here today, so it might be valuable one day, she's quite famous. Anyway, I've got it for my granddaughter, even though she'd most likely prefer something signed by those longhaired Liverpool lads ... er, what's their name?'

'The Beatles,' replied Jean, totally surprised that she knew the answer. She smiled at the old lady then added, 'I think you may be right. Perhaps I'll get a copy for my son.'

'I don't think it'll be his cup of tea,' the old lady cackled, 'not really a boy's story I'm thinking.' Given it was about the war, Jean had no idea why she had said that, but suddenly reaching a decision, she smiled her thanks and clutching her bags of shopping joined the end of the queue. Somehow she felt she just had to have a copy, especially if it was written like a diary. She used to keep one herself, knowing that one day she would like to read and remember all the little things that had happened, mostly about Jack growing up. She had not written in it for years and thinking about it, was not sure what she had done with it. 'I must look it out when I get home,' she thought.

Keeping an anxious eye on the time, Jean shuffled towards the bookshop until at last she was standing with all her shopping bags in front of Margaret Made. She could see the woman did not remember her, no reason why she should, of course, but it was a huge relief to Jean that this woman, who gave her these strange butterflies in her stomach, viewed her as just another stranger in the queue.

'Is it for you? What name should I write?' the author asked, her pen poised over a new copy of *Tomorrow We Can Tell.*

'Yes, it's for me. My name is Jean Hargreaves, but please would you add my son's name too, Jack, he'd like that. Thank you.' Jean watched as the author wrote inside the book: *For Jean and her son Jack, with best wishes, Margaret Made,* her pleasant smile already directed at the next person in the queue as she reached for another book.

On the way home on the bus, Jean opened up the bag and dipped into the first few pages of the book she had just bought, feeling guilty at what it had cost. As her gaze alighted on the first page, the noise of the bus and the chattering passengers seemed to disappear.

> *May, 1943*
> *Despite being taken to the top of the world, away from all living souls, my heart soared once I realised they were going to let me carry my baby to term. I knew I would surely die if they had made me have an abortion. I believed throughout those early weeks of my banishment that you would arrive and tell me we were to be married and that I'd been dreaming and everything they told me was untrue. I never ever believed you had run away, David. Gone to*

fight in the war, they said, yet why would they say that if it wasn't true? I keep asking Mother and Mrs Thrift, the woman who has been hired to look after me, and Lizzie, my maid, but they never answer the question. What hurts so much is that we loved each other you and I. Did you not tell me so all those times when we were as close to each other as any human beings can possibly be? I allowed you to do those beautiful things to me, because I loved you and I believed you loved me too. And yet you left without even saying goodbye and before I could tell you I was carrying your child. I am trying to be brave as I wait for you to return home and come and collect us. I say us, because by the time this wretched war is over, it will be us.

September, 1943
It has been several days since I opened my diary to write, I've felt nauseous and worse. I don't think I have the kind of body that is good for child bearing. Mrs Thrift and Lizzie are being very kind, but I just want to go home and see you, except they tell me you are not there. I can't write anymore today, the sickness is killing me. Please come and get me ... please!

Five days have passed since I last wrote and my hand still trembles and my eyes are so puffy I can barely see out of them. I have learnt that I am to stay here in this far away cottage forever. My hateful father has had me banished from Satchfield Hall. You may wonder how I know this; I overheard Mrs Thrift talking to our driver,

Mr Brand. So I asked Mama, who visits me as often as she can, and she said it was true, I am to remain here indefinitely. Father will never let me come home. How I hate him. I asked her about you, but she will not mention your name. If only I knew where you are, then I know I could cope, but I know nothing anymore. I had thought that if I kept myself occupied, by this I mean writing my diary and helping out in the house and garden, I would soon be rescued and return to be with you at Rookery House, but this is not to be. I want to find a way to resolve this, but as I get heavier and heavier, and the sickness will not leave me, I am unable to do anything about my situation at the moment. You cannot imagine a more desolate place than where they have sent me, apart from Lizzie, Mrs Thrift and hundreds of bleating sheep, who clearly do not suffer from vertigo, there are no other living souls up on this mountainside. Until I was brought here, I never realised just how loud clocks tick - thunder by comparison is quiet!

I can feel our baby moving around as I write, I know in my soul it's a boy. It almost feels like he is trying to force his way out, but I am so afraid that when he does begin to arrive ... but no, I can't write these thoughts down, they hurt too much to even think about. Though, if this baby does not come soon, I think my body will explode. I did not think it was possible that anybody could grow so grotesquely huge as I am now. My biggest fear is how I am going to give birth. Our baby is surely too big to be born.

November, 1943
I return to my diary, though it has been three days since I last penned my thoughts. Today, for the first time I have not been sick and because of this, my thoughts stray to holding my baby. I cannot wait. Despite my fear of the birth, my heart leaps at the thought of holding him. I have decided to call him Ashton, David. I hope you will approve.

December, 1943
Since I last held my pen, I have been to hell and back. In fact it would be true to say I have repeated the journey so many times and know the road so well I could now travel it blindfold. Sadly, I feel there is nothing left to live for. My baby has gone and so have you and I just want to die. Even as I write, my hand is shaking and my heart is broken, nothing will ever be able to repair what has happened to me. When my baby was born, I tried to reach out to touch him, but as I stretched out my hand with all the strength I could muster, to feel his brand new body, he was snatched away from me and wrapped in a white towel. At first I did not think too much about it all, I just assumed he was being washed ready for me to hold, but I knew he was perfect, so I had expected him to be placed in my arms. Then I heard his cries and I screamed out his name, but no one took any notice. And you know, I never even saw his face and no one ever said his name, only me as I cried in an attempt to call him back. And no matter how I tried to

struggle out of the bed, which was almost impossible after all the hours I had spent giving birth to him, Mrs Thrift pushed me back and would not let me move, and all this time my baby was being taken away from me. I screamed and screamed and screamed, but nobody paid any attention to my pleas. Oh David, our baby has been taken away. I do not know where and nobody will tell me.

Even though my mind was in turmoil with having just given birth and what was happening, I wasn't allowed to have my eyes open anymore. They sedated me for days afterwards and because of this, it took every ounce of my strength to remember what the date was: the date I had brought Ashton into a world that I was not allowed to be a part of with him. It was the nineteenth of November. This date I know will be etched on my heart for as long as I live.

After all the pain I never saw my baby again. Each day without him is torment. I live for the day when I will see you again and perhaps together we can find our little boy.

With tears streaming down her face, Jean closed the book and put it back in her bag. They had said it was sad, but this was more than sad, it was agonising. She had no idea who Margaret Made was other than the author of the book, but whoever she was, it disturbed her greatly and now, after reading only the first few pages of *Tomorrow we can Tell,* Jean could see too many coincidences linking her life with the harrowing saga told by Margaret Made. Her mind racing, she clutched her bags on her lap and wished the miles away. She could not wait to get home and continue reading the book. She should have a few hours to herself before the men came home for their supper. She would put a stew on as soon as she got back so it would be ready for them.

With these thoughts, Jean got off the bus and lugged her shopping back to the cottage. Throwing together a beef hotpot and leaving it to stew gently on top of the Rayburn, she sat herself down in their rarely used front room and once again turned to the book, re-reading the first chapter and continuing to the next. The more she read, the worse became her fears.

Twenty-five years ago, she and Tom had been paid to keep silent about the child. In the envelope handed to them by Mrs Green they had found an extra wad of cash with a note to say it was for their continuing silence. If the child lived to maturity, they must ensure he never looked for his birth mother. Back then she and Tom had puzzled about why they had been paid so well to take in a baby they would have given their eye teeth for without payment, particularly since, as they had been told, the mother did not want the child in the first place. They had not wanted the money, but it had been thrust at them.

Now, with all these thoughts racing though her mind, Jean feared she was beginning to understand why. Deep down, she had always felt that something about it was not right, but at the time they had both been so overcome with happiness at the chance of having a baby that it had never crossed their minds to question what Mrs Green had said. Recalling all the words again in her mind, Jean could see, reading this book that revealed so much, that it was highly likely everything was not as they had been told. It would most certainly add up with the money she and Tom had been given to keep silent all those years ago.

She did not need a diary to remind her of the day their new born son had been brought to their home. The baby in the book was born on the 19th November, the exact same day their baby had arrived, only hours old and swaddled in a white towel. And then there was the coincidence of

Margaret Made turning up at the cottage all those years ago and then again in Pendleham of all places. As incredible as it seemed, Jean could not escape her growing belief that by sheer chance she had met the mother of her son.

As shadows began to gather in the front room, she looked up at the clock on the mantelpiece and gasped. She had been so absorbed the time had gone by without her noticing. Her menfolk would be home soon. She tucked the book under the seat cushion to finish later and went through to the kitchen to check on the stew, but her mind would not stop working.

Maybe the author, clearly upper class and from a rich, influential family judging by the references to 'Satchfield Hall', a maid and a driver, was indeed Jack's birth mother. If so, she had wanted him desperately, not like they had been told. Jean's heart lurched thinking about how the baby had been wrenched away from his mother. What upset her even more was that Margaret Made had never even seen her baby's face. Nobody could make all that up; all that pain when her baby was taken away.

On the other hand, thought Jean, picking up the ladle to stir the stew, it was just a book and she could be allowing her imagination to run away with her, yet somehow she did not think so. No, she thought again, nobody could make all that up. And even if she had, why did it all seem to fit so well with their own circumstances? *Could* it just be coincidence? But on top of all that was the strange feeling she'd had, both times she had seen Margaret Made, that she knew her.

In a sudden flash of insight, such a shock that she dropped the ladle into the stew and scalded her hand as the hot gravy splashed up, it came to Jean that it was the author's faint resemblance to Jack when he smiled that had gripped her heart with icy fingers that first time, and then again today. She had recognised the smile; Jack's smile. *That* was why the woman had seemed so familiar. *Why* hadn't she seen it before?

And then, her eyes streaming with tears, Jean knew there could be no doubt.

Drawing the curtains and switching on the light, she thrust her burnt hand under the cold tap for a moment, dried it on the tea towel then laid the table and cut up the fresh loaf of bread she had got in the market. She had only bought the book out of curiosity and that was because she had recognised the author as the woman who had once stood in her garden and asked her the way to the school. At the time it had set her heart racing in fear, afraid the stranger was snooping around to take Jack away, but when she had driven away and Jean had never seen her again she had thought no more about it. Until today. But if she was Jack's birth mother, why had she never come back? There was no answering these questions, but the chief one that now bothered Jean was what could or should she do about it?

She heard Tom and Jack laughing as they came walking up the path to the back door. Forcing everything to the back of her mind and moulding her features into a cheery smile, Jean reached for the ladle to dish out the stew, hoping they would not notice she had been weeping.

Later, when Tom and Jack had gone up to bed, knowing Tom would be dead to the world the minute his head hit the pillow, Jean sneaked back into the front room and was soon reabsorbed in Margaret Made's diary.

The faint light of dawn was stealing into the room when she finally put down the book after reading the last page. Once again she studied the photograph of the author on the back cover. 'So much suffering, so much sadness,' she whispered to the silent room 'and all because of one despicable man.' Though if she were to believe her own thoughts, Jean knew she and Tom were part of it all too, and because of this, she realised that she must talk to Jack before she did anything else. She just hoped he would agree with what she had in mind and that all of this would not change things between them, she could not bear the thought of losing him. And now, as she remembered those times when his head had been full of questions about adoption, Jean wondered how this woman, Margaret Made, had found the strength to carry on. Because she knew if she had lost Jack her world would have ended. Equally, she knew something had to be done, for she could not live with herself if she did not try to make some recompense for all the years that poor woman had suffered.

Chapter FOUR

After reading her mother's letter from beyond the grave on that distant day in 1953, it had taken Celia two years to track down her firstborn son. The obvious thing, she now knew, would have been to look for the name 'Hargreaves' on the electoral registers for the Pendleham area, but back then, even had she been able to do that without David's knowledge, it had simply not occurred to her. With an infant who kept her busy all day and much of the night, she was constantly weary, so she had done nothing about it until little Ashton – the name she had chosen for her first baby, but which David had liked so much he had given to their second son - was a year old and she could bear to leave him in the capable hands of Lizzie Rainbow. The maid had happily moved back to Satchfield Hall once the Squire – Celia could no longer think of him as her father - had been locked up for twenty years: three proven cases of rape had seen to that even without the additional charge of corruption.

Not knowing how else to go about her search, Celia had begun to trawl the primary schools in the area of Pendleham. She was convinced that with one look she would know her son and be able to tell if he needed her. If he did not then she could stop worrying and let him live his life without her. It was a lie and she knew it: what she had really wanted was to find him and hold him to her as tight as she could and never let him go, but of course, she would never do that.

Celia had not realised just how many schools there were in the area of Pendleham, but she had persevered, gradually extending the area of her search on days when David was out on business so she did not have to lie about where she was going, but the weeks, months and then a whole year had gone by and she had drawn a blank. Then she had realised that she should now be seeking her son in secondary school, which was much easier since they were fewer. In fact there were only two in Pendleham, which was the catchment area for many of the villages around about.

She had never forgotten her first sight of her son. The boy who walked out of the school on that particular day transported her back to when she had met and fallen head over heels in love with David. His son was so like him it had taken all the breath from her body and by the time she had recovered her wits, he had gone. Thereafter, she had repeatedly gone back to the school, sometimes taking little Ash with her. There was no question that her firstborn son was happy: she had watched him laughing and joking with his friends as he kicked around a football, very clearly healthy and strong and without a care in the world. She had loitered outside the school like some of the other mothers waiting there, and had fed on the sight of his face, wanting so very much to say 'Hello, I'm your mother and at last I have found you,' to hug him and kiss him. Knowing that for his sake she must not was an exquisite torture, but like an irresistible drug she kept going back just to see him.

A year later, she had fallen pregnant with her third child. It had been a difficult pregnancy and David, concerned for her health had asked her not to drive out by herself, and so her regular visits to the school had stopped. By the time her daughter, Clara, was born and old enough to leave in Lizzie's care, Celia had gone back to the school on three occasions, but had not seen her son. Terribly anxious, she had been on the point of going in to see the headmaster when it dawned on her that he was now over fifteen and must have left school. She was filled with despair because she had no idea where he lived and she had lost him all over again.

Concerned by her obvious depression, David had tried all sorts of ways to divert her to no avail, until the day he had said, 'I hope you don't mind, my darling, but I happened to mention your diary to a friend of mine, Anthony Phipps, he's a literary agent. He says it's just the sort of thing that would sell like hot cakes and if you'd like to turn it into a book, he'll see if he can get it published.'

Jolted out of her despondency, Celia remembered how she had once conceived the same idea herself. She had long ago worked out that the man who had orchestrated her suffering would have ensured the people who adopted her son were ignorant of his true parentage. Even if by now her son knew he had been adopted, a man who could be so cruel as to banish his daughter and have her baby snatched away at birth would have gone to any lengths to prevent him from ever knowing her name and finding her. There had to be another way.

Sitting on the tree stump in Ridge View Cottage garden, so long ago now that it seemed like another life, she had formed a plan: she would write her diary like a book and one day get it published, and somehow, her son's mother would read the story and know it was about her adopted baby. Surely no woman could withhold information from a mother about her son if she knew how he had been taken from her and how much she had suffered? But it was such a long shot that Celia had eventually decided she was simply fantasising to feed a false hope, and over time she had let the idea die. Then, years later, David, without realising it, had given it back to her.

Writing had become her solace, just as it had before in Ridge View Cottage. In fact, she had declined to publish her diary at first. Unable to face the thought of sharing the extremely personal anguish of her early life she had put it off and instead had written three novels in quick succession. Anthony Phipps had liked them and found her a publisher and to her perpetual amazement they had become best-sellers. Eventually, however, yearning for her long-lost son, she had turned back to her original plan and today, at long last, it had come to fruition. Here she was in Pendleham, signing *Tomorrow We Can Tell*, the story of her lost baby and the circumstances of his birth.

Throughout the entire one-and-a-half hours, as she enjoyed chatting to her readers, she kept a watch for the only person she had really come to Pendleham to see, carefully asking each customer his or her name, hoping against hope that one of them would be 'Hargreaves'. She had not thought beyond that, refusing to listen to the little voice in her head that said, *'And then what?'*

'It's for my mum,' said an elderly lady, 'she loves reading and she'll never believe I've got her a signed copy.' Celia looked up at the person talking to her and was astonished. The old dear looked at least seventy herself!

'She'll be ninety next week,' the old lady added, 'she was brought up in the workhouse because her mother had her out of wedlock.' She looked straight at Celia, 'So she'll understand.'

Celia nodded and smiled, not sure what to say, but the old lady said nothing more, just picked up her signed book and went to the counter to pay and have it gift-wrapped.

As the queue of enthusiastic readers dwindled, Celia was unable to shake off the feeling of guilt that she was a fraud to these people. Because, in her heart, the only book she truly wanted to sign was the one that belonged to the mother of her lost son, Jack Hargreaves. She knew his name was Jack because she had heard his friends calling out to him in the school playground.

Coming here to Pendleham for the launch of her book was always going to be a gamble: it was too long a shot that her son or his adoptive mother would come into the bookshop, but Celia had hoped nonetheless. She had spent quite some time convincing both her agent and publisher that it was as good a place as any for her to make an appearance and that the best day would be on a Wednesday, the day when lots of people came into town from the villages all around. 'Market day would draw a bigger crowd, much more than on an ordinary day,' she had insisted.

'Celia, I can't help thinking there is more to this than you are prepared to tell me,' Anthony Phipps had said. He had become a personal friend and knew all about her past. 'I want to help and any publicity is good publicity, but I don't want you going off on a wild goose chase, building up your hopes and then getting hurt.'

'I'll risk it,' she had told him.

'You think your son is somewhere in the Pendleham area?' Anthony had asked directly, never one to beat about the bush.

'I know he is in the Pendleham area. I have known it for years, I just don't know exactly where. I just want the launch to be there and maybe he ...' She had not finished her sentence, because even to her ears it sounded lame. What did she expect from being there? That he would come into the shop and recognise her? Or his mother ... but then, what if she did? Celia had asked herself. How would she even know if it was the right Mrs Hargreaves? It was not an uncommon name. Celia could only hope that *if* the right Mrs Hargreaves came in and *if* she bought the book and read the story, she would know her adopted son had been born to an author named Margaret Made and *maybe* would seek her out through her agent or publisher, both of whom were acknowledged in the book. 'Long shot' was more than an understatement, Celia had thought ruefully: far too many ifs, buts and maybes. But it was what she had long ago planned and she was not going to stop hoping now.

'Well, if you're sure,' Anthony had said, but Celia had seen his look of dismay.

After signing the book for a young boy, who insisted he was buying it for himself, 'Things like this interest me, Miss,' he said and then added, 'my nan said you can learn a lot from reading. My paper round paid for this,' he tapped the book.

'Did she?' asked Celia as she scribbled a note and handed it to him. 'Your nan's a wise lady. Take this note to the counter with your book and the lady will let you have it free of charge. I would like you to have it as a gift from me and if you like it, you might want to buy my next one.' She smiled at him, 'I hope I'll see you again.'

With his eyes wide open, the book in one hand and his paper-round money in the other, the boy grinned. 'Coor, thanks Miss Made. I promise I'll love it.' She watched him walk up to the counter and because of this did not notice the woman approach to the table.

When she looked up and was about to ask her standard question, 'Is it for you?' her heart skipped a beat and her words hung in the air as if frozen. Celia recognised her instantly as the woman she had once asked the way to a village school, in her ignorance not realising it was closed for the summer holidays. Clearly the woman had not recognised her, which was hardly surprising. When she gave her name as, 'Jean Hargreaves,' Celia kept her face blank. Even though all her instincts were screaming at her that this was the 'right' Mrs Hargreaves, her head told her that it might not be. And then she said her son was called 'Jack' and it was too big a coincidence to ignore. Fighting back the urge to jump up and say, 'I am the mother of your son!' she wrote the name 'Jack', wanting desperately to add more words, but knowing she couldn't do that. She was a stranger to this woman and her son. She was simply the author of this book: a book in which this woman's son was the main character!

When Celia handed the signed book over to Jean, she smiled, but it was a smile that stifled a cry, a cry that wanted to ask a million questions and couldn't.

'Thank you,' Jean said as she took the book. Celia held on to it for the fraction of a second longer than was necessary before letting go. In anguish she watched as the woman who had raised her son read the words she had written then went up to the counter, paid and walked out of the shop.

Her heart pounding like a steam hammer, Celia wondered if she had done the right thing by coming to Pendleham. Would it all end in tears? It struck her as an extraordinary coincidence that fifteen years ago, without knowing how close to finding her son she had been at that moment, she had happened on Jean Hargreaves hanging out her washing. Had Jack been there that day? If so, she had not seen him.

She was brought up short by the next customer, who was eyeing her with concern, 'Are you all right, Miss Made?'

'Oh yes, sorry. Is the book for you?' she asked automatically, picking up her pen.

At last the queue came to an end and Celia, reassuring Anthony Phipps that yes, she was perfectly well even if she did look as though someone had just died, and no thank you, she did not want to be taken home, her driver was waiting, but she would catch up with him in the next day or two, Celia escaped out of the bookshop to anonymity.

She made her way to the ancient churchyard and sat quietly on a bench in the sunshine. As much as she hoped Jean Hargreaves would put two and two together and look for her after reading her book, she could not *expect* it to happen. She needed to think about how to try and talk to Jack's mother without frightening her, but she would wait a while. It occurred to Celia that by sheer chance she at least knew where the Hargreaves lived, assuming they had not moved, of course, but it would be so much better if Jean made the approach rather than the other way round.

The book launch had left her feeling utterly drained. Her fatigue had nothing to do with the number of books she had signed; there had not been that many compared to the big town events she had attended in the past. She was fully aware that her exhaustion was down to the emotional trauma of seeing Jack's mother; of being so close and yet so far from her son. It had been unbelievably hard not to give in to her impulse to jump up, hug the pretty woman and thank her for being a good mother to Jack. Not being able to had made Celia's heart ache. She had long ago accepted that her son was gone from her life, but despite this it had never stopped her from hoping that by some miracle they would one day be reunited and seeing his adoptive mother standing there in front of her had reawakened all her hopes, only to dash them again as she realised that nothing would most likely come of it.

After sitting in the churchyard struggling to calm her troubled thoughts, she wandered slowly back to where her driver had parked the car. David insisted that she allow herself to be driven most of the time these days and usually she was more than happy to concur. She liked Tony; he had been her driver for a number of years, ever since George Brand had retired. Celia had quickly discovered that he knew a great deal about her past, but perhaps that was not surprising since he was George's nephew and a great favourite of Gladys'. It did not trouble her; he had become a friend over the years and trusting his discretion she spoke freely to him.

'Sorry to have kept you waiting Tony. I just needed a bit of fresh air,' she said, as he held the door open for her.

'Is everything ok? You don't look so good.' He frowned with concern as she settled herself into the back seat. 'Not a good signing in Pendleham?'

'As a matter of fact, it went rather well. I'm just a little tired. The book signings take it out of me, smiling at all those anxious faces and trying to think of different ways to say the same thing to each person. It always surprises me that they are nervous about meeting me when it's really the other way round and I'm the one who is shaking like a leaf wondering what on earth they will think about my book.'

Closing the door, Tony went round to the driver's seat and started the car. He smiled at her in the rear view mirror, 'Go on; you've signed enough books over the last few years to fill a library. You don't usually come away looking so unhappy about it, though.'

Looking out of the side window at the countryside gliding past, Celia was surprised at how low she felt, but then, she asked herself, how had she thought she would feel? As Tony slowed the car down to give way at a T-junction, she leaned forward, 'You know me too well, Tony! As a matter of fact I met the woman who adopted my son and it took every ounce of strength I possess not to say something to her.'

'Ah, so that's what's upset you. I knew there was something. But didn't you say that was what you were hoping for?'

'Yes, but I'm not sure anymore what I'd hoped for, in fact I wish now I'd never gone to Pendleham. It was a mistake. I should have listened to Anthony Phipps' advice, he warned me not to go.'

Tony swung the car to the left and changed up a gear, 'I expect what you are feeling is anti-climax. It's like that sometimes when you really hope something will happen and then when it does it isn't like you thought it was going to be.'

'I daresay you're right. I'll feel better when I get home.' *I have been patient for so many years,* thought Celia, *I can be patient a while longer.* Jack was a grown man now; she could only hope that one day she could meet him without causing too much pain.

Chapter FIVE

Arriving home from work, Jack saw to his dismay that his mum had been crying again. He hated to see her so sad. His dad had been gone almost three months now and they had both been struggling to come to terms with their grief, but his mum so rarely cried – at least, not when he was around to see it. All through his life he could only remember her being cheerful and smiling. Even when they had buried his father, she had managed to smile through her tears. 'I have been twice blessed,' she had whispered as they stood huddled together in the front pew of the crowded church - almost everyone from the village had wanted to pay their last respects to Tom Hargreaves. 'He was the only man I ever loved and I loved him more each day. I had the best husband in the world and if that were not enough for any woman to hope for, the best son too. Your dad is at peace now, Jack, and he wouldn't want us to be sad. It will be hard, but we will learn to be without him,' and she had squeezed his hand, knowing he was close to tears. At the time her words had comforted him, but not a day went by that he did not miss his dad.

She looked up at him has he came through the door, shrugging out of his coat and bending to take off his boots. Her eyes were all red and puffy and she was sitting on the sofa holding a book, which surprised him. Not that she was reading – she often had her nose stuck in a library book – but not usually at this time of day when normally she would be busy getting his tea.

'You shouldn't read it if it makes you sad, Mum. What is it anyway? It looks new,' he hung up his coat on the back of the door, slid his feet into his slippers and walked across to kiss her cheek, feeling it moist beneath his lips.

'It is, I bought it for you just before your dad died. I want you to read it.'

Jack was amazed; he could not remember her ever buying a book, which made the scene in front of him even stranger. As he sat down next to his mum, he could see the book had a sepia photograph on the front cover. The picture depicted a young woman pushing a pram, but it was clear there was no baby inside. In the background there was a large building that looked very grand. Jack read the title, *Tomorrow We Can Tell*. His instinct was that it was not a book for him. When he was younger and had more time to read, science fiction and battling knights were the books that once he had got his nose into he had found impossible to put down, but these days he rarely opened a book. Why would this one make his mum sad enough to cry? It was a question that hung off of his lips, dangling in mid air, waiting to be spoken out loud, but at that moment it sat on the fence of hesitation. Not wanting to hurt her feelings, he said awkwardly, 'Oh, well thanks.'

'You'll never believe this, Jack, but the author signed this book especially for me.'

Craning his neck to see as she opened the book and pointed at the inscription, which was finely written in blue ink on the title page, he read: *For Jean and her son Jack, with best wishes, Margaret Made.* 'I started reading it on the bus on the way home and couldn't put it down,' his mum said. 'I was going to give it to you when I'd finished it, but then your dad ... well, that was when ...' Her voice faltered and she sniffed, reaching for a handkerchief.

Jack felt instinctively that it was not just the pain of his dad's death that was troubling her; she was clearly struggling not to weep. He stared at her, bewildered as she said in a low voice, 'When I met her the first time she was a total stranger, yet I had the weirdest feeling that I knew her. She came into the garden to ask me directions, said she was looking for the school. You were only ten, so it must be all of fifteen years ago. Then just before your dad passed away I saw her again in the bookshop and it felt just the same. She didn't recognise me when she wrote those words, but I knew her straight away. She has a face you could never forget, beautiful but full of sadness.'

'You'd probably seen her in the newspaper, famous people get everywhere these days,' Jack put his arm around his mum's shoulders and hugged her to him. She felt tiny in his big hands. When had it changed, he wondered? It used to be his mum's comforting arms around his childish body, now he was the one holding her in his strong adult arms. It was like they had changed places.

'You're probably right,' she dabbed at her eyes. 'I must be a bit run down to let a book upset me like this.'

'Why did you want me to read it, Mum?'

She moved out of his encircling arms to look up into his face, 'Because it is all about a lost baby.'

Jack gaped at her, wondering for a moment if her grief about his beloved dad had unhinged her. Thinking he should humour her, he grinned, 'Well that's not something I would normally read about, but I'll give it a try, thanks Mum.' He took the book from her hand, idly turned it over and with a sudden thrill of shock recognised the author's photograph. 'That's extraordinary. I've seen her before; lots of times.'

He felt his mum flinch, 'When and where?' she gasped.

Unnerved by her sudden anxiety, Jack thought back. He had often wondered about the woman he had seen looking into the school playground from time to time. She had appeared out of the shadows for as long as he could remember. The first few times he had seen her, he had thought she was the mother of one of the other kids at his school, but then later he was not sure, because she never seemed to collect anyone, just stood there watching him. He remembered thinking he should perhaps say something to his teacher, but what? That a woman sometimes stood looking into the playground? They'd have thought he was daft. Then she had suddenly stopped coming. He had looked out for her, but not seen her again, so it had seemed pointless to say anything after that. He had forgotten all about it until now.

He became aware that his mum was all tensed up and gazing at him, eyes wide with alarm. He shrugged, 'Years ago. I used to see her hanging around outside the school.'

'Did she ever speak to you?

'No, just smiled sometimes.'

'Why haven't you mentioned this to me before?'

'Why would I? She wasn't doing any harm. I didn't know she was an author or anyone special or I might have done. What does it matter now?'

'Did it never occur to you she'd come to see you?'

Jack was not entirely sure what was going on here or why his mum was being so odd. 'Don't be daft, Mum, why would she want to see me? She was most likely waiting for her son or daughter to come out of school, there was nearly always a little boy with her.'

He smiled as his words brought back a memory. The little boy and his mother had been walking past the playing field where he and his friends were having a game of football. He had kicked the ball too hard and it had bounced over the fence. The little boy, who could only have been about four, had run after it and with all his strength thrown the ball back over the railings. Catching it, Jack had grinned at him, 'That took some doing. Thanks.'

Jack had heard the woman call, 'Ashton, don't be a nuisance, darling. Come away now.'

Ignoring his mother, the boy had said, 'Can I come and play football with you?'

Before Jack could reply, Ashton's mother had looked across and smiled at him then pulled the little chap away from the railings, bending to wipe the mud off her son's face and hands, spitting on her handkerchief in the horrid way that mother's do. Jack remembered he had winked in sympathy at little Ashton, who had grinned back at him. How odd that he should remember such a trivial incident; even odder that the woman was the same person who, so many years later, had signed his mum's book.

'Anyway, he said, 'she stopped coming before I was in my final year and I never saw her again, so I don't know why you're so worried about it.' He looked at his mother's careworn face and saw that she had leaned back against the sofa her eyes closed. 'You look tired, Mum,' he squeezed her hand. 'Let me make you a cup of tea. If it's so important to you, I'll read the book later, promise.'

And so he had, although it had taken more than a fortnight to finish it, his awareness growing with each chapter as to why his mother had found the book so painful to read. Clearly this Margaret Made had suffered dreadfully, he could see that. He still could not fathom why his mum had been so keen for him to read it. Because it was about adoption maybe? But he knew that unlike in the story, his own birth mother had not wanted him; it was one of the few things his dad had confided to him about his adoption. He remembered the conversation as if it was yesterday, though it was a good few years ago now. Jack had long known he was adopted; it had never occurred to him to ask his parents about it. Aside from the fact that he was entirely happy with his lot in life, he would never have done anything that would cause either of them hurt, but one time, after they'd had a visit from a rep trying to sell them an insurance policy and his mum had gone into one of her usual panics, he had asked his father why she acted that way every time a stranger came to the door.

'Don't blame her, son. Your mother has never ceased to worry that someone will come looking for you and take you away.'

It had taken Jack a moment or two to realise what his dad meant by that. 'You mean my birth parents?'

'Yes, but it's never going to happen. When you were brought to us as a baby, we were told your mother was a girl from a village several miles away - no one we knew or had heard of. She ...'

Jack remembered that his father had coughed and looked embarrassed. 'She what?' he had prompted, suddenly curious.

'Well, I don't want you to feel bad, Jack, but we were told that the young girl had been rather too free with her favours to the American soldiers and she had no idea who the father might be, so she wanted rid. You're a grown man now, you know how these things happen. Your mother and I had no reason to disbelieve what we were told and we both wanted a baby so bad - it was my fault we couldn't have one, we'd been trying for years and just about given up when you came along just hours old. To us it seemed like you were heaven sent and we both thanked God for it, so I don't want you ever thinking you weren't wanted.'

'I never have,' Jack had reassured his dad, 'you and mum are the best parents anyone could wish for and I've been happy all my life, so whoever my mother was – or is – she did me a favour.' He had grinned at his dad, who had hugged him, his eyes suspiciously moist. They had never spoken of it again, but reading Margaret's Made's book had made Jack remember that conversation and had him really thinking about his birth mother for the first time.

On Sunday, when he finished the book, he carried it downstairs and placed it on the table, where his mum was dishing up a roast.

'What did you think of it?' she asked.

'Sad. I still don't understand why you got it for me, though.' He waded into the delicious slice of beef and smiled up at her as she sat down opposite. It was still so strange that there were just the two of them. The Sunday roast had been one of the few occasions when they all sat down together in the daytime.

'Do you ever wonder about the woman who gave birth to you, Jack?'

'Not often,' he answered, his mouth full. 'Dad told me she didn't want me.'

'That's what we were told and it's what I've believed all your life, until I read this book. I've always wondered about how she could bear to let you go and I never stopped being afraid she'd come to take you back. I still am.'

'You're paranoid,' he grinned, 'if she was ever going to, she'd have done it by now. And anyway, like I said, she didn't want me, so why would she? Besides, it may have escaped your notice, but I'm a grownup now. Nobody can take me anywhere I don't want to go. Smashin' dinner, Mum, the roast potatoes are just how I like them,' he loaded up his fork.

'Don't you think it's strange that Margaret Made's baby was born the same day as you? Did your dad not tell you that you were only hours old when you came to us? And did you not wonder why she came looking for the school that day and then all those years later you saw her loitering outside your playground?'

Jack almost choked on his mouthful of potatoes. Still coughing, he put down his knife and fork and stared at his mother. 'Are you saying what I think you're saying?'

For the first time she smiled, 'That depends on what you think I'm saying!'

'You think she's my real mother, don't you?'

'I think there is a distinct possibility, yes. More than that: you look a tiny bit like her. And if she is, then I have a very great deal to thank her for.'

'You and me both.' Jack considered that for a moment then surprised himself by saying, 'Well if you're going to look for her, I'd like to help you.'

His words hung in the air and for a moment his mum did not speak. Then she nodded. 'We can do it together. I suspect "Margaret Made" is not her real name, it sounds like a made-up name to me. It may take a while to find out who she really is.'

'Are you sure that's what you want? Suppose you're wrong?'

'Then it won't matter, will it. Anyway, whatever the outcome, you will always be *my* son; nothing will change that for me. I love you so much, Jack.'

'I know, I have always known,' he said, thinking that nothing would change for him either. 'You and dad always said I was special, but that's only partly true, I'm special because I have you. You'll always be my mum. Even when you don't want to be, especially when I make you mad,' he added this to make her smile, because he knew they were both too close to tears for comfort.

That night, after he had gone up to bed, Jack looked long and hard at the photograph on the back of Margaret Made's book. 'Are you my real mother?' He held the book up beside his face and stared at both in the mirror, but could see not even a faint resemblance. 'And if you are, why didn't you talk to me all those years ago?' He thought back to when he had last seen her. Had he ever suspected the woman outside his school had something to do with him? Maybe, fleetingly, when he was younger and had fantasised for a time that she was rich and famous and would shower him and his parents with all her riches. It occurred to him that part of his distant fantasy had come true: she was famous, and judging by the things she said in her book, rich too. It also occurred to him as he drifted off to sleep, that Ashton, the little chap with the football, might be his brother!

Chapter SIX

After Jack had gone up to bed, Jean, grappling with a tumult of thoughts and knowing she would never be able to sleep, lingered on by the fire. Since she had bought her signed book from the author, Margaret Made, she had not had a moment's peace; her mind had not stilled from one day to the next. Soon after that fateful Wednesday in Pendleham, Tom had been taken seriously ill with pneumonia and within a few days, she had lost the one man she had loved all her adult life and missed more than even she could have imagined, though for Jack's sake, she tried to be strong. Losing her husband had driven all other thoughts from Jean's mind until long after the funeral, when she had come across *Tomorrow We Can Tell* in the front room, having gone in there to clean the windows. They did not need cleaning, but her only means of keeping her tears at bay was to keep busy, so much so that she was often weary to the point of exhaustion.

Picking up the book she had sat down with it and forgetting all about the windows had read it again. A few days later she had read it yet again, from cover to cover, until she had begun to think the ink would wear away and the paper turn to dust, so much had she handled each page. Each time she read it, the story reduced her to tears. Knowing that it might change their lives forever, Jean had thought long and hard about giving it to Jack, but she could no longer go on feeling as she did. Not now she was so sure Jack was the baby Margaret Made had lost; wrenched away from her before she had even seen his face.

Now, a few weeks after Jack had read it and they had talked about it, and Jean had agreed they should try to make contact with the author, she was conscious that she had still done nothing about it. Just thinking about it sent qualms of icy fear racing up her spine. Sitting with her son on the sofa in front of the log fire in their cosy living room, Jean, feeling a tad guilty, brought the subject up again.

'I'm sorry I haven't got around to looking for Margaret Made yet. It's not that I don't want us to meet her, but ...' her voice faltered and then the words came out all in a rush, 'I'm so afraid you'll love her more than me and I will lose you.'

'Oh, Mum! What a thing to say; don't even think it. If Dad was here he'd be telling you you're a daft old biddy!' Putting his arms around her, he smiled, 'Nothing or no one will *ever* take me away from you. It's just not possible. As I said before, I am curious about her, but not at the cost of you worrying, so let's just forget all about it.'

Reassured and enjoying the feeling of her son's strong arms about her, Jean let him hug her. 'I'm not sure I can. What do you think I should I do, Jack?' He held her tight as he thought about her question and she could tell from the way he then spoke that he was choosing his words with care.

'I suppose I would like to know more about her and the life she's had. Her book was such a very sad story, her father was unbelievably cruel ... God! I suppose he's my grandfather! It doesn't bear thinking about. I wonder if he's still around. I don't much fancy coming face to face with him.'

Recalling the way the author's father had acted, banishing her and arranging for her baby to be stolen away, Jean shuddered. Could he still be a danger to Jack? The thought screwed her up inside. But he must be an old man by now and her son was so big and strong, yet you never knew what could happen.

For a moment they sat in silence then Jack said, 'I don't know, Mum, I just wonder sometimes if meeting Margaret Made would actually make everyone happy.' He shrugged and looked down at her, 'On the other hand, like I said, I would quite like to, not just to satisfy my own curiosity, but because I know that if we don't you are just going to go on worrying about it and get no peace.' He paused, bit his lip, 'One thing I've been thinking is that when she found me at school all those years ago, she could have approached me and didn't. She couldn't have been sure if I knew I was adopted and it was like she was just wanting to satisfy herself I was all right, but without shocking me or causing us any pain. I can think of no other reason for her going to all the trouble of finding me and then not saying who she was, can you?'

Speechless at her son's logic, Jean shook her head.

'Don't laugh,' he went on, 'but I've even started to wonder if she wrote her book especially for us to read, maybe she wanted me to know that she didn't give me up out of choice. Perhaps she is even hoping it will prompt us to look for her so the approach comes from us rather than her.' He shrugged, 'But it's such a long shot, I expect it's just my imagination running riot.'

Jean had entertained similar thoughts: it had seemed too much of a coincidence that the author had chosen to sign her book in that tiny bookshop in Pendleham where she knew Jack had gone to school. Gazing at her beautiful, sensitive son Jean wanted to cry; he was so precious to her. Did his kind and wonderful nature come from her and Tom? She hoped so, but wherever it came from she was so very proud of him.

'So, Mum, all in all, I think you *should* try and contact her. I know there's a risk it'll open doors we might not want to look in or even go through, but I think we should do it all the same.' He got up from the sofa and bent to kiss her, 'Well, I'm for bed. Try not to worry about it, eh? Let's face it, we can't be absolutely certain she's my birth mother anyway. The whole story might be fiction and everything else just a coincidence.'

Jean knew that was not true, and how could she help worrying about it? But despite tossing and turning all night long, the next morning, she took the bus into Pendleham. It wasn't a Wednesday, so not market day, but what she needed to do had nothing to do with shopping and more with research.

In the office of Margaret Made's agent, the post had piled up to the point of overflowing the in-tray. The office junior had been off sick and there was no one else to do the task. The four people who worked in the office were rushed off their feet and opening the post was the last thing they had time to deal with. So when at last the office junior returned to work, she had the task of sorting the huge pile of envelopes, most of them containing unsolicited manuscripts headed for the slush pile because nobody had time to read them.

Catching the in-tray with her hip, she knocked the pile of unopened envelopes onto the floor. In a state of anxiety, aware that her boss was looking at her with ill-concealed irritation, she hurriedly bent down and scooped up the runaway envelopes. Two or three had managed to go right under the table and as she scurried around in a bid to bring them back into the fold, she saw that one of them was handwritten. It stood out against the numerous typed foolscap envelopes and curious, she retrieved it and read the bold words written across the top: *Private and Confidential – for the attention of Margaret Made only.* Intrigued, the junior stood up and fingered the envelope wondering who might have written a personal letter to their top author. Not that she would open the envelope, goodness, her job was far too important to her to do such a stupid thing, but she would love to know what it contained.

Looking over the top of his half-moon spectacles, Anthony Phipps watched the office junior fingering the envelope. 'Susan; is it your intention to read the letter through the envelope or open it and see what really is inside?' He knew he sounded exasperated. He was, but not at her.

The girl's head jerked up at the tetchy voice of her employer, 'Sorry Mr Phipps; I'd like to open it, but it says it is only to be opened by Margaret Made.' With a nervous smile she walked over to Anthony Phipps' desk and handed him the envelope.

'Thank you, Susan.' He took it from her and said nothing more, but the curt nod of his head and pointed look had the girl scuttling back to her work.

Examining the handwritten address and the two-week old postmark, Anthony had a good idea who this letter was from and that he needed to talk in private to Celia Gillespie. Just as Susan had sat down at her own small table, which substituted for a desk, he asked her to go and make a pot of tea. 'Not too strong this time,' he called. Watching her head out of the door on her way to the small back kitchen along the corridor, he lifted the phone and dialled Celia's number.

Five minutes later, he placed the phone back down and getting up from his chair, pulled his coat from the rack in the corner and walked out of the office. He almost collided with Susan carrying a small tray of freshly brewed tea, her face bearing a comical expression as she realised he had no intention of staying to drink it. He nodded his thanks, but saying nothing continued out of the office.

Chapter SEVEN

'Thank you, Anthony, I'll see you shortly.' Celia, her hand to her mouth, replaced the receiver and stared down at it, her breath coming in short gasps as her agent's words continued to sound in her head. 'Celia? I'm sorry to disturb you. You know I wouldn't trouble you if I didn't think it was important, but a letter has been delivered to the office marked for your personal attention and I believe it might be the one you have been hoping to receive. I think you need to see this in the privacy of your own home. If you'd like me to, I'll bring it straight over. I just don't want it to upset you.'

Celia supposed she should not be surprised that he sounded so concerned. Not only were they professionally acquainted, but over the years, Anthony had become her trusted friend and she knew he worried about her. She began to pace backwards and forwards across the room where she did her writing. It had once been her father's study but was no longer recognisable as such; before she could even bring herself to go in there, she had arranged for it to be stripped, redecorated and completely refurbished, eradicating all trace of him.

The forty-five minutes it would take her agent to drive to Satchfield Hall crawled by. Celia was glad that for once she was alone in the house: Tony had driven Lizzie into town to do some shopping; the housekeeper had the day off to go and see her sister; the children, of course, were at school, and David had gone to a business meeting in London and would not be back for a couple of days.

She still wrestled with her conscience about David. If the letter Anthony was bringing her did indeed concern Jack then she was going to have to tell her husband. They so rarely discussed their firstborn son and sometimes she wondered if David had forgotten all about him. It would not be easy to confess to him that she had gone behind his back all these years. Perhaps she wouldn't have to. Perhaps she could let him assume their son had found her out of the blue ... but no. Even at risk of hurting the man she had married and loved so very much, she had never lied to him and was not going to start now.

Celia was waiting at the door when Anthony finally arrived. She did not need to look at the handwritten envelope to know it was the one she had been waiting for; the letter she had hoped and prayed would arrive one day and now, more than two decades later, it had. Looking into his eyes as he handed it to her, Celia saw pity. It was not what she had expected and to her surprise it upset her.

'You know I've always been fond of you, Celia, I just hope I've done the right thing bringing this to you and that whatever is in the envelope will bring you some measure of peace, because you deserve it.' Anthony's tone was subdued as he placed the letter into her outstretched hand. 'I know I'm only the messenger, but I don't want to see you crushed with disappointment if it's not what you have hoped for and dreamed of for so long.'

'Stop worrying about me, Anthony, there's really no need,' Celia said more lightly than she felt. She pulled the front door wider, please come in. Can I offer you a glass of something?'

Anthony hesitated, 'Er, no thanks, I'm a bit pushed for time – and anyway, I feel this is something you need to do on your own. You know I'll always come running if you need me,' he smiled.

With the envelope almost crushed in her hand, Celia knew he was right and that she did need to be alone. Grateful for his sensitivity, she leaned forward and brushed her lips against his cheek, 'Thank you for bringing it to me and for being so kind and considerate and more importantly, for being my friend.'

'It's my pleasure. Be sure to call me if you want to talk or if I can be of any help,' Anthony turned away, almost running down the steps to where his car was parked on the wide driveway.

Celia stood and watched until the car disappeared through the large electric gates and into the lane that would take Anthony back to his office. Clutching the envelope, she walked down the spacious hallway and back to her study. The heat from the log fire blazing in the grate hit her as soon as she stepped through the door. The fire always created an ambience of comfort and calm in this room she called her sanctuary, the only child-free zone in the house, where she came to find peace and quiet. The atmosphere never failed to give her inspiration with her writing, but today she felt anything but peaceful.

Sitting not at her desk, but in the leather wing chair by the side of the huge stone fireplace, Celia gazed into the crackling flames. They seemed to bow to the cast-iron dog-grate, licking the burning logs as if in some exotic dance before reaching to stretch up the chimney. Celia always saw things in the flames if she concentrated on them. In the past she had seen some of the characters that had helped to make her books best sellers. Today she saw not people, but another blazing fire: the one that had made the tiny living room at Ridge View Cottage so hot and stuffy. Inevitably her mind travelled back to the day she had given birth to her baby, the boy she now knew as Jack, who had lived a life so very different from her own; one that might be about to be made known to her.

Staring down at the neat inscription on the envelope, Celia judged it had been written by a woman's hand. For an instant she wondered how she could be so certain it was Jean Hargreaves' writing, even hoped that perhaps she was mistaken. The enormity of what could be written inside the small white envelope almost overwhelmed her. Celia knew that once it had been slit open, the letter unfolded and the words read, then everything would change; nothing could be undone and for the first time in all the years she had waited for this moment, she was afraid of the consequences of what she had set out to achieve. For a split second, sick with fear that her son wanted nothing to do with her, she almost threw the envelope into the flames so she did not have to read the words she dreaded to see.

For several minutes she continued to stare at the envelope wondering if she had the courage to open it. Her son was now twenty-five. Not a day had gone by that she had not thought of him. The 19th November each year had been particularly painful, each anniversary of his birth taking her further away from the child she had borne. Over the years she had almost, but not quite, convinced herself that her son knew nothing of her and had no need of her; that he was happy and loved by the only family he had ever known. She had told herself repeatedly that should she ever try to get involved in his life, it would cause anguish for him and his family, yet despite reminding herself of all of these things, she had never give up hope that one day she would be reunited with her lost child. And now, at last, she held in her hand the longed for contact and yet was too scared to open it. How stupid was that?

She saw from the postmark that it had been posted two weeks earlier; it had doubtless been sitting in Anthony's office ever since. Despite its tardy delivery, it seemed somehow significant that today was a Wednesday, exactly sixteen weeks to the day since she signed Jean Hargreaves' book in Pendleham. Sixteen weeks! So long ago she had given up all hope that anything would come of it. Was the timing a good omen, she wondered?

Her hands shaking and her heart racing, Celia slit open the envelope and pulled out the one sheet of folded paper. For a moment she looked down at it and then, drawing a deep breath, she carefully unfolded it and read what was written in a few short lines.

She read them again and again. Only when too blinded by tears to read them anymore did she place the letter she had waited nearly all her life to receive, down on her knee then closing her eyes, she wept.

Eventually, drained, Celia went to her desk and wrote a brief note in reply, thanking Jean Hargreaves for her letter and expressing her extreme sympathy for her recent loss.

She signed it 'Celia Gillespie'.

Chapter EIGHT

Jean woke early that morning, though in fact she had barely slept a wink all night. When she heard Jack's alarm go off in the bedroom next to hers, she was relieved that the long night had finally come to an end.

Jack's sandwiches for his lunch were made, wrapped and ready for him to take to work. She had made them last night. He usually ate them sitting in a field or sheltering in the barn, his tractor never too far away. Ever since Jack had started work at the age of fifteen, she had made his sandwiches every night before she went to bed. Alternate days of ham and cheese, except on Mondays when he had cold meat left over from Sunday's roast, and always with lashings of pickle. He always took a flask too, hot tea in the winter and cold tea in the summer; he was a creature of habit, was Jack, like his dad. Jean wondered how much longer she would have the happy task of getting her son's sandwiches ready; she was unsure now that he was courting. She smiled as she thought about his fiancée, Susan, a real nice girl. Jean had known it was serious for a long while; Jack had talked about marriage more than once before he eventually popped the question and Jean was already looking forward with happy anticipation to becoming a grandmother one day, God willing.

As she placed her feet into her slippers, she heard Jack's footsteps as he made his way downstairs to the kitchen. The stairs always creaked loudly first thing in the morning. That was how it sounded to her, anyway. Maybe it was because the house was so still and quiet at that time of the day. Too quiet, she thought, as she slipped her thick dressing gown on and tied the belt around her waist. Not as trim as she used to be, she reflected. Middle-aged spread had a lot to answer for. She shivered. The mornings where still cool, despite spring having long gone. She had asked Jack and Susan to come and live with her in the cottage after they were married, it was big enough for the three of them, but both of them had been polite and said, 'Thanks, but can we think about it?' It seemed they still were thinking about it, as they had not mentioned it for over a week. But then, they'd had other things to think about: today for a start.

As Jean made her way down to the kitchen she knew Jack would be making his breakfast. That was something he did each day before he went to work. 'I have to get up far too early to have you looking after me,' he always said. 'I can just about manage to put cereal in a bowl or stir my porridge, Mum!' Lately, he had taken to making her a cup of tea at the same time and she enjoyed sitting there, still in her dressing gown, watching him eating his breakfast, her heart filled with pride at the beautiful young man everyone knew as her son. She only hoped that after today this would not change. They had talked until there was nothing left to say about her meeting with the woman who had brought him into the world, but unlike Jean, her son was surprisingly calm about it.

'I'm interested to meet her, who wouldn't be, I've a lot of questions, but for me, you are and always will be my mum. Nobody could take your place.' He had said this so often now that Jean dared to believe it and as she watched him getting ready to go to work, she just knew that what she had planned for today was the right thing to do.

The reply to the letter she had sent to Margaret Made care of her literary agent, whose name was inside the book and whose office address she had found out from the girl behind the counter in the Pendleham bookshop, had confirmed her thoughts. Margaret Made, or Celia Gillespie, as Jean now knew she was called, was indeed Jack's natural mother – not that she had ever doubted it. The letter had been a very polite and humbling one, placing no pressure on Jean, even though she knew how desperate the author must be to meet her son and his family, but suggesting that they might meet in Pendleham for a cup of tea. Jean, convinced it was time for all of them to put the ghosts of the past to rest, was happy to agree and had dropped a note back – addressed to Satchfield Hall, no less! – confirming the day and time. She knew Celia Gillespie could never have the years that she and her Tom had enjoyed watching their only child grow from a tiny helpless new born baby into a handsome, strong man, who without hesitation called her 'Mum'. Nothing could take those years away. Bolstered by these thoughts, Jean had agreed to meet the woman who had brought her son into the world.

Neither rich nor privileged, Jean had lived in tied farm cottages all her married life. Her husband had worked all hours God sent to put food on the table and she'd had to count every penny to make sure it went round. There had never been any money left over; all her life it had been make-do-and-mend, and yet for all that, Jean did not feel a lesser person to Jack's wealthy, famous mother. If she felt anything, it was that she was the one who had been blessed. Now, just hours away from meeting the woman who, without knowing it, had cast such a huge shadow over her life, Jean prepared herself for the most important cup of tea she would ever likely drink.

Celia had given up trying to sleep and had sat in her study since three a.m. trying to write her new book, but the only words that came to mind were those written on the letter she had received from Jean Hargreaves over a week ago agreeing to a meeting. The day before yesterday she had at last summoned up the courage to tell David and to her joy and relief, far from being upset and annoyed, he had been delighted, hugging her to him and telling her she was a silly goose not to have said anything before. Of course he had not forgotten their son! The single reason he had never talked about him and had asked her not to try to trace him was because of his fear that it would cause her yet more pain and she had suffered enough. He had always thought that one day, when their boy was grown to manhood, they would somehow find him.

Celia chided herself for being surprised. She might have known her darling, sensitive husband would react in that way. He had told her to go ahead and meet Jack's mother on her own. He would wait, he had said, knowing that eventually he too would meet her and make himself known to their son. In the meantime, he would take on the task of explaining to their two other children that they had an older brother, which would no doubt take the wind out of their sails, if only for a moment!

Now, as she walked down the street where almost six months ago she had stepped out of her car to sign books in the small bookshop on the corner, her emotions were in just as much turmoil as they had been on that day. She was overwhelmed at Jean Hargreaves' generosity in agreeing to meet her, knowing how she would feel were their positions reversed. Celia knew she would not be seeing her son today; Jean had written in her note that he was looking forward to meeting her, but wanted to wait until after this first meeting to be sure everyone was comfortable with it.

If she hadn't been so nervous, Celia would have laughed at herself. She had spent twenty-five years waiting for this moment and now it was here, she was terrified. Before her nerves could get a further hold, to her surprise and delight she saw the woman who had given her son a family, a home and everything she had not been able to give him, walking towards her. Even from this distance she could see the woman was as nervous as she was herself.

Jean Hargreaves stopped dead in her tracks when she saw her son's natural mother approaching. Despite everything she had told herself about wanting to meet the smartly dressed author again, she was suddenly conscious of how down at heel she must look in her old-fashioned coat and shoes, a headscarf covering her grey hair, and wished the ground would open up and swallow her without trace.

'Mrs Hargreaves,' she heard the woman call as she drew near. 'Hello ... Mrs Hargreaves.'

Just as Jean was about greet her, Celia Gillespie smiled – and there it was: Jack's smile! It took her breath away and she could not speak.

'Thank you so much for agreeing to meet me, Mrs Hargreaves. I can't tell you just what it means to me.'

To Jean's consternation, she saw that the woman she had been so nervous about meeting looked equally nervous and what was more, close to tears. Instinctively, her own eyes blurring, she took hold of Celia Gillespie's trembling arm and guided her into the adjacent tearooms in which they had agreed to meet, steering her over to a table near the back and sitting down.

'I'm sorry,' the author murmured, 'I didn't mean to dissolve into tears, but it's just so amazing to meet you at last,' she half-laughed, added, 'although it is actually our third meeting, of course.'

'I thought you didn't recognise me,' Jean said, dabbing her eyes to hide her own emotion.

'Oh yes, I recognised you from the first time, though I didn't know who you were back then, not until you said your name in the bookshop. But I didn't want to distress you by saying anything then. You see, I knew my baby had been taken in by a couple named Hargreaves who lived somewhere near Pendleham – my mother found that out, but she never told me. Instead she wrote it in a letter to be opened after her death. She's been gone sixteen years now. That's why I was looking for the school that day. I looked at so many ...' she broke off, fresh tears coming to her eyes.

Jean tried to speak, but it took several breaths before she managed to utter a word, and by then the waitress was standing at their table. Coughing gently to find her voice, Jean ordered tea and cake for them both, not believing for a moment that either of them would be able to eat or drink anything the waitress brought to their table.

It was only then that Jean, with a sense of shock, realised how much older she was than Celia Gillespie. Strangely, it made her feel she had an advantage. Not in the sense of superiority so much as a feeling of responsibility. Her maternal instinct coming to the fore, Jean, to her surprise, felt she would be able to talk to the woman whom for so many years she had feared. It was hard to take in. The attractive young woman sitting opposite her looked barely old enough to be Jack's mother, but of course, she had been only seventeen. Even when Celia Gillespie's eyes were swimming with tears, Jean could see they were Jack's eyes too. In a strange way it hurt to see this, because to her, Jack had always looked like Tom. 'You're your father's son,' she used to say to him when father and son had conspired to do something together, so alike in their ways and their colouring that no one would ever have known they were not related by blood.

'Thank you for agreeing to meet me, I owe you so much,' Jack's mother said. 'The silly thing is that now, having for so long wanted to talk with you, I don't know where to begin.'

'I feel the same,' Jean said. 'I loved your book, Mrs Gillespie, it broke my heart and since reading it I haven't stop thinking about you. I admit, I am scared of getting to know you, but my Jack said I needn't be.'

Celia reached over and put her hand on Jean's. 'Oh, please, call me Celia, and I hope you don't mind if I call you Jean?' In a voice that was thick with emotion, she said, 'Thank you, thank you from the bottom of my heart ...'

Sometime later, the waitress returned with a second pot of tea, but as she approached the table, she knew it would go cold and not get drunk just like the first pot she had brought over an hour ago. Whatever the two ladies were talking about, it had made both of them cry a lot. She only hoped that it would end happily, although by the look of them, they were old friends.

She caught a snatch of their conversation as she drew near: 'We were told you didn't want him and we believed it. We wanted him desperately and loved him on sight. For us he was heaven sent ...' the older one was saying. The younger one's eyes were streaming, but she was nodding and smiling through her tears.

The waitress placed the fresh pot on the table, noted the plate of uneaten cakes, looked from one woman to the other, neither of whom noticed her, then shrugged and picking up the cold pot of tea, left them to talk undisturbed.

Chapter NINE

They talked for what seemed like hours, speaking words that Jean had believed could never be voiced. Somewhere in the course of their conversation, weeping, she had met Celia's gaze across the table and seen that she was weeping too. As they smiled through their tears into each other's eyes, Jean reached across the cups of cold tea and uneaten cakes to clasp Celia's hand, giving it a gentle squeeze. In that moment she knew she had found someone who would have a special place in her heart for as long as she lived. It was so unexpected that she was surprised into saying, 'It's so strange. All these years I have thought about you and worried that you would come and take my Jack away and now I feel as if I have always known you and we have always been friends.'

'I feel the same,' Celia sobbed, 'it is not only our son that we have in common, Jean. If I had been able to choose someone to raise my baby, it would have been you.'

Two days after that fateful meeting, Jack finally met the woman who had given birth to him. Jean had invited Celia to her home, for although she was aware that it was very likely a long way off what Celia was used to in terms of luxury or space, she had wanted to be on home territory when Jack met his natural mother for the first time.

Jean heard the tyres pulling hard on the unmade track that led to their cottage long before she saw the car stop outside their gate. Wringing her hands and listening to the sound of the engine running outside, she knew that from now on nothing would ever be the same again, but to her surprise, she found that she welcomed it. It was the end of fear and questions: fear of a stranger turning up and announcing she was the mother of Jack and taking him away; questions asked for which there would never be an answer or if there was, she might not want to give it or hear it. Jean was not so foolish as to imagine there would not be rocks in the road ahead. There had to be consequences when you took on a baby someone else brought into the world, but between the three of them they would find a way round whatever problems awaited them. She knew that now.

She wished with all her heart that her Tom was still here to share all of this with her. Had it not been for the woman who was now bringing her car to a stop outside their gate, she and Tom would never have been parents. She knew he had loved every moment he had spent with his son and as memories flashed unbidden through her mind, it took all the effort she could muster to stop herself from crying. All those years ago, nothing had prepared her for Tom being unable to give her a child, but thanks to Jack, they had survived it. Nothing had prepared her for being a widow either, she thought sadly, but she was surviving that too. If there was a God, she just hoped He was looking down with Tom now and smiling, for despite how her life had turned out so far, she was one of the lucky ones.

Looking through the kitchen window and seeing Celia getting out of her car, Jean finished putting the cups and saucers onto the tea tray before placing the kettle on the Rayburn. Then slipping off her apron she clasped her hands in front of her and prepared to welcome their special guest.

Jack was standing in the front room, just close enough to the window to look out, but far enough away so that he could not be seen from outside. As he stared out at the scene he loved, fields and more fields, he could hear his mother in the kitchen. The lid on the teapot had been put on and taken off twice, he had counted. He smiled as he heard several clatters as cups landed on saucers. He knew she was nervous and he would have offered to pour her a sherry, but she'd only cry out with horror. 'Goodness Jack, I can't be having alcohol on my breath at such a time!' Funny, he thought, he would have expected it to be him who was the nervous one, but he wasn't. He was just curious. Nothing could change what had happened all those years ago and he could not imagine having better parents than the ones he'd had. His dad was dead, but that changed nothing. His mum had told him that his natural father was called David and was still alive. It would be nice to meet him, but Tom Hargreaves would always be his dad.

He turned to look at his mum as she walked back into the front room. He could see her anxiety for him written all over her face and knew that at any minute she would be clasping him to her and hugging him tight, just like when he was a child and had scraped his knee. He forestalled her with a broad smile, 'It's all right, Mum, stop worrying. I'm fine.'

Together they watched as the woman Jack had seen many times over the years, but only recently discovered her identity, stepped out of her car and took the few steps to the gate. He could feel his mum shaking beside him. 'You said she was ok when you met her the other day, so why are you so nervous?'

'You can have no idea,' she said. And he had to agree, but before anything more could be said, his mum was hurrying out to the front door and pulling it open.

Celia saw Jean and smiled, and then she saw Jack standing behind his mother. She was overwhelmed and try as she might she could not speak. She had spent most of her life waiting for this moment, rehearsing what she would say, and now it was here she was speechless. Then to her amazement Jean stepped to one side and said, 'Celia, please come in and meet our Jack.'

And there was her son, her long lost baby, who looked so much like David that had she not been weeping she would have laughed. She put out her hand and to her great relief, Jack took hold of it. 'You have a brother and sister who can't wait to meet you,' she said, to cover her confusion, because all she wanted was to hug him to her the way she had always imagined, but whilst with every fibre of her being she *knew* him as her son, to him she was only a stranger and she must resist lest she embarrass him.

'I would like that,' he said shyly. Then he smiled at her, a broad grin that was the image of Ashton's. 'Thank you for coming ... and thank you for ...'

He didn't finish; quite simply, her longing to hold him would not be denied. Giving way to it, Celia took Jack in her arms and after the briefest hesitation, she felt him hug her back. It was a moment she knew she would treasure for as long as she lived – and beyond.

Watching their embrace, knowing that Celia was weeping as many silent tears as she was herself, Jean did not feel threatened, she felt happy for the mother of her son who had suffered so much, and happy that Jack would learn about his blood family. And yes, happy because she knew in her bones that all her fears had been for nothing.

'Take your mother into the front room, Jack,' she said quietly. 'You have so much to talk about. I'll make the tea.'

Walking into the kitchen, Jean picked up the framed photo on the dresser, looked down at it and smiled. 'It's going to be all right, Tom, my love. It's going to be all right. We'll never lose our boy.'

Epilogue

As Tony swung the car into the lane leading to Ridge View Cottage, Celia's mind was in a spin, so much of the past played back to her. She shook her head in an attempt to clear it, but today of all days, when her father had been laid in the ground – if not to rest - she knew it would be almost impossible to stop the past creeping into the present. It held so much and had ultimately shaped her life. But before the memories of those darker days jostled once again to take hold of her, she needed to bring her thoughts back to the present and away from the pain of all those years. Yet even the news she wanted to give Jack would push open the doors of the past; everything was so intrinsically entwined, no amount of division or separation could ever tear them apart.

Smiling at the irony of her thoughts, Celia said as lightly as she could, 'You'll never guess where I've been invited to go to do signings for my latest book?' As she spoke, she gently tapped the ribbon-bound manuscript that sat in the pocket of the armrest dividing the rear seat. She focused on her son's beloved face and saw his brow wrinkle as he tried to guess. 'It's a rhetorical question,' she laughed, 'I've been asked to go to Pendleham. It seems they still like my books there even after all these years.'

'Why doesn't that surprise me?' he smiled. 'It's nice to have such a clever mother, Mother!'

They both laughed. Soon after they had met for the first time and Jack and his mum had been to Satchfield Hall to meet David, Ashton and Clara, he had grasped Celia's elbow and whispered, 'What should I call you both? I can't call you Mr and Mrs Gillespie and Celia and David doesn't feel right.'

'Well we wouldn't mind a bit if you called us Celia and David, but if you're uncomfortable with that, why not Mother and Father?' she had suggested, conscious that Ashton and Clara were giggling in the background at Jean, who had taken one look at Ashton and gasped, 'Two peas in a pod! If I didn't know better I'd think I was in one of those time slip thingamajigs and looking at Jack at the same age.' Their laughter had broken the tension and remembering it now, Celia smiled. 'Mother' she had become and Jean, as always, was 'Mum', which Celia knew had been a relief to her. It had been a happy solution, all sorted out with just two words: mother and mum.

'I'm not clever, Jack, just extremely lucky,' she glanced up at him and added, 'in more ways than one.'

Looking at his mother and seeing the love standing in her eyes, Jack grinned at her. He was so proud of her and as his heart swelled with affection, he reached for her hand and held it, knowing what she was thinking. Had it not been for her first book signing in Pendleham, things would have turned out very differently for all of them. So much had changed for them both since that fateful Wednesday sixteen years ago, but as much as he loved his mother, nothing would change the fact that Tom and Jean Hargreaves, who had devoted their lives to raising him with so much love and kindness, were and always would be his mum and dad. He bore their name as did his own two sons, and had made him the man he was. It still hurt that his dad wasn't around and would never know his grandsons or they him. He still missed him so much.

'Don't be so modest, Mother, you're as bad as my dad, he never rated himself either. He'd have loved you. I wish ...'

'I know,' his mother said, as if she had just read his mind. 'I know.'

When Lizzie Rainbow heard the car pull up outside Ridge View Cottage, she flung open the door and hurried down the path to see the woman who had once been her employer, but who over the years had become more than just a friend, as close to her as any loved sister. Even Celia's children all called her 'Auntie Liz.'

When she had retired, not long after both George and then Gladys had passed away within six months of each other, Celia had asked Lizzie if she would like to stay at Satchfield Hall, where she would always have a home, or whether she would prefer to live in the cottage. She had been thrilled; she loved it up here with all the lovely country all around, and she loved the cottage too, especially since it had been all done up. It suited her better than the big old Hall, although she had been happy there. The cottage had electricity now, a telephone and oil-fired central heating. The old cess pit had been replaced with a septic tank that hardly ever needed emptying. Only the water supply was the same, piped into the header tank from the pure mountain springs, and in Lizzie's view tasted the better for it.

Earlier that morning, feeling a little guilty because she knew Celia wanted her company at the interment, she had telephoned to say she didn't feel well enough to go. She knew how important it was for Celia to witness the end of his life on this earth, but for Lizzie, the truth was, she couldn't face being anywhere near that man even if all that was left of him was his rotting corpse. What he had done to her had never left her; she still had nightmares about it. When he had come out of prison she had been terrified, but thankfully he had gone to live abroad until the last few months of his life, since which time he had been bedridden in a nursing home. Even then he had refused to make his peace with his daughter. Well now he was dead and gone and good riddance. Today Lizzie knew they could at last put the past behind them, but even knowing this, she still had not been able to bring herself to be there.

As the doors of the car opened, Lizzie, her emotions running high, saw Jack was with Celia and knew he must have been with her at the burial. It delighted her: a fitting end to that wicked man who had done everything he could to stop a mother and her son from ever meeting. She hoped he could see them now from wherever he had gone; and if he still had feeling, she hoped it hurt.

'Hello Jack,' she said as he hugged her, 'how's your mum and your family? I've not seen them for ages.'

'Sorry, Auntie Liz, I'll bring them over soon, I promise. They are all fine. Actually,' he murmured in her ear, 'I haven't told anyone else yet, so keep this under your hat, but Susan is expecting. If it's a little girl she's going to have the longest name in the history of daughters and one of them will be Elizabeth.'

She smiled up at him, her eyes twinkling. 'That's wonderful news,' she whispered, 'I won't tell a soul.'

'What are you two whispering about?'

'Oh, nothing much,' Jack said grinning at his mother and letting Lizzie go.

She turned to Celia and the look that passed between them travelled down the years to those dark times and back to the present in a split second; it needed no words. They both understood.

Rushing over to her, Celia put her arms around her and they hugged each other fiercely, both with tears in their eyes. 'Lizzie, my dearest friend; it's over. It's finally over and at last we are free.'

THE END

Printed in Great Britain
by Amazon